NEGOTIATING SCIENCE AND RELIGION IN AMERICA

Science and religion represent two powerful forces that continue to influence the American cultural landscape. *Negotiating Science and Religion in America* sketches an intellectual-cultural history from the Puritans to the twenty-first century, focusing on the sometimes turbulent relationship between the two. Using the past as a guide for what is happening today, this volume engages research from key scholars and the author's work on emerging adults' attitudes in order to map out the contours of the future for this exciting, and sometimes controversial, field. The book discusses the relationship between religion and science in the following important historical periods:

- from 1687 to the American Revolution
- the revolutionary period to 1859
- after Darwin's 1859 *On the Origin of Species*
- 1870–1925: the rise of religious modernism and pluralism to the Scopes Trial
- from Scopes to 1966
- the present: 1966 to 2000
- the third millennium: the voices of Stephen Jay Gould, Richard Dawkins, and Francis Collins
- the future and its contours.

This is the ideal volume for any student or scholar seeking to understand the relationship between religion and science in society today.

Greg Cootsona is Lecturer in Comparative Religion and Humanities at California State University, Chico, USA. He is the author of *Mere Science and Christian Faith: Bridging the Divide with Emerging Adults* (2018) and *C.S. Lewis and the Crisis of a Christian* (2014).

NEGOTIATING SCIENCE AND RELIGION IN AMERICA

Past, Present, and Future

Greg Cootsona

LONDON AND NEW YORK

First published 2020
by Routledge
2 Park Square, Milton Park, Abingdon, Oxon OX14 4RN

and by Routledge
52 Vanderbilt Avenue, New York, NY 10017

Routledge is an imprint of the Taylor & Francis Group, an informa business

© 2020 Greg Cootsona

The right of Greg Cootsona to be identified as author of this work has been asserted by him in accordance with sections 77 and 78 of the Copyright, Designs and Patents Act 1988.

All rights reserved. No part of this book may be reprinted or reproduced or utilised in any form or by any electronic, mechanical, or other means, now known or hereafter invented, including photocopying and recording, or in any information storage or retrieval system, without permission in writing from the publishers.

Trademark notice: Product or corporate names may be trademarks or registered trademarks, and are used only for identification and explanation without intent to infringe.

British Library Cataloguing-in-Publication Data
A catalogue record for this book is available from the British Library

Library of Congress Cataloging-in-Publication Data
Names: Cootsona, Gregory S., author.
Title: Negotiating science and religion in America : past, present, and future / Greg Cootsona.
Description: New York : Routledge, 2020. | Includes bibliographical references and index.
Identifiers: LCCN 2019037622 (print) | LCCN 2019037623 (ebook) |
ISBN 9781138067394 (hardback) | ISBN 9781138068537 (paperback) |
ISBN 9781315157856 (ebook)
Subjects: LCSH: Religion and science--United States--History.
Classification: LCC BL245 .C665 2020 (print) |
LCC BL245 (ebook) |
DDC 201/.650973--dc23
LC record available at https://lccn.loc.gov/2019037622
LC ebook record available at https://lccn.loc.gov/2019037623

ISBN: 978-1-138-06739-4 (hbk)
ISBN: 978-1-138-06853-7 (pbk)
ISBN: 978-1-315-15785-6 (ebk)

Typeset in Bembo
by Taylor & Francis Books

For those in America who work at negotiating the relations between "the force of our religious intuitions, and the force of our impulse to accurate observation and logical deduction" (A.N. Whitehead)

Negotiate, transitive verb: "to deal with a matter or issue that requires skill for its successful handling"

CONTENTS

Preface	*x*
Foreword	*xii*
Elaine Howard Ecklund	

1 Introduction: the topic   1

A way not taken 1
Whitehead's Challenge 3
How to respond to Whitehead's Challenge: some critical terms 5
Outline of chapters 8

2 The problems of defining science and religion   13

Definitions and their limitations 13
*How do science and religion relate? Adapting Ian Barbour's
typology 17*
A brief meditation on science and religion in America 19

3 From 1687 to the American Revolution   29

*The importance of the Enlightenment, the Reformation, and the
conquest of the New World 29*
The Spanish conquest 31
The Puritans' colonizing 32
The Great Awakening and its ongoing importance 35
Jonathan Edwards: a brief case study 36

viii Contents

4 The revolutionary period to 1859   43

The deism of Thomas Paine 43
Blending science and religion with Common Sense Realism 46
The early 1800s and a brewing discontent 48
Key words and critical shifts 51
Brief notes on antebellum America, race, and slavery 52

5 Post-Darwin   57

Setting the break with Darwin's Origin of Species *57*
What Darwin's theory really meant for American religion 59
John William Draper, Andrew Dickson White, and the circumstances
  surrounding them 63
Reconciliation and rejection: Asa Gray, Charles Hodge, and
  others 65

6 1870–1925: from the rise of religious modernism and pluralism to the Scopes Trial   73

Modernism and pluralism in late nineteenth-century America 73
Fundamentalism 77
The fundamentalist-modernist split 78
The expansion of eugenics in America 81
The 1925 Scopes Trial 84

7 From Scopes to 1966   93

Major scientific discoveries: relativity and the quantum revolution 93
Science and shifting worldviews 96
1930–1966: the Great Depression, WWII, the Nuclear Age, and
  the Eisenhower Revival 98

8 The present: 1966 to 2000 (more or less)   106

Slowing down the narrative 106
The Sixties: turbulence 109
The 1970s: broadening the dialogue 113
The 1980s: growth and collaboration 116
The 1990s: consolidation and counter-narratives 118

9 The present: the third millennium and three representative voices   126

A new century for science and religion 126
Stephen Jay Gould 129

Contents ix

Richard Dawkins 130
Francis Collins 131

10 The future and its contours: religious individualism and
tinkering   134

How emerging adults are accelerating a venerable American
  tradition 134
A sketch of emerging adulthood in America 135
Streaming spirituality versus LP religion 137
Signs pointing in opposite directions? 141
Top eleven topics today and for the future 144

11 The future and its contours: major trends   156

The perils of prediction 156
A decreasing influence of Christianity and a splintering of American
  religious life 157
A rise in atheism and agnosticism 160
With the nones' increase, antipathy both increases and decreases 161
Toward new modes, new models 164
Toward a truly pluralist model 166
Final thoughts on what I've learned 168

Appendix A: Summary of Negotiating Science and Religion in
              America   *175*
Appendix B: 2020 notes on topics today and for the future   *178*
Index   *201*

PREFACE

Why I wrote this book

As a rule, I avoid writing prefaces. Besides the fact that few read them, I'm not always sure what purpose they serve, except as another chapter. Why not just call it "Chapter One"? And if the material is important enough to communicate, why not just include what's here in the book proper?

Nevertheless, this time a preface seemed useful because some of the reasons for writing this book might be unclear, and I want you, as readers, to know why I took time (more than I expected) to write on science and religion in America in its past, present, and future forms (at least as far as I can discern the latter).

The simple answer is that I haven't seen another similar attempt. Certainly, there are outstanding titles in American religion, the history of science, as well as science and religion. The bibliographies at the end of each chapter list many of those. Nevertheless, I can describe my impetus for writing this monograph through the subtitle of Edward Larson's superb Pulitzer Prize-winning *Summer for the Gods—America's Continuing Debate Over Science and Religion*. Could I add to our understanding of this debate, or discussion, or dialogue? Larson leaves many questions, and sections of our history, unaddressed. (As inevitably, in a book of this scope, I have as well.) Still, sheer enthusiasm for the subject, perhaps with a measure of hubris or naïveté, made this seem like a worthy goal. And for what I've also left unaddressed there is a concomitant hope that it might spur on many similar projects in response.

This has been a challenging and entirely engaging book to write because the topic is so capacious. In the process of charting how our country has negotiated the relationship of religion and science, the hardest part was making decisions about what to research and thus what to include. In the text that follows I offer a rubric—essentially what serves my main narrative—but I realize my decisions about inclusion and exclusion aren't perfect. As I present in the text, negotiating the place of science and religion is central to American culture, and so this could almost be simply another history of our country. Thankfully my publisher also offered a directive, namely a word count, which provided another helpful guide.

On two related notes: in the bibliographies that follow each chapter I could list everything ever written on the subject, but frankly I find extensive bibliographies that include texts only tenuously related to the main topic tedious and a bit pretentious. Instead I've only included the books and articles that readers would find helpful in going deeper. Frankly, I read some of my sources so many years ago that they've become part of my thinking, even if they weren't my insights originally. In sum, the bibliographies are sufficient, but not entirely exhaustive. Second, since many readers don't want to bother with footnotes (which can be found in each chapter), I've used them almost entirely to identify scholarly support for my assertions and not to carry on a separate conversation. Ultimately it's a decision of writing style. I don't want you to have to flip from the text to notes to hear everything I'm trying to say. My goal is that it's possible simply to read the text.

Finally, a preface is the place to thank my many dialogue partners who won't appear in the bibliography and footnotes but who have contributed to this book nonetheless. I have benefited from conversations with my colleagues in the Science, Technology, and Religion program unit at the AAR, especially my co-chairs, Josh Reeves and Sarah Fredericks, as well as my colleagues at Chico State University, particularly those who have participated in various ways in the almost yearly conferences on science and religion, Joel Zimbleman, Sarah Pike, Dan Veidlinger, Brian Oppy, and Dawn Clifford (the latter now at Southern Arizona University). Additional conversations with Drew Rick-Miller, Zach Ellis, Dave Navarra, Justin Barrett, Rebecca Dorsey Sok, Sarey Martin, Ric Machuga, Dan Barnett, Gary Fugle, Elaine Howard Ecklund, Geoff Mitelman, Denis Alexander, Ruth Bancewicz, Deborah Haarsma, Leslie Wickman Se Kim, Curtis Baxter, Jennifer Wiseman, Joshua Swamidass, Josh Moritz, Braden Molhoek, Ted Peters, and Robert John Russell through various grant projects; work with the Center for Theology and the Natural Sciences; Biologos; AAAS's Dialogue on Science, Ethics, and Religion (DoSER); the American Scientific Affiliation; the Faraday Institute, the Religion and Public Life Program; and various other science and religion events—as well as the monthly Chico Triad on Philosophy, Theology, and Science meetings—have proven extremely beneficial in clarifying my positions and expunging wooly ideas. I also treasure all the informal conversations at home with my brilliant wife, Laura, and equally able daughters, Lizzie and Melanie.

To all (and those I inadvertently forgot), thank you.

FOREWORD

Elaine Howard Ecklund

I am not always a fan of interdisciplinary work; sometimes it becomes a lowest common denominator, where scholars in no single discipline are entirely satisfied with the results. This is because truly rare is the person able to learn the tools of more than one discipline at the level required to do scholarship that truly cuts across disciplines.

Greg Cootsona is that rare scholar.

In *Negotiating Science and Religion in America,* Cootsona provides us an overview of the past, present, and future of the relationship between science and religion. Perhaps most important to me as a sociologist, he helps us understand the evolution of the sometimes fraught relationship between religious and scientific communities, helps us understand their present interactions, and guides us toward what might need to happen to gain the future relationship between these communities that we might like to see.

It is my firm conviction that examining this complex relationship ought to be a central topic of university scholarship in the years to come. Religion and science are *the* dominant ways of meaning-making in the late-modern world. While theologians and philosophers have built an impressive body of work on how science and religion *should* relate, we know little about how contemporary people *actually do* understand the science and religion interface. And the body of scholarship that is starting to build in my own field, of the sociology of science and religion, rarely draws on the impressive body of scholarship developed by historians who have examined how intellectual elites previously connected scientific and religious ideas.

Cootsona's work is the first contemporary book I have read that marshals a true intellectual history in the service of situating where we are now as a society in terms of the relationship between science and religion.

This is consequential work.

During the past 15 years, while doing empirical sociological scholarship on how contemporary people view the science and religion relationship, I have met Christian parents whose worries about what the science professors they will encounter will say about faith have an impact on which colleges and universities these parents choose for their children. Some groups of US Christians, Jews, and Muslims worry about certain medical technologies and research; whether, for example, new technologies involving the human genome are ethical and whether they take into account the uniqueness of the human being and what it means to be made in the image of God. I have met Christians who are generally afraid of how science will have an impact on their faith and how scientists will influence religion and its place in society. My work shows clearly that, even though philosophers, theologians, and historians say there does not have to be a conflict between religion and science, there very much still is one. Although scientific technologies are quickly changing, viewing the current religion and science landscape through the twinned lens of intellectual history and current social science will allow Cootsona's work not to become quickly dated. Through his comprehensive intellectual history, "the study of intellectuals, ideas, and intellectual patterns over time,"[1] Cootsona starts to show us exactly how such contemporary US dynamics may have occurred.

But Cootsona does not stop in the past.

He then uses contemporary social science to show us the present, explaining current dynamics clearly through existing surveys and his own collection of interview data. He digs into the modern landscape in a way that moves us beyond the focus on conflicts between *Christianity* and science, (a concern of much scholarship), to help his readers think through how what he calls the "pluriform religious landscape"—which includes Muslims, Hindus, atheists, non-religious, neopagans and other traditions—is re-situating the relationship between science and religion.

And the real benefit of being steeped in multiple disciplines, as Cootsona is, comes out toward the end of the book, where he starts to make predictions. He presents contours of the future more boldly than I would as a social scientist, but his ideas are grounded in solid social scientific work nonetheless. My favorite section is indeed that last section of the book where he "looks for sources and signs to discern the contours of the future." In some ways Cootsona gives us enough to chart a potential research agenda for the future. He leaves us with questions like; will Christianity really gray away and, if it does, what impact will this have on the importance of and type of relationship between religion and science? Cootsona provides a more nuanced appraisal of the impact the increase in nones, agnostics, and atheists will have on the future religion and science landscape, arguing that they may lead to an increased antipathy toward the collaboration of science and religion in the culture at large "out there" and a decreased tension between science and an individual's personal religion or spirituality "in here," what I see as a wise and nuanced insight. It is this kind of helpful and testable prediction that speaks to the depth of Cootsona's book; it is a book that offers its readers the best of history, sociology, and grounded scholarly prediction all in one highly readable volume.

Note

1 See Peter Gordon, 2012, "What is Intellectual History?" http://projects.iq.harvard.edu/files/history/files/what_is_intell_history_pgordon_mar2012.pdf

1

INTRODUCTION: THE TOPIC

A way not taken

I was tempted to introduce this book as follows:

In 1925 the Harvard scientist and philosopher Alfred North Whitehead commented that the future of our civilization depended, to some degree, on how effectively we were able to relate religion and science, that is, "the force of our religious intuitions, and the force of our impulse to accurate observation and logical deduction."

We can hope the science will prevail. In light of Whitehead's Challenge, it's increasingly clear that religion has failed and led emerging adults in America today to conclude that religion is anti-science, outdated, irrational, prejudiced against sexual minorities, and regularly prone to violence. This book is an answer to why this is the case through narrating a cultural-intellectual history of America focused on science and religion as a way to chart their future relationship.

The past provides us with a guide to the present and future. Even if what we today call *science* and *religion* don't map exactly onto our history, nonetheless, as we look backward in time, we surely see enduring tensions between a recalcitrant religion and a burgeoning science. What then is "the past"? I'll define it as approximately 1687 (Newton's *Principia*) to 1966 (Ian Barbour's *Issues in Science and Religion*), with a division of 1859 (Darwin's *Origin*) as midpoint. I freely admit that every historical division is clunky, somewhat arbitrary, and therefore distorting; nonetheless, between Newton and Darwin the United States was officially founded, and, in that time, it maintained a tensive relationship between rationality and religious "affections," to use Jonathan Edwards's term—but in a country founded by the religiously zealous (such as the Puritans), the latter most often triumphed. A growing Enlightenment rationality marked the late eighteenth century and features

2 Introduction

prominently in our nation's core documents (indeed, a time of a remarkable flowering of free thinkers like Thomas Jefferson), while also embodying a warmth of emotional life that is no less characteristic of America and that tamped down our release from religious shackles.

I then chart how, starting in the late nineteenth century, Charles Darwin freed us from William Paley's facile Watchmaker deity and the last vestiges of theological control over our institutions of higher learning and leading intellectual culture through characters such as Andrew Dickson White, William Draper, Robert Ingersoll, Charles Hodge, and Asa Gray, as well as through events like the 1925 Scopes Trial and the fundamentalist-modernist split. Christianity, in order to maintain its integrity, had to retreat from the public sphere. Indeed, America was coming of age intellectually and culturally, and continued to find an uneasy relationship with religion. It is undeniable, however, that gradually science grew in power and persuasion, and though religion fought the inevitable, it lost cultural and intellectual sway. Put another way, though there was both scientific growth and religious expansion—the predominant theme of this 100-year period is simply stated: *scientific advance and religious retreat.*

With Barbour's book, the present academic study of religion and science begins and increasingly the hegemony of Protestant America is shattered from the 1960s to our present day, when a variety of religious traditions became more mainstreamed and atheism, agnosticism, and "no religious affiliation" (or "nones") ascend. Broadly speaking, this takes us to the new millennium where religion becomes more pluralized and individualized. I look at how the early twenty-first century interaction of religion and science brought the increasing importance of technology, sexuality, global climate change, and religious pluralism. It also highlights new voices—notably scientists and not theologians—such as Francis Collins, Stephen Jay Gould, and Richard Dawkins.

To understand the future I analyze research from key scholars on emerging-adults' attitudes about religion and science as signposts for the future. I conclude by analyzing these views as a way to discern the contours of the future of science and religion in America: first of all, a world in which evolution will continue as an acid to eat away at traditional religious dogmas, and concerns about topics such as sexuality, climate change, technology, AI, and transhumanism will rise in importance. Fewer and fewer will look to religion and religious ideologies since they are decreasingly presenting meaningful or valuable insights. Second, Christianity will continue to wane in influence. And, third, we will see an ongoing and marked increase of the religious nones and other religious and spiritual traditions with a corresponding uptick in atheism and agnosticism. One might hope that these trends represent a conclusive answer to Whitehead's Challenge—i.e., that human reason and science will demonstrate the repressive force of religion—but we will have to wait.

Still, the trends are evident. Science and technology will increasingly guide the minds and the future of America, while religion, as a vestige of our country's Puritanical past, will continue to retreat and find distorted forms like fundamentalist

Introduction **3**

congregations and the political actions of the religious right. Gradually it will gradually wither away, like a dying branch on a vibrant tree.

This represents one way I could have introduced this book, but the problem is that it's largely inaccurate—entirely too simplistic and, therefore, distorting. The actual narrative of negotiating science and religion in American is much more nuanced and vastly more interesting.

Whitehead's Challenge

Let me start again in how negotiating the relationship between science and religion has worked historically in *America* (a term I'll be using synonymously with the *United States of America* ... more on that below). Science and religion need to keep talking, but their talking may actually be an argument, and that's not a bad thing.

Alasdair MacIntyre has argued that a *living tradition* is "an historically extended, socially embodied argument, and an argument precisely in part about the goods which constitute that tradition."[1] In the pages to come, I'll follow MacIntyre's definition and at times substitute *common good* for MacIntyre's "goods which constitute that tradition," and for Thomas Jefferson's glorious phrase in the *Declaration*—and which has become central to our national identity—"life, liberty, and the pursuit of happiness." With that in mind, it remains worth discussing the cultural traditions that constitute America, particularly how science and religion relate. A fair reading of American history demonstrates that our county has been at its best when we bring these two cultural forces together. And, as far as I can tell, that's the direction of the future, as emerging adults, and their attitudes on religion and science, increasingly lead us. From my vantage point, this direction is largely a good thing because ultimately I believe it's best for our country when these two, religion and science, learn how to get along. Our future will be better without the warfare of religion and science.

Whitehead did most of his academic work in England, focusing on the mathematics, especially in its relation to physics. He even offered his own version of relativity theory. He also loved the great questions that human beings ponder through philosophical reflection and worked on *Principia Mathematica* with his most brilliant student at Cambridge, Bertrand Russell. After a long career in science he retired at 63 and shortly thereafter, in 1924, received an invitation from Henry Osborn Taylor of Harvard University to teach philosophy in light of the transformations of scientific thought wrought by evolution and relativity. Perhaps Harvard wanted Whitehead to offer a more nuanced version of how to relate science and religion there than Andrew Dickson White had done at Cornell about five decades earlier. And so Whitehead moved to Cambridge, Massachusetts, and wrote the philosophical and metaphysical texts like *Process and Reality*[2] for which many in the field of science and religion know him best.

4 Introduction

The great English mathematician and Harvard philosopher addressed his assembled audience in the Philips Brooks House almost a century ago, and presented what I call Whitehead's Challenge:

> When we consider what religion is for mankind and what science is, it is no exaggeration to say that the future course of history depends upon the decision of this generation as to the relations between them. We have here the two strongest forces (apart from the mere impulse of various senses) which influence men, and they seem to be set one against the other—the force of our religious intuitions, and the force of our impulse to accurate observation and logical deduction. [3]

Admittedly his challenge finds earlier precedents in James T. Bixby's urgent exhortation, as a Unitarian speaking to the Lowell Institute in 1876, "The future of Religion would be vastly more sure and prosperous if she could make science an ally instead of a rival."[4] And yet Whitehead's is more noteworthy. It was February 1925. That summer the infamous Scopes Trial would set conservative Christianity in a legal battle with evolutionary thought (tinged as it was with eugenics), and the former would retrench and, as we are prone to say today, "rally its base." In that same year Whitehead presented a reasonably bleak assessment: "Religion is tending to degenerate into a decent formula wherewith to embellish a comfortable life."[5]

To be sure, we are far from Whitehead's generation, but his challenge still has merit because we know that the "conflict thesis" endures in popular imagination. As Lawrence Principe writes, "Although rejected by every serious historian of science today, the 'conflict' or 'warfare' model for the historical interaction of science and religion remains not only widespread but naturalized as a 'fact' in popular culture."[6]

It is true that many people think science and religion are bad for each other, and, even more critically, at least one is ruinous for our country. The sooner we get rid of one—religion for the "cultured despisers" and science for proponents of "old time religion"—the better off America will be. Sometimes the hegemony of religion or science presents the impetus for conflict and for one side to whine. The religionist proposes, "God said it. I believe it. That settles it." Or similarly, but with more subtlety, scientists represent themselves as James Franck did in a 1945 letter with other scientists to President Truman, as "a kind of international brotherhood, comparable in many ways to a religious order."[7] But that hardly seems like a workable solution, nor can it strike an unbiased reader of American history (or even a biased one, for that matter) as a defensible idea.

Following Whitehead, I pose these questions: is a détente possible between these two cultural forces in the coming 20 to 30 years? Or, more generally, what will this interaction look like in the future? How has American responded to Whitehead's Challenge?

How to respond to Whitehead's Challenge: some critical terms

How to respond is my first concern. I want to know where this argument about the common good is headed. The partners in this argument constantly shift, and I am seeking to discern the contours of the future of the interaction of science and religion based on the views of emerging adults (age 18–30) because they will increasingly define this discussion. Incidentally, I am broadly employing, along with many other commentators, Jeffery Arnett's category of *emerging adulthood*, as a stage of life that is not still adolescence but neither is it adulthood. I am not committing to all the implications of Arnett's theory, but find this to be a highly usable paradigm.[8] Yet I am also not forgetting our past. Whatever I write about the future finds roots in the past and the American story of negotiating the relationship between science and religion. Because emerging adults will increasingly become the thought leaders for our country (and admittedly they already are), this book will utilize the best demographic research available, as well as my own interviews and surveys of emerging adults, to assist in discerning future trends. It is also worth adding that I am not writing about what I *hope* will be the future. Instead, with the research data we possess, and by making reasonable judgments, what defensible claims can I make about what is to come?

I have used the phrase *cultural forces* (echoing Whitehead's language of "forces" and Alister McGrath's "cultural and intellectual forces"[9]) and will sometimes employ "sets of cultural forces" as epithets for science and religion. But why? Drawing from John H. Evans's *Morals Not Knowledge: Recasting the Contemporary U. S. Conflict between Religion and Science*, most problems between science and religion consist more often in morality than a "systematic knowledge conflict."[10] True enough. As Stephen Jay Gould remarked, in considering the limits of science,

> Morality is a subject for philosophers, theologians, students of the humanities, indeed for all thinking people. The answers will not be read passively from nature; they do not, and cannot, arise from the data of science. The factual state of the world does not teach us how we, with our powers for good and evil, should alter or preserve it in the most ethical manner.[11]

Many scientists do not heed Gould's boundaries. So often, however, the line of analysis for comparison that scholars of religion take follows a handbooks for our guild, *The HarperCollins Dictionary of Religion* in its entry on *science and religion*: "The problem for scholars is to clarify the nature of the relationships between these forms of knowledge."[12] All this is partly the fault of social location, that much of the discussion about science and religion has focused on "epistemic conflict" rather than a "social/moral conflict."[13] In other words, those who write about science and religion represent a cultural elite, namely those who hold PhDs in academic fields. As Evans puts it, "This elite reasoning can be described as an 'ideology' or 'worldview.'"[14] And the work of elites resides in their ability to see whether their worldviews and ideologies are consistent.

6 Introduction

But, the public has much less logical consistency than elites do. This is not an insult but a matter of sociological realism. The reason for the difference is that the only people who have the time and motivation to develop airtight, logically consistent beliefs all the way back to first principles are those rewarded for doing so. Academics are rewarded for this with tenure—analytic philosophers are an extreme case.[15]

And so the study of science and religion has gone askew.

This ethical conflict rears its head in the *cause célèbre* of science and religion, the fundamentalist rejection of evolution. As John Whitcomb and Henry Morris assert in their vastly influential 1961 creationist text *The Genesis Flood,*

> The morality of evolution, which assumes progress and achievement and "good" come about through such action as benefits the individual himself or the group of which he is a part, to the detriment of others, is most obviously anti-Christian.[16]

When we read this the cover is ripped off and we see that the warfare between "creation" and "evolution" is no longer solely cognitive. Or when H.L. Mencken summarized the 1925 Scopes Trial, he clearly framed it as titanic cultural forces with a clear villain and an equally identifiable champion, "It was [Clarence] Darrow who carried the main burden, and Darrow who shaped the final result. When he confronted [William Jennings] Bryan at last, the whole combat came to its climax. On the one side was bigotry, ignorance, hatred, superstition, every sort of blackness that the human mind is capable of. On the other side was sense. And sense achieved a great victory."[17] Both left and right seem to agree: this indeed is about the soul, and not simply the mind, of America.

Nevertheless, I can't avoid stepping into producing something like an intellectual history, drawing from what Peter Gordon has written for the Harvard Colloquium: "Broadly speaking, intellectual history is the study of intellectuals, ideas, and intellectual patterns over time."[18] He clarified that this is not simply a "history of ideas" for these reasons:

> Intellectual history is often considered to be different from the history of ideas. Intellectual history resists the Platonist expectation that an idea can be defined in the absence of the world, and it tends instead to regard ideas as historically conditioned features of the world which are best understood within some larger context, whether it be the context of social struggle and institutional change, intellectual biography (individual or collective), or some larger context of cultural or linguistic dispositions (now often called "discourses").[19]

In keeping with this approach I am working hard to embed this story of science and religion in America as not simply disembodied ideas—even focused on

Introduction 7

intellectuals—but on cultural forces and cultural leaders. To state the obvious, religion, and certainly its leaders and practitioners, are dominant forces in American culture.

And yet I am stepping back even further. I believe we are addressing what I've come to see as "the dream of America," a recasting of "the American Dream" I sometimes employ to describe the grand vision for the good, even the best, of what our country has to offer. It certainly does not entirely represent reality, but an almost religious vision—or, better, a vision that has often been fueled by religious narratives and passions. And for this reason I have titled this book *Science and Religion "in America"* rather than *"in the United States."* In other words, what is the experiment of America and the goods implicit in our common good?

I've also been inspired by Andrew Delbanco's brilliant (and, to my mind, under-appreciated) reflection on our country from 1999, *The Real American Dream: A Meditation on Hope,* [20] in which he argues, as the subtitle suggests, that our search for hope has powered the American Dream. And now I'll return to why I'm using "America" throughout this book. I do realize the problems—because there are many "Americas" in our hemisphere—but the word has enduring and irreplaceable value because "America" is also a symbol of our hopes. It's partly an idealized form or at least an aspirational future. In that light, Delbanco offers a three-part typology through the first 200 years with the Puritans, who grounded their hope in a covenant with God, the nineteenth century (broadly speaking), where Nation became our guiding light, and in the ending of the twentieth century, which focused our attention on Self. He found the final stage of this search for hope insubstantial. We cannot set the entire hope of our country in search for self-expression.

The specifics of Delbanco's argument are brilliant and brilliantly articulated, but my interest does not lie there. Instead, I have learned from him the impor-tance of hope and even more a story[21] and vision for what makes the good life, for what constitutes the American Dream. My rephrasing of that search as *the dream of America* is intended to demonstrate that our country's yearning extends beyond financial mobility (as important as that is for the lower economic strata), to a gleaming vision for America as a concept and inspiration. Following MacIntrye, I pose the question again in a slightly different mode: how are science and religion involved in an argument over the common good of America yes-terday, today, and tomorrow? And so to repeat: what is the experiment of America, and what are the goods implicit in our common good? Who will be included? I'm not sure any generation has presented definitive answers to these questions, but I believe some are better than others. And that they have sig-nificant cultural implications for our country.

One way to make this argument is to present an alternative question: if, indeed, religion and science are critical to our country, where is their future relationship? (This would be a worthwhile question without its centrality, but that centrality intensifies the need for an answer.) What do we do with the fact that about 70% of Americans see ultimate conflict between the teachings of science and religion, but that same percentage of believers don't see their personal faith disagreeing with

8 Introduction

science?[22] The past will provide us with a guide to the present. And as we look at the past, we do see tensions between the two and yet a profound struggle to integrate them.

Outline of chapters

How then to sort out these various subplots and to arrive at an idea where the American drama of science and religion is headed?

In writing a narrative that brings us to the current state of science and religion in America, my rubric will be this: *I will focus on the thought leaders, events, and ideas that set up the story of science and religion in the present with an ongoing cultural impact.* Therefore, before I look at the present state and future trends in science and religion, I need to take time to view the past and how it establishes both where we are today and where we are headed.

In order to tell this story well I will have to first set the context. In the next chapter I address some necessary concerns: how to define key terms such as religion, science, and technology, then to Ian Barbour's noteworthy 50-plus-year-old typology on how to relate science and religion, and finally to a meditation for how these two actually do interact in America. All starting points require decisions, and in this book I have decided to begin with the seventeenth-century Puritans in the American colonies—partly because they responded to the European Reformation, Scientific Revolution, and Enlightenment.[23] In addition I will only briefly touch on the massive religious changes in Europe that preceded our country's founding.

But, even more, I will let science set the agenda; I'll set the starting date around Isaac Newton's *Principia Mathematica* in 1687 and end with Ian Barbour's *Issues in Science and Religion* (1966), with Charles Darwin's *On the Origin of Species* (1859) as the midpoint. In the process I will also sketch a cultural and intellectual history of the United States in the eighteenth century around the theme of religion and science and use the brief case studies of Jonathan Edwards and Thomas Paine. In subsequent chapters, I will turn to the changes Darwin wrought in the late nineteenth century and present brief treatments of Charles Hodge and others. Hodge and Edwards both looked at religion and science with intellectual rigor and, in many respects, similar theology, but around them the culture had shifted so dramatically that their voices sound radically different.

In moving toward the present, I cannot help but note, in Chapter Six, the key twentieth-century events in the interaction of science and religion, not least of which is the 1925 Scopes "Monkey" Trial, but certainly includes more than simply the twisted and oft-discussed narrative of the Butler Act, *Civil Biology*, John Scopes, William Jennings Bryan, H.L. Mencken, Clarence Darrow, and Dayton, Tennessee.

A necessary note on recounting our past: in order to understand where the interaction of science and religion is today, and where it's headed, I have to chart how we arrived here. This study briefly charts this interplay in America since the eighteenth century. Please be aware that I am not trying to sketch all of American history or offer a comprehensive treatment of our intellectual foundations. In this light, I am emphasizing general themes and even (if I may use the term) "great thinkers." My main intent is to weave together a narrative in this first part that sets up the present state of science and religion so that we can discern its future contours. The road that has led us here should offer us a sense of what our future journey will look like. At least one can hope.

In Chapter Seven I decelerate my narrative and move to the second part, "the present," which begins, for the purpose of this book, with Barbour's 1966 *Issues in Science and Religion*. It is set as the twenty-first century dawns, where a new chapter in the story of science and religion begins. Barbour set the agenda for the contemporary study of science and religion right at the time that "American religion" certainly began to mean more than "Protestants, Catholics, Jews."[24] I peer into the twenty-first century proper, in which Dawkins, Gould, and Collins are able spokespeople for the revised typology of Barbour I have constructed. As I have mentioned above, though, I will use this intellectual tripod to take a picture of the contemporary environment and will be free to edit it and offer additional ways to proceed with my analysis. Two key notes about our century: the religious landscape is pluriform, consisting not simply of Christians, Muslims, Wiccans, and neopagans, but sometimes a mixing of those traditions (and more) all together; and the conversation has moved from purely science and religion to science, *technology*, and religion. In that latter regard I cannot help but mention the work of transhumanism and posthumanism, which is currently exploding.[25] Here the pace of the book eases, as I sketch out the past 50 years or so and bring the narrative of science and religion to the present day. In the process, it is important to underline, I'll lean on cultural leaders, intellectuals, and religious more often than specific scientific discoveries, although I'll work to note those where they are significant for the conversation. My intention is for this to establish how we've arrived at our contemporary *Sitz im Leben* as I then move into considering where religion and science in the United States is headed.

The future fascinates me, and thus, in the final two chapters, I begin by assessing recent surveys and analyses conducted by key sociologists and social scientists—such as Elaine Howard Ecklund, Christopher Scheitle, Jonathan Hill, Christian Smith, and Robert Wuthnow—as well as the findings of my qualitative interviews and quantitative surveys with emerging adults. I conclude by analyzing these views as a way to discern the contours of both the present state and future directions of science and religion in the United States, a world in which evolution and creation will be present but where concerns about sexuality, climate change, technology, AI, and transhumanism will rise in importance. There will also be a reduction of the influence of the Christian church, a notable rise in the influence of atheism, agnosticism, and especially the nones, or "none of the above"—those who identify as agnostics or atheists, or any religion they practice is "nothing in particular,"[26] as well as other religious and spiritual traditions. Nonetheless—and here's my most potentially contentious claim—the interaction of science and religion will most likely find a decrease in the antipathy that's often been promoted between the two.

10 Introduction

One might wish that I am presenting a conclusive answer to Whitehead's Challenge—to find the final cultural reconciliation, or perhaps a détente, between science and religion. It's most likely, however, that we'll hear another set of responses in an ongoing historical process. The final chapter, in making the boldest claims and outlining the problems facing the dialogue, stretches my role beyond observer and analyst. I realize the dangers. Still it seems to me that the future will not yield a clear winner, and, despite whatever problems and/or challenges lie before us, the sketch of this variegated interaction of science and religion remains more interesting than any simple caricature.

Of course, all these statements await support in the chapters to come.

Notes

1 Alasdair MacIntyre, *After Virtue*, 2nd edition. (Notre Dame, IN: University of Notre Dame Press, 1981), 222.
2 A.N. Whitehead, *Process and Reality: Corrected Edition*. David Ray Griffin and Donald W. Sherburne, eds. (New York: Free Press, 1978 [1929]).
3 Whitehead, *Science and the Modern World*, 181.
4 Jon H. Roberts in Jeff Hardin, Ronald L. Numbers, Ronald A. Binzley, eds., *The Warfare Between Science and Religion: The Idea That Wouldn't Die* (Baltimore: Johns Hopkins University Press, 2018), 145; citing Bixby, *Similarities of Physical and Religious Knowledge* (New York: D. Appleton, 1876), 10–11.
5 A.N. Whitehead, *Science and the Modern World* (Cambridge, 1926), 188.
6 Lawrence Principe, in Hardin et al., eds. *The Warfare Between Science and Religion*, 6.
7 Cited in James Gilbert, *Redeeming Culture: American Religion in an Age of Science* (Chicago: University of Chicago, 1997), 42.
8 Cf. Jeffrey Arnett, "Emerging Adulthood: A Theory of Development From the Late Teens Through the Twenties," *American Psychologist* 55. no. 5 (2000): 469–80.
9 Alister McGrath, *Science and Religion: A New Introduction*, 2nd edition. (Oxford: Wiley-Blackwell, 2010), 1.
10 John Evans, *Morals Not Knowledge: Recasting the Contemporary U.S. Conflict Between Science and Religion* (Oakland: University of California Press, 2018), 84.
11 "Nonmoral Nature," *Hen's Teeth and Horse's Toes: Further Reflections in Natural History* (New York: W.W. Norton, 1994), 42; cited in McGrath, *Science and Religion: A New Introduction*, 3.
12 Jonathan Z. Smith, William Scott Green, eds., *The HarperCollins Dictionary of Religion* (San Francisco: HarperCollins, 1996), 965.
13 John Evans, in Jeff Hardin, et al., eds. *The Warfare Between Science and Religion*, 325.
14 Ibid., 334.
15 Ibid., 335.
16 John C. Whitcomb, Jr. and Henry M. Morris, *The Genesis Flood: The Biblical Record and Its Scientific Implications* (Phillipsburg, Presbyterian and Reformed Publishing Company, 1961), 447; cited in Evans, *Morals Not Knowledge*, 82.
17 H.L. Mencken, *Baltimore Evening Sun,* 1925, "full text of Coverage of The Scopes Trial by H.L. Mencken," retrieved June 20, 2019, https://archive.org/details/CoverageOfTheScopesTrialByH.l.Mencken
18 Peter Gordon, "What is Intellectual History?" 2012, retrieved June 20, 2019, http://projects.iq.harvard.edu/files/history/files/what_is_intell_history_pgordon_mar2012.pdf
19 Ibid.
20 Delbanco, *The Real American Dream: A Meditation on Hope* (Cambridge, MA and London: Harvard University Press, 1999).

Introduction   **11**

21 Ibid., 1.
22 Kyle Longest and Christian Smith, "Conflicting or Compatible: Beliefs About Religion and Science Among Emerging Adults in the United States," *Sociological Forum* 26, no. 4, (2011): 846–69; Elaine Howard Ecklund, and Christopher P. Scheitle, *Religion vs. Science: What Religious People Really Think* (Oxford: Oxford University Press, 2018).
23 Along the way I can untangle this history from enduring myths, especially around, but not limited to, the Galileo trial, that need to be sorted out before proceeding. See, for example, Ronald Numbers, ed., *Galileo Went to Trial and Other Myths* (Cambridge, MA: Harvard University Press, 2010).
24 To lift the phrase from Will Herberg's influential book, *Protestant—Catholic—Jew: An Essay in American Religious Sociology* (Chicago: University of Chicago, 1983), originally published in 1955.
25 Some examples are the ongoing American Academy of Religion engagement with religion and transhumanism, e.g., in the program unit I co-chair, Science, Technology, and Religion, as well as two 2014 issues dedicated to these topics in the journals *Zygon* and *Theology and Science*.
26 Paraphrasing Michael Liptka, "Millennials Increasingly are Driving Growth of 'Nones'." Pew Research Center, retrieved May 23, 2019, http://www.pewresearch.org/fact-tank/2015/05/12/millennials-increasingly-are-driving-growth-of-nones.

Bibliography

Arnett, Jeffrey. "Emerging Adulthood: A Theory of Development From the Late Teens Through the Twenties." *American Psychologist*, 55, no. 5 (2000): 469–480.

Barbour, Ian. *Issues in Science and Religion.* San Francisco, CA: HarperCollins, 1971 [1966].

Delbanco, Andrew. *The Real American Dream: A Meditation on Hope.* Cambridge, MA: Harvard University Press, 1999.

Ecklund, Elaine Howard and Christopher P. Scheitle. *Religion vs. Science: What Religious People Really Think.* Oxford, UK: Oxford University Press, 2018.

Evans, John H. *Morals Not Knowledge: Recasting the Contemporary U.S. Conflict Between Science and Religion.* Oakland, CA: University of California Press, 2018.

Gilbert, James. *Redeeming Culture: American Religion in an Age of Science.* Chicago, IL: University of Chicago, 1997.

Gordon, Peter. "What is Intellectual History?" (2012 paper), retrieved June 20, 2019, http://projects.iq.harvard.edu/files/history/files/what_is_intell_history_pgordon_mar2012.pdf

Hardin, Jeff, Ronald L. Numbers, Ronald A. Binzley, eds. *The Warfare Between Science and Religion: The Idea That Wouldn't Die.* Baltimore, MD: Johns Hopkins University Press, 2018.

Herberg, Will. *Protestant—Catholic—Jew: An Essay in American Religious Sociology.* Chicago, IL: University of Chicago, 1983 [1955].

Liptka, Michael. "Millennials Increasingly are Driving Growth of 'Nones'." Pew Research Center, retrieved May 23, 2019. http://www.pewresearch.org/fact-tank/2015/05/12/millennials-increasingly-are-driving-growth-of-nones

Longest , Kyle and Christian Smith. "Conflicting or Compatible: Beliefs About Religion and Science Among Emerging Adults in the United States." *Sociological Forum*, 26, no. 4 (2011): 846–869.

MacIntyre, Alasdair. *After Virtue.* 2nd Edition. Notre Dame, IN: University of Notre Dame Press, 1981.

McGrath, Alister. *Religion and Science: A New Introduction.* 2nd Edition. Oxford, UK: Wiley-Blackwell, 2010.

12 Introduction

Mencken, H.L. "Full text of Coverage of The Scopes Trial by H.L. Mencken," *Baltimore Evening Sun*, 1925, retrieved June 20, 2019. https://archive.org/details/CoverageOfTh eScopesTrialByH.l.Mencken

Numbers, Ronald, ed. *Galileo Went to Trial and Other Myths*. Cambridge, MA: Harvard University Press, 2010.

Principe, Lawrence. *The Scientific Revolution: A Very Short Introduction*. Oxford, UK: Oxford University Press, 2011.

Smith, Jonathan Z. and William Scott Green, eds. *The HarperCollins Dictionary of Religion*. San Francisco, CA: HarperCollins, 1996.

Whitcomb, John C. Jr. and Henry M. Morris. *The Genesis Flood: The Biblical Record and Its Scientific Implications*. Phillipsburg, NJ: Presbyterian and Reformed Publishing Company, 1961.

Whitehead, Alfred North. *Process and Reality: Corrected Edition*. Edited by David Ray Griffin and Donald W. Sherburne. New York: Free Press, 1978 [1929].

Whitehead, Alfred North. *Science and the Modern World*. New York: Free Press, 1925.

2

THE PROBLEMS OF DEFINING SCIENCE AND RELIGION

Definitions and their limitations

To define is to separate and, one hopes, to clarify. Sometimes, however, definitions also create problems. In the last chapter I wrote as if *religion* and *science* represent two things. Lurking in my words may lie a desire to reify science and religion as one thing each because then we would have a singular relationship between them. And who wouldn't want that? If we simply could help these two dance in a beautifully orchestrated duet, life might be beautiful. But that convenient pairing was a convenient fiction, a useful heuristic device I employed to move things along. I have to concede that neither *science* nor *religion* enjoys a particularly stable definition, which makes their relationship complicated. Thomas Dixon in his lapidary overview of the field has commented rather provocatively, but not without merit: "There has certainly not been a single and unchanging relationship between two entities called 'science' and 'religion.'"[1] And that makes this book more complex, variegated, and therefore more interesting.

Let me begin with *science*. Certainly, it did not exist as a discrete field for most of American history (and of course for centuries before that). The Latin word for knowledge, *scientia*, was used more generally for a variety of disciplines. What we understand as science was often called *natural philosophy*. This shift in naming had collateral effects. In his brief treatment of the Scientific Revolution, Lawrence Principe offered this analysis:

> Natural philosophy is closely related to what we familiarly call *science* today, but is broader in scope and intent. The natural philosopher of the Middle Ages or the Scientific Revolution studied the natural world—as modern scientists do—but did so within a wider vision that included theology and metaphysics. The three components of God, man, and nature were never insulated from one another.[2]

14 Problems of defining science and religion

The change in nomenclature signaled a shift in scope.

Not until 1833 did the Cambridge University historian and philosopher of science William Whewell coin the term *scientist* to replace such terms as *cultivators of science* (more below in Chapter Four). Indeed, even today there is no one Science with a capital S. In fact—as is the case in French and other languages, but not in English—we would do better to refer to "the sciences" (or *les sciences*) or the "science of x," such as physics, biology, or—to follow Thomas Torrance— even the "science of theology." A.D. Ritchie offers this in his *Studies in the History and Methods of Sciences*, "there is no Science in the singular, for there are only sciences."[3] And "There is no one scientific method that is universally applicable."[4] The failure of the Logical Positivists in the 1920s to sustain their assertion of *verification* and then Karl Popper's later revision, also a failure, to promote *falsification* demonstrate that the "scientific method" of fourth grade science fairs provides no real aid in comprehending what scientists actually do. By the middle of the twentieth century Thomas Kuhn's "paradigm shifts"[5] and Paul Feyerabend's *Against Method* (a book title that apply describes its ethos and tone)[6] further solidify the chaos. For my part, I'm most convinced by Imre Lakatos's "research programme"[7] as well as Peter Lipton's Inference to the Best Explanation[8] as meditating theories between the putative Scientific Method and scientific anarchy, which I'll leave aside for now.[9]

Despite these challenges, defining science represents the less complicated side of the ledger. The term *religion* also has no single consensual definition in the academic guild, nor among its practitioners. The classic five "world religions" of Judaism, Christianity, Islam, Buddhism, and Hinduism all tolerate at best an uneasy relationship with the moniker *religion*. For example, Stephen Prothero has written, "One of the most common claims among Hindus in the West is that 'Hinduism is a way of life' rather than a religion ... *Sanatana Dharma* (Eternal Law),"[10] and many Christians will say that their faith is "a relationship, not a religion." And when one includes Native American cultures, the discussion becomes particularly intriguing. Severin M. Fowles has noted that there is no good word for "religion" among the Southeast Pueblo peoples, but instead the best rendering is "doing," and so he titles his study of their practices and beliefs *An Archaeology of Doings*. [11] I'll stop there, but the citations could certainly be multiplied. It is no less difficult to find an accepted definition among scholars (as I will in a moment). This fact provoked Alister McGrath in his introduction to religion and science to concede, "there is no generally accepted definition of religion."[12] While I appreciate McGrath's intellectual humility, I cannot take recourse to this approach because I need to let the reader know what I mean by these terms.

Peter Harrison has argued that some definitions that we take for granted have only existed in the past 300 years or so. In that sense they are arguably "modern"—i.e., post-Enlightenment—concepts. For that reason he would rather talk of the "territories" of religion and science, not their definitions.[13] Referring to the historic alterations in defining *science*, Harrison writes on the shift from emphasizing an approach to focusing on what it produces:

Overstating the matter somewhat, in the Middle Ages scientific knowledge was an instrument for the inculcation of scientific habits of mind; now scientific habits of mind are cultivated primarily as an instrument for the production of scientific knowledge.[14]

Harrison then describes how views of religion have changed since the time of Thomas Aquinas in the twelfth century: "Between Thomas's time and our own, *religio* has been transformed from a human virtue into a generic something typically constituted by sets of beliefs and practices."[15]

This prodigious and erudite work, which represents Harrison's 2011 Gifford Lectures, is fundamentally discipline-changing and will influence how I describe these two terms in my reconstruction of historical American views on religion and science. Nonetheless, Harrison repeatedly focuses on "beliefs and practices," which is inadequate for grasping contemporary definitions of religion. True, one of the greatest minds in the sociology of religion, Émile Durkheim, offered this definition in his 1912 *Elementary Forms of Religious Life*: "A religion is a unified system of beliefs and practices relative to sacred things, that is to say, things set apart and forbidden— beliefs and practices which unite in one single moral community called a Church, all those who adhere to them."[16] But a great deal has changed in the past 100 years in the study of religion, and any number of more recent commentators such as Robert Bellah, Wilfred Cantwell Smith, Huston Smith, Clifford Geertz, Robert Orsi, and Stephen Prothero do not solely emphasize beliefs and practices.[17] Prothero is perhaps clearest in presenting his "four Cs" of religion: "creed, cultus, code, and community."[18] Obviously beliefs ("creeds") and practices ("cultus") can be found in this palette, but these two do not exhaust his list. Similarly, Orsi, in his ground-breaking *The Madonna of 115th Street: Faith And Community In Italian Harlem, 1880–1950*, coined the term *lived religion* as including "the work of social agents/actors themselves as narrators and interpreters (and reinterpreters) of their own experiences and histories, recognizing that the stories we tell about others exist alongside the many and varied story they tell of themselves."[19] At this point I'll add *myth* or story—narratives about how the world works and our place in it—as central to what a religion does. Its narratives and practices form us. Or, put differently, as George Lindbeck pointed out in his brilliant *The Nature of Doctrine*, [20] religious teachings do not simply express internal states of piety (the experiential-expressive model), but form how we experience life and the world.[21] Lindbeck, appropriating the later Wittgenstein, summarized his *cultural-linguistic alternative*: "a religion can be viewed as a kind of cultural and/or linguistic framework or medium that shapes the entirety of life and thought."[22] Finally, these comments lead to two related definitions—*theology*, "the systematic study and development of religious beliefs and theory,"[23] and *theologians*, those who produce theology.

In addition, what I hope is clear then is that these scholars do not equate religion with belief in a supernatural being.[24] Buddhism, as is commonly known, has many nontheistic forms and it is not even clear that the Buddha himself had much use for a god. Belief in God or many gods may of course be a component of religion in

16 Problems of defining science and religion

the sense that I'm using the word, but there's much more. The scholarly definition of *religion* brings us much closer to *spirituality* in common parlance, especially among emerging adults who play a major role in this book and my methods, which makes it difficult to interpret "I'm spiritual, but not religious." Roughly speaking, to be spiritual is to be religious in the academic study of religion.

From Harrison I've learned a sensitivity to the ways in which the terms *religion* (or *religio*) and *science* (or *scientia*) have changed during the past 300 years in the story I am telling. He thus highlights the problem of *essentialism*, which Joshua Reeves also raises,[25] that there are enduring essences in religion and science, or, put another way, that these two are *natural kinds*; i.e., ones that exist in nature and not simply in the socially constructed world of human beings.[26] Related to the issue of essentialism is the question *Who speaks for a particular religion?* I often tell my introductory to religion students that, in a lecture on Islam, for example, I'm offering general contours for the religion as a whole, but they shouldn't think that this applies to every single 1.8 billion Muslims. If religion is a "thing," then all who participate in this "thing" *ipso facto* agree. But it's not that simple. Religion, like truth, resists simplicity.[27]

Jettisoning essentialism can lead to significant problems, as Reeves admits,

> If one rejects essentialism—if one gives up the assumption that unique features unite science across time and disciplines—then there is no straightforward way to prove the "scientific" nature of theological claims or to assert the cognitive parity of theology and science.[28]

He's right. Although essentialism makes a scholar's life easier, it's deficient. In addition to mourning the loss of essentialism, and as I will continue to argue through this book, we cannot comprehend the relationship of science and religion solely as cognitive categories. And yet, even if I don't swallow anti-essentialism whole in this book—or that we best grasp religion and science as sources of systematic knowledge (alluding to John Evans[29])—I note these critiques as a way to chasten any overly enthusiastic conclusions. And below I will even propose two working definitions.

Finally, before asserting that I can propose those definitions I will further complicate the binary mode of science *and* religion by gradually slipping in a third term (one that admittedly does not even make it into my title): *technology*, which is replacing elements of what has been defined as *science* in the minds of many.[30] In agreement with the comments by Willem Drees, technology is increasingly central to the science and religion dialogue: "The practice of science is culturally and technologically embodied...."[31] In studying the mindset of 18–30-year-olds,[32] I have discovered that *technology* and *science* are closely related. That these two terms appear conjoined merits no particular power for determining their definitions. Nevertheless, we cannot comprehend Artificial Intelligence or genetic engineering, as two examples, except as both scientific and technological pursuits. Moreover, technology and science are actually quite close, and what affected the historical interaction of "science and religion" was not only Charles Darwin's *Origin of Species* but also the development of geography and shipbuilding that brought the English and Spanish to the Americas and thus Darwin to the Galapagos.

With these considerations in mind I arrive at my working definitions—or, perhaps better, as heuristics—of my two key terms.[33] *Science* is "knowledge about or study of the natural world, framed in theories based on observation, which are tested through experimentation." Science studies nature. *Religion*, which is an even trickier term than science, doesn't just "study God," but it can be defined as "the belief in God or in many gods or Ultimate Reality, as well as an organized system of beliefs, ceremonies, sacred stories, and ethical guidelines used to relate to God, a plurality of gods, or Ultimate Reality."[34] Finally I define *technology* as "the use of science in industry, engineering, etc. to invent useful things or to solve problems" and "a machine, piece of equipment, method, etc. that is created by the use of science."[35]

How do science and religion relate? Adapting Ian Barbour's typology

The received wisdom on how best to frame the relationship of science and religion—and thus emerging-adults' attitudes—is the typology constructed by the doyen of this discipline, the late physicist-theologian Ian Barbour. [36] His work has set the agenda for the modern study of religion and science in the past 50 years or so—a topic to which I will return at the end of the book—although there are certainly further nuances to be made. And so I will start with Barbour and later give his work greater nuance. For example, having learned from Evans, the relationship between these two forces is not about a "systematic knowledge conflict" between two elite groups (i.e., scientists and theologians), but more often about moral questions asked by the American populace.[37]Barbour's book, *Issues in Science and Religion,* mitigates Evans's telling critiques in analyzing the wider cultural and intellectual influence of science and religion on America.

Although I will still employ Barbour's typology because of its remarkable staying appeal, I will modify it a bit, particularly in excising his category of *dialogue*, which has always struck me as an uneasy midpoint on the road to integration (where, it seems, Barbour was really headed). Put simply, to dialogue is already to *integrate* at some level. Accordingly I have found that a good place to start is by dividing how Americans relate science and religion into three main categories, *conflict, independence* (or *independent co-existence*), and *collaboration*. After unfolding this critical typology I will also be quick to assert—what I hope to elaborate, if not actually prove, in this book—that the actual future is much more complicated and needs different categories. Still, I will begin here.

Barbour's first category is *conflict*, in which religion and science will never agree. Richard Dawkins certainly represents a key thought leader and perhaps the leading spokesperson of this type. According to Elaine Howard Ecklund and Christopher Scheitle's study of 10,541 participants, 27% of American adults take this view (with

18 Problems of defining science and religion

14% affirming "I'm on the side of religion" and 13% "I'm on the side of science").[38] Consistent with these findings, some students I've interviewed and/or teach are hard-core adherents to the "warfare thesis" promoted in the late nineteenth century by such classic texts as Andrew Dickson White's *A History of the Warfare of Science with Theology in Christendom* and William Draper's also best-selling *History of the Conflict between Religion and Science* [39], and contemporary books by Jerry Coyne, Richard Dawkins, Ken Ham, and Philip Johnson. [40]

Even though the concept of the warfare of science and religion has not survived an onslaught of scholarly critique,[41] it has remarkable staying power in popular culture.[42] As one student, Evelyn, commented in an interview with me, "I think that science and religion will always be in conflict because science and religion will never be able to agree, and there are such contradicting views."[43] This book does attempt to solve one intellectual and culture problem: the disparity of why the warfare thesis has met considerable resistance academically but seems to continue to thrive popularly. A partial answer is that, though historians and academics don't see the conflict, there's a *perception* of conflict at the popular level. For example, conservative Protestants, who represent about 20% of the American populace, do see a conflict with science, and the media over-represent their views because it is effective journalism.[44] Conflict sells even as it distorts.

Ecklund and Scheitle found that 35% of US adults hold the second view, *independence*, or *independent co-existence*, which understands religion and science as two completely different ways to look at the world that ought to remain separate. Stephen Jay Gould and his Non-Overlapping Magisterial Authority (NOMA) is its most well-known proponent.[45] I love this from Gould: "Science and religion do not glower at each other … [but] interdigitate in patterns of complex fingering, and at every fractal scale of self-similarity."[46] I love this citation because I'm not entirely sure what it means. He's more clear when he writes that religion and science each possess a domain of teaching authority that does not overlap with the other.[47] Similarly, the 1981 policy statement of the National Academy of Science phrases it this way: "Religion and science are separate and mutually exclusive realms of human thought whose presentation in the same context leads to misunderstanding of both scientific theory and religious belief."[48] (Again, worthy of note is that NAS emphasizes that these are "realms of human thought," where the relation, and especially conflict, may lie in morality.)

Certainly, given the differences between science and religion, independent coexistence makes a great deal of common sense. My study and research also indicate that many take this approach when they are not really sure what they believe. In addition, this generation has been nurtured in pluralism and one of its most important coping mechanisms, tolerance. With this in mind I can make sense of one student's description of the atmosphere at my university (California State University at Chico) and thus this position: "Science is science, and religion is religion. Not much of a blend between the two." For many, blending results in an odd-tasting cultural smoothie.

Third, the largest slice of Americans in Ecklund and Scheitle's survey, at 38%, endorses an *integration* or *collaboration* of science and religion. In other words, both disciplines need to make a difference to each other by collaborating and learning from the other. Here one thinks of Francis Collins, who brings his evangelical Christian faith to mainstream science, "I find that studying the natural world is an opportunity to observe the majesty, the elegance, the intricacy of God's creation."[49] Or Pope Paul II's notable letter to George Coyne, "Science can purify religion from error and superstition; religion can purify science from idolatry and false absolutes. Each can draw the other into a wider world, a world in which both can flourish."[50] But, frankly, I'm most astounded by John Calvin's comments about taking in the insights from non-canonical authors. Whatever Calvin's particular views on science were, this theoretical framework stoutly supports an integrationist model, "If we regard the Spirit of God as the sole fountain of truth, we shall neither reject the truth itself, nor despise it wherever it shall appear, unless we wish to dishonor the Spirit of God."[51] Note Calvin's word—not simply *forget* or *evade*, but *dishonor*!

There are some ways to massage and nuance these types. Emerging adults—and an emerging view in our country—recommend exploration or a creative choosing of components from each. One of the students I interviewed was nurtured by her father's Catholic background and Buddhist spiritual practice to embrace all forms of spirituality, including those that come directly from science. In a phrase that one commonly hears, "Everyone has the right to their own beliefs."

Indeed, it's tempting to cherry pick and create a unified narrative, but in fact there is no one type that perfectly summarizes American negotiation of science and religion. In fact, following the careful historical analysis of John Hedley Brooke, I agree with his *complexity thesis* and that the adjective *complex*—rather than *warring* or *harmonious*, or a host of others—best represents the way that science and religion have related, especially in our country. Brooke offers a needed correction to the primness of all these categories when he writes, "Serious scholarship in the history of science has revealed so extraordinarily rich and complex a relationship between science and religion in the past that general theses are difficult to sustain. The real lesson turns out to be the complexity."[52] Complexity and a variegated tapestry best describe the relationship of these two titanic forces, and so I am indeed persuaded by Brooke's analysis, even if it is much harder to advocate as an approach to science and religion than a simple conflict or harmony mode. It represents the interpretation that undergirds this book.

With these comments in mind—and the promise of returning to them in the final pages of this book—I can turn to where science and religion have fit in the history of our country.

A brief meditation on science and religion in America

America has often exhibited a dialectical relationship with science and religion, often expressed with rationality and order in conversation, feeling, and intuition. In

20 Problems of defining science and religion

James Gilbert's view, science and religion "are words suggesting two great and opposing philosophic systems—materialism and idealism—that, in a variety of forms, operate as polarities in American culture."[53] And since I begin this study with seventeenth-century European colonies in the south-west and particularly the north-east, it is even anachronistic to speak of "America" or "the United States." Nonetheless, a tensive—and sometimes contentious—relationship exists between these two forces, which of course continues to the present day.

One of Robert Jenson's comments (as he unfolds the thought of Jonathan Edwards) struck me, "America has been more than other nations undone by alternate fear of science itself and capitulation to usually jejune science-inspired ideologies."[54] For a nation as unusually religious as ours—we are outliers as a developed country—any uneasy antiphonal response to science merits our attention. Or, to use Whitehead's categories above, as Americans we are often poised between "the force of our religious intuitions, and the force of our impulse to accurate observation and logical deduction,"[55] feeling a compulsion to decide between them. From the citation, it would sound perhaps that religion is solely emotional. And that notion is worth challenging. Whitehead does later comment in the chapter devoted to "Religion and Science" (from which this quote emerges),

> Religion is the vision of something which stands beyond, behind, and within, the passing flux of immediate things; something which is real, and yet waiting to be realised; something which is a remote possibility, and yet the greatest of present facts; something that gives meaning to all that passes, and yet eludes apprehension; something whose possession is the final good, and yet is beyond all reach; something which is the ultimate ideal, and the hopeless quest.[56]

That is to say religion seeks to put us in connection with a broader Reality behind the reality we see. It is not simply an emotion, but an intuition of Something or Someone greater than we are.

Some take recourse in a common cliché (even Whitehead's Challenge contains hints): science and religion depict the contrast of "head" and "heart." That idea is somewhat distorting since, at least minimally, we know that emotions and rationality are intertwined and take place in various functions of our wonderfully complex and often chaotic brains. For the past decade or two, affective neuroscientists like Antonio Damasio have noted the close connection between emotion and decision-making,[57] and Luiz Pessoa encapsulated the trend lines of recent research on emotion and cognitive science when he wrote, "there are no truly separate systems for emotion and cognition because complex cognitive-emotional behavior emerges from the rich, dynamic interactions between brain networks."[58] And yet the head/heart dichotomy begins to bring us to the right position in understanding our heritage in the United States. Historically, we want either to be warmed in our feelings about the world around us—to see meaning and order and beauty—or to have our thinking kindled—to analyze the particulars of how things fit together.[59] The eminent historian of American religion Claude Welch labels the three main threads in the eighteenth century "pietism, rationalism, and romanticism." In my view, the former and latter are both cut from similar human cloth. In addition, Romanticism is often a secularized religion, and rationalism weaves the thread of science in our culture.

How to make the decision about what to include in this story? My training is intellectual and religious history as well as philosophical and comparative theology, and so that offers me direction. I'll focus on American religious and cultural history and how science contributed. In addition, I learned from Robert McCauley in *Religion is Natural and Science is Not* that our human cognition is drawn to story and ritual—the stuff of religions—while the actual work of science is complicated and unnatural (as is the systematic formulation of religious teaching we call "theology.") As human beings with malleable brains we can learn unnatural ways to think, such as the rigorous methods of science. But they are not natural and therefore remain the interests of the scientifically trained. This means that when science has truly affected our culture, it's not the experiments but the larger story of ourselves and our world—the religious aspects perhaps. Albert Einstein's special relativity theory is amazing science, but when we hear that time dilates, that's an astounding story. Charles Darwin's theory of evolution through natural selection is ground-breaking science, but what influences culture is that we are more similar to chimpanzees, and less special, than we thought. And so, in the following pages, I'll not only note the science for science's sake, but science for culture's sake. And that indeed is what interacted most with religious life in America.

The story I'm telling finds its roots in the past, brings us to the present of science and religion (from the mid-1960s to the early decade or so of this millennium), and then looks at the future of religion in the United States. This might be a spoiler alert, but mine is a narrative in which no generation ever arrives at a fixed relationship between these two cultural forces (or sets of forces), but one in which we continually negotiate how religion and science will relate. It's less clear but, to my mind, more exciting. And as Gilbert wrote in his study of religion and science in the United States, it's very American.

> The dialogue between science and religion in America expresses essential ideas and deep-seated structures of culture. It reveals a theological problem and a profound concern of philosophy; it also shapes a significant portion of everyday popular culture. It provides categories for thinking about modern existence: to structure the world as divided between science and religion, or to imagine it united with their convergence.[60]

To take this conversation up a notch intellectually then, in some ways this book represents my contribution to American intellectual and cultural history. And this brings me to a few considerations. By *culture*, I'll proceed with *Webster's* first entry, "the customary beliefs, social forms, and material traits of a racial, religious, or

22 Problems of defining science and religion

social group."[61] Talcott Parsons has further clarified that culture "consists in those patterns relative to behavior and the products of human action which may be inherited, that is, passed on from generation to generation independently of the biological genes."[62] Biology is nature, and when I speak of "human culture" it is what human beings *cultivate* in their various spheres of life. And when I talk of "American culture" I'm referring to the second definition primarily. Finally, it's impossible to talk about culture (at least for me) without referring to Clifford Geertz's iconic definition of "culture," "historically transmitted patterns of meanings embodied in symbols, a system of inherited conceptions expressed in symbolic forms by means of which men communicate, perpetuate, and develop their knowledge about and attitudes toward life."[63]

Michel Foucault called a period of intellectual history an *episteme*, [64] which "defines the conditions of the possibility of all knowledge."[65] Helen Longino offers a succinct explanation: Foucault employed *episteme* "to refer to the systematically interconnected set of vocabulary, formation rules, rules of truth, and the like that constitute, generate, and sustain a discourse about a domain." Foucault, in a more elaborated form, offers this additional definition, which also demonstrates a sensitivity to the nuances of the term *science*:

> I would define the *episteme* retrospectively as the strategic apparatus which permits of separating out from among all the statements which are possible those that will be acceptable within, I won't say a scientific theory, but a field of scientificity, and which it is possible to say are true or false. The *episteme* is the "apparatus" which makes possible the separation, not of the true from the false, but of what may from what may not be characterized as scientific.[66]

Epistemes do not neatly separate like to fists abutted, but often overlap *in patterns of complex fingering* (to appropriate an image from Gould's playbook). One period gradually recedes while another advances, and for a time they overlap. This is certainly accurate for grasping the intellectual climate of pre- and post-Darwin. (And yet I must observe that, even today, religions often operate in a pre-Darwinian *episteme*, while the scientific community is decidedly post-Darwinian.)

At the same time, my periodization below—sometimes as simple as divisions by decades—is admittedly an overly neat transition. I do not subscribe to some Hegelian *Zeitgeist*, which would render this project an attempt to discern a particular "spirit" in each age and, *voila!*, out comes the right intellectual history. To be sure, the periods I propose are not arbitrary, and some I have discovered as standard designations. But they are primarily heuristics, to be used lightly but ultimately to create a positive *theoria,* which I'm using in its root meaning as something designed to help us see more clearly.

C.S. Lewis, in his 1955 inaugural lecture at Cambridge University, began by remarking on the combination in the newly created chair, "Medieval and Renaissance English," that scholars increasingly saw little antithesis between these periods. He then made a broader point about the limits of periodizing. He cited G.M. Trevelyan,

"Unlike dates, periods are not facts. They are retrospective conceptions that we form about past events, useful to focus discussions, but very often leading historical thoughts astray." Lewis commented:

> The actual temporal process, as we meet it in our lives (and we meet it, in a strict sense, nowhere else) has no divisions, except perhaps those "blessed barriers between day and day," our sleeps. Change is never complete, and change never ceases. Nothing is ever quite finished with; it may always begin over again.... And nothing is quite new; it was always somehow anticipated or prepared for. A seamless, formless continuity-in-mutability is the mode of our life. But unhappily we cannot as historians dispense with periods.[67]

He added a few sentences later, "There is nothing in history that quite corresponds to a coastline or a watershed in geography."[68] I am not an historian—and this is not, strictly speaking, a book of history—but in creating this historical sketch I will necessarily make divisions. As Whitehead phrased it, "The guiding motto in the life of every natural philosopher should be, 'Seek simplicity and distrust it.'"[69]

Moreover, in writing this book I have become convinced that we have done best as a culture when we have held both religion and science together. It's my related conviction that human beings are at their best with this same combination. My intent in this book, however, is primarily to observe and not to promote. And a way of understanding this study is to ask how these two cultural forces interrelate, as well as to chart on this spectrum the key thinkers and movements. And yet it almost immediately becomes more complicated because those who privilege science and rationality may seek to bring feeling under its aegis. Worth noting, as we seek to take in the intellectual history of the United States in this way, is that *science* and *religion* are often symbols in wider cultural currents and are not only what scientists and religious leaders practice and teach about. As I've written above (and is worth at least one repetition per chapter), what we today call "science" and "religion" doesn't map exactly onto our history.

One final point (which may have already been in your mind as a reader). There's one thing I need to warn you about – the religion I'm addressing, especially in the initial chapters on the history of our country, may strike the reader as unquestioningly singular, that is to say, Christian. You might ask, how can I possibly begin with the term *religion* in the singular when today it is a pluralized and multiform reality? I'm endeavoring to understand what to do with religion today and, especially, in the future within the United States of America. This is not to deny that Native American religions had been present for centuries before Protestant or Catholic conquests, nor that many African slaves who were forced to come to the United States were Muslim. And, in fact, these voices have gained strength over the past several decades. Admittedly this book studies the dominant cultural narrative. It needs to be complemented by other texts. Nevertheless, in order to focus I'll take it as a pardonable restriction that I can focus on Christianity, and my primary story remains Christian in the early centuries of our country as a group of

24 Problems of defining science and religion

colonies, or perhaps a "pre-nation" (if you'll allow me to use that term), and then as a nation. More broadly, the interaction of modern science and its rise in Europe naturally makes its interaction with Christianity more extensive. Nonetheless, the presence and gradual growth of religions outside of Christianity has a steady build in my narrative, and certainly in the present (which I define as 1966 to today) and the future the discussion about religion must be pluralized. The future—to which I am heading—will certainly contain a variety of voices beyond Christianity.

Notes

1 Dixon, *Science and Religion: A Very Short Introduction* (Oxford: Oxford University Press, 2008), 3.
2 Lawrence Principe, *The Scientific Revolution: A Very Short Introduction* (Oxford: Oxford University Press, 2011), 27.
3 Thomas Torrance, *Theological Science* (Oxford: Oxford University Press, 1969), 106.
4 Ibid., 107.
5 Thomas Kuhn, *The Structure of Scientific Revolution*, 4th edition. (Chicago: University of Chicago Press, 2012 [1962]).
6 Paul Feyerabend, *Against Method,* 3rd edition. (London: Verso, 1993).
7 Imre Lakatos, "Falsification and the Methodology of Scientific Research Programmes," in *Criticism and the Growth of Knowledge*, ed. Imre Lakatos and Alan Musgrave (Cambridge: Cambridge University Press, 1970), 91–106.
8 Peter Lipton, *Inference to the Best Explanation*, International Library of Philosophy (New York: Routledge, 2004).
9 I'll return to this topic in the final section when I consider Joshua Reeves's new book, *Against Methodology in Science and Religion: Recent Debates on Rationality and Theology*, Routledge Science and Religion Series (Oxfordshire: Routledge, 2018).
10 Prothero, *God Is Not One: The Eight Rival Religions That Run the World* (San Francisco: HarperOne, 2010), 135.
11 Severin Fowles, *Secularism and the Study of Pueblo Religion* (Santa Fe, NM: School for Advanced Research Press, 2013).
12 Alister McGrath, *Religion and Science: A New Introduction*, 2nd edition. (Oxford: Wiley-Blackwell, 2010), 5.
13 Peter Harrison, *The Territories of Science and Religion* (Chicago: University of Chicago Press, 2015), chapter 1.
14 Ibid., 15.
15 Ibid., 16.
16 Émile Durkheim, *The Elementary Forms of the Religious Life*, trans. Karen E. Fields (New York: Free Press, 1995), 44.
17 Here I think of my first reading of Wilfred Cantwell Smith's *The Meaning and End of Religion* (Minneapolis, MN: Fortress, 1991), which made the definition, and study, of religion both more problematic and more interesting.
18 Prothero, *God is Not One*, 324.
19 Robert Orsi, *The Madonna of 115th Street: Faith And Community In Italian Harlem, 1880–1950* (New Haven, CT: Yale University Press, 2002), xxxix.
20 *The Nature of Doctrine: Religion and Theology in a Postliberal Age* (Philadelphia: Westminster Press, 1984).
21 Ibid., chapter 2, especially 31ff.
22 Ibid., 33.
23 This is my definition, assembled from a variety of sources. I will apply the term often to Christian theologians and to other traditions when it applies.

Problems of defining science and religion **25**

24 James Turner's study of the rise of unbelief ("the continuing absence of a conviction that any such superhuman power exists") runs therefore in a slightly different direction from this study (*Without God, Without Creed: The Origins of Unbelief in America* [Baltimore and London: Johns Hopkins, 1985]), xv.

25 Reeves, *Against Methodology*, e.g., 122ff.

26 "To say that a kind is *natural* is to say that it corresponds to a grouping that reflects the structure of the natural world rather than the interests and actions of human beings," *Stanford Encyclopedia of Philosophy*, "Natural Kinds," March 15, 2007, retrieved July 31, 2019, https://plato.stanford.edu/entries/natural-kinds, https://plato.stanford.edu/entries/natural-kinds.

27 An adaptation of a phrase attributed to John Green, retrieved June 24, 2019, https://www.goodreads.com/quotes/335186-truth-resists-simplicity.

28 Reeves, *Against Methodology*, e.g., 124.

29 John Evans, *Morals Not Knowledge: Recasting the Contemporary U.S. Conflict Between Science and Religion* (Oakland: University of California Press, 2018), 87ff.

30 This emerged from a study, funded by the John Templeton Foundation (JTF), of 18–30-year-olds I conducted in 2014–2015 called SEYA (Science for Students and Emerging Adults), http://www.scientistsincongregations.org/seya. More on that study in subsequent chapters. The opinions in this book are mine, not necessarily those of JTF.

31 Willem B. Drees, "Techno-secularity and Techno-sapiens: Religion in an Age of Technology," *Zygon: Journal of Religion and Science* 48, no. 1 (2013): 6, retrieved June 20, 2019, www.zygonjournal.org/technology.html.

32 Greg Cootsona, "Some Ways Emerging Adults Are Shaping the Future of Religion and Science." *Zygon: Journal of Religion and Science* 51, no. 3 (2016): 557–72.

33 These are the definitions I have adapted from various dictionaries and standard texts in the field, which I then reworked and finally employed in teaching religion and science to undergraduates (i.e., 18–23-year-olds). So far these definitions have worked reasonably well, and so I will employ them in this book.

34 I've cobbled together this definition from a variety of sources (e.g., Prothero, Smith). Still, the sources for my definition aren't responsible, but neither is it an entirely *de novo* creation from my brain.

35 Merriam-Webster Dictionary, s.v. "technology," definition for English Language Learners, retrieved May 21, 2019, www.merriam-webster.com/dictionary/technology.

36 See Ian Barbour, *Issues in Science and Religion* (San Francisco: HarperCollins, 1971 [1966]).

37 See, for example, Evans, *Morals Not Knowledge*, 84.

38 Elaine Howard Ecklund and Christopher Scheitle, *Religion vs. Science: What Religious People Really Think* (Oxford: Oxford University Press, 2018), 64, summarized in Table 4.4.

39 Andrew Dickson White, *A History of the Warfare of Science with Theology in Christendom* (BibiloLife, 2009 [1896]) and William Draper's best-selling *History of the Conflict between Religion and Science* (BibiloLife, 2008 [1874]). Worth adding here is that some commentators note that these are still two of the most widely read texts on science and religion.

40 Philip Johnson, *Darwin on Trial*, 20th anniversary edition. (Downers Grove: IVP Books, 2010), and Ken Ham, Answers in Genesis, retrieved June 20, 2019, https://answersingenesis.org.

41 Jeff Hardin, Ronald L. Numbers, and Ronald A. Binzley, eds., *The Warfare Between Science and Religion: The Idea That Wouldn't Die* (Baltimore: Johns Hopkins University Press, 2018) and Ronald Numbers, ed., *Galileo Goes to Jail and Other Myths about Science and Religion* (Cambridge, MA: Harvard, 2010). For a wider context, see also Gary B. Ferngren, *Science and Religion: A Historical Introduction* (Baltimore: Johns Hopkins University Press, 2002); David C. Lindberg and Ronald L. Numbers, eds., *Where Science and Christianity Meet* (Chicago: University of Chicago, 2003); Thomas Dixon, Geoffrey Cantor, and Stephen Pumfrey, eds., *Science and Religion: New Historical Perspectives* (Cambridge: Cambridge University Press, 2010).

42 Besides a few adherents in scholarly work, e.g., Roland Bénabou, Davide Ticchi, and Andrea Vindigni, "Forbidden Fruits: The Political Economy of Science, Religion, and

26 Problems of defining science and religion

Growth," 2013, retrieved June 23, 2019, https://www.princeton.edu/~rbenabou/papers/Religion%20December%201g_snd.pdf, the conflict thesis is prevalent in popular treatments, e.g., Jerry Coyne, *Faith Versus Fact: Why Science and Religion Are Incompatible* (New York: Penguin, 2016) and Richard Dawkins, *The God Delusion* (New York: Mariner, 2008).

43 These quotes from students, and those that follow, are all taken from my qualitative interviews partly for the SEYA project, but also for continuing personal research.

44 John Evans, in *The Warfare Between Science and Religion*, 330ff.

45 A quite short but entirely useful version can be found here: Stephen Jay Gould, "Non-overlapping Magisteria," *Natural History* 106 (1997): 16–22.

46 Stephen Jay Gould, *Rock of Ages: Science and Religion in the Fullness of Life* (New York: Ballantine Books, 2002), 63.

47 Gould, "Nonoverlapping Magisteria."

48 National Academy of Sciences, "Compatibility of Science and Religion," retrieved June 20, 2019, http://www.nas.edu/evolution/Compatibility.html.

49 In David van Biema, *God vs. Science*. Time 168 (2006, November13): 50.

50 Pope John Paul II, quoted in Robert John Russell, William R. Stoeger, and George V. Coyne, eds., *Physics, Philosophy, and Theology* (Notre Dame, IN: University of Notre Dame Press, 1988), 13.

51 John Calvin, *Institutes*, 2.2.15.

52 John Hedley Brooke, *Science and Religion: Some Historical Perspectives* (Cambridge: Cambridge University Press, 1991), 5.

53 James Gilbert, *Redeeming Culture: American Religion in the Age of Science* (Chicago: University of Chicago, 1997), 12.

54 Robert W. Jenson, *America's Theologian: A Recommendation of Jonathan Edwards* (New York: Oxford University Press, 1988), 34.

55 A.N. Whitehead, *Science and the Modern World* (New York: Free Press, 1925), 181.

56 Ibid., 191–2.

57 Antonio Damasio, *Descartes' Error: Emotion, Reason, and the Human Brain* (New York: Grosset/Putnam, 1994).

58 Luiz Pessoa "On the Relationship between Emotion and Cognition," *Nature Reviews Neuroscience* 9 (2008): 148.

59 Claude Welch, *Protestant Thought in the Nineteenth Century*, 2 vols. (New Haven and London: Yale University, 1972, 1985), I: 22.

60 Gilbert, *Redeeming Culture*, 322.

61 Meriam-Webster's Dictionary, "culture," retrieved June 24, 2019, https://www.merriam-webster.com/dictionary/culture.

62 Talcott Parsons, *Essays in Sociological Theory* (Glencoe, IL: Sagwan Press, 1949), 8.

63 Clifford Geertz, *The Interpretation of Cultures* (New York: Basic Books, 1973), 89.

64 Helen Longino, *The Fate of Knowledge* (Princeton: Princeton University Press, 2002), 86. Longino is referring to Foucault's *The Order of Things: An Archaeology of the Human Sciences* (London: Tavistock, 1970) and *The Archaeology of Knowledge*, trans. A. M. Sheridan Smith (New York: Pantheon Books, 1972).

65 *Les Mots et les choses*, 179, my translation. See *The Order of Things*, 168.

66 Foucault, *Power/Knowledge: Selected Interviews and Other Writings, 1972–1977*, Colin Gordon, ed. (New York: Pantheon, 1980), 197.

67 C.S. Lewis, *They Asked for a Paper: Paper and Addresses* (London: Geoffrey Bles, 1962), 10–11, citing Tevelyan, *English Social History* (London, 1944), 92.

68 Lewis, *Paper*, 11.

69 A.N. Whitehead, *The Concept of Nature* (Cambridge: Cambridge University Press, 1920), 46.

Bibliography

Barbour, Ian. *Issues in Science and Religion*. San Francisco, CA: HarperCollins, 1971 [1966].

Bénabou, Roland, Davide Ticchi and Andrea Vindigni. "Forbidden Fruits: The Political Economy of Science, Religion, and Growth." (2013). Retrieved June 23, 2019. Available at https://www.princeton.edu/~rbenabou/papers/Religion%20December%201g_snd.pdf

Brooke, John Hedley. *Science and Religion: Some Historical Perspectives*. Cambridge, UK: Cambridge University Press, 1991.

Calvin, John. *The Institutes of the Christian Religion*. Edited by John T. McNeil. Translated by Ford Lewis Battles. Two volumes. Philadelphia, PA: Westminster, 1960 [1559].

Cootsona, Greg. "Some Ways Emerging Adults Are Shaping the Future of Religion and Science." *Zygon: Journal of Religion and Science*, 51, no. 3 (2016): 557–572.

Coyne, Jerry. *Faith Versus Fact: Why Science and Religion Are Incompatible*. New York: Penguin, 2016.

Damasio, Antonio. *Descartes' Error: Emotion, Reason, and the Human Brain*. New York: Grosset/Putnam, 1994.

Dawkins, Richard. *The God Delusion*. New York: Mariner, 2008.

Dixon, Thomas. *Science and Religion: A Very Short Introduction*. Oxford, UK: Oxford University Press, 2008.

Dixon, Thomas, Geoffrey Cantor and Stephen Pumfrey, eds. *Science and Religion: New Historical Perspectives*. Cambridge, UK: Cambridge University Press, 2010.

Drees, Willem B. "Techno-secularity and Techno-sapiens: Religion in an Age of Technology." *Zygon: Journal of Religion and Science*. February 2013. Retrieved June 20, 2019. www.zygonjournal.org/technology.html

Durkheim, Émile. *The Elementary Forms of the Religious Life*. Translated by Karen Fields. New York: Free Press, 1995.

Ecklund, Elaine Howard and Christopher P. Scheitle. *Religion vs. Science: What Religious People Really Think*. Oxford, UK: Oxford University Press, 2018.

Ferngren, Gary B. *Science and Religion: A Historical Introduction*. Baltimore, MD: Johns Hopkins University Press, 2002.

Feyerabend, Paul. *Against Method*. 3rd edition. London: Verso, 1993.

Foucault, Michel. *The Archaeology of Knowledge*. Translated by A.M. Sheridan Smith. New York: Pantheon Books, 1972.

Foucault, Michel. *Les mots et les choses: une archéology des sciences humaines*. Paris: Gallimard, 1966.

Foucault, Michel. *The Order of Things: An Archaeology of the Human Sciences*. New York: Vintage, 1973.

Foucault, Michel. *Power/Knowledge: Selected Interviews and Other Writings, 1972–1977*. Edited by Colin Gordon. Translated by Colin Gordon, Leo Marshall, John Mepham, and Kate Soper. New York: Pantheon, 1980.

Fowles, Severin. *Secularism and the Study of Pueblo Religion*. Santa Fe, NM: School for Advanced Research Press, 2013.

Geertz, Clifford. *The Interpretation of Cultures*. New York: Basic Books, 1973.

Gilbert, James. *Redeeming Culture: American Religion in an Age of Science*. Chicago, IL: University of Chicago, 1997.

Green, John. "Truth Resists Simplicity." Retrieved June 24, 2019. https://www.goodreads.com/quotes/335186-truth-resists-simplicity

Ham, Ken. "Answers in Genesis." Retrieved June 20, 2019. https://answersingenesis.org

Hardin, Jeff, Ronald L. Numbers, Ronald A. Binzley, eds. *The Warfare Between Science and Religion: The Idea That Wouldn't Die*. Baltimore, MD: Johns Hopkins University Press, 2018.

Harrison, Peter. *The Territories of Science and Religion*. Chicago, IL: University of Chicago Press, 2015.

Jenson, Robert W. *America's Theologian: A Recommendation of Jonathan Edwards*. New York: Oxford University Press, 1988.

Johnson, Philip. *Darwin on Trial*. 20th anniversary edition. Downers Grove, IL: IVP Books, 2010.

Kuhn, Thomas. *The Structure of Scientific Revolution*. 4th Edition. Chicago, IL: University of Chicago Press, 2012 [1962].

Lakatos, Imre. "Falsification and the Methodology of Scientific Research Programmes." *Criticism and the Growth of Knowledge*. Edited by Imre Lakatos and Alan Musgrave. Cambridge, UK: Cambridge University Press, 1970, 91–106.

Lewis, C.S. *They Asked for a Paper: Paper and Addresses*. London: Geoffrey Bles, 1962.

Lindbeck, George A. *The Nature of Doctrine: Religion and Theology in a Postliberal Age*. Philadelphia, PA: Westminster Press, 1984.

Lindberg, David C. and Ronald L. Numbers, eds. *Where Science and Christianity Meet*. Chicago, IL; University of Chicago, 2003.

Lipton, Peter. "Inference to the Best Explanation." *International Library of Philosophy*. New York: Routledge. 2004.

Longino, Helen. *The Fate of Knowledge*. Princeton, NJ: Princeton University Press, 2002.

McGrath, Alister. *Religion and Science: A New Introduction*. 2nd edition. Oxford, UK: Wiley-Blackwell, 2010.

Merriam-Webster Dictionary. "Technology." Retrieved May 21, 2019. www.merriam-webster.com/dictionary/technology

Meriam-Webster's Dictionary. "Culture." Retrieved June 24, 2019. https://www.merriam-webster.com/dictionary/culture

National Academy of Sciences. "Compatibility of Science and Religion." Retrieved June 20, 2019. http://www.nas.edu/evolution/Compatibility.html

Numbers, Ronald, ed. *Galileo Goes to Jail and Other Myths about Science and Religion*. Cambridge, MA: Harvard University, 2010.

Orsi, Robert. *The Madonna of 115th Street: Faith and Community in Italian Harlem, 1880–1950*. New Haven, CT: Yale University Press, 2002.

Pessoa, Luiz. "On the Relationship between Emotion and Cognition." *Nature Reviews Neuroscience*, 9 (2008): 148–158.

Principe, Lawrence. *The Scientific Revolution: A Very Short Introduction*. Oxford, UK: Oxford University Press, 2011.

Prothero, Stephen . *God is Not One: The Eight Rival Religions That Run the World*. San Francisco, CA: HarperOne, 2010.

Reeves, Joshua. *Against Methodology in Science and Religion: Recent Debates on Rationality and Theology*. Routledge Science and Religion Series. Oxford, UK: Routledge, 2018.

Russell, Robert John, William R. Stoeger and George V. Coyne, eds. *Physics, Philosophy, and Theology*. Notre Dame, IN: University of Notre Dame Press, 1988.

Science for Students and Emerging Adults study project (SEYA). Retrieved June 20, 2019. http://www.scientistsincongregations.org/seya

Smith, Wilfred Cantwell. *The Meaning and End of Religion*. Minneapolis, MN: Fortress, 1991.

Stanford Encyclopedia of Philosophy. "Natural Kinds." February 15, 2017. Retrieved July 31, 2019. https://plato.stanford.edu/entries/natural-kinds

Turner, James. *Without God, Without Creed: The Origins of Unbelief in America*. Baltimore and London: Johns Hopkins University Press, 1985.

Welch, Claude. *Protestant Thought in the Nineteenth Century*. Two volumes. New Haven and London: Yale University Press, 1985 [1972].

Whitehead, Alfred North. *The Concept of Nature*. Cambridge, UK: Cambridge University Press, 1920.

Whitehead, Alfred North. *Science and the Modern World*. New York: Free Press, 1925.

3

FROM 1687 TO THE AMERICAN REVOLUTION

The importance of the Enlightenment, the Reformation, and the conquest of the New World

In 1608 the eyeglass maker Hans Lippershey applied for a patent on his newly created invention, a *kijker*, which meant "looker" in Dutch and was what we would call a rudimentary telescope.[1] The application proved unsuccessful, but the news of his invention spread and within a few years a far more useful version emerged with a convex objective lens and eyepiece lens. By 1655 Christiaan Huygens had constructed powerful but cumbersome Keplerian telescopes with compound eyepieces. Of course, these discoveries enabled Galileo Galilei's observations and his promotion of heliocentrism. And by 1688 the prodigious Isaac Newton is credited with incorporating the first reflector into his telescopes.

Seeing the world in a new way represents a cardinal principle of the Enlightenment, but it could be argued that more important than an alternative means to view the heavens was how that ability helped Europeans to move around the globe. The conquest of the Americas, and especially North America, only occurred because of scientific and thus technological innovations that allowed Europeans—whether Spanish, English, or French—to travel to the New World. This certainly involved telescopes, cartography, shipbuilding, medicine, and firearms, but that is hardly an exhaustive list. It also represented a confidence in manipulating the material world through technology that allowed Christopher Columbus to set sail for the New World and its treasures—with the blessings (financial and otherwise) of Queen Isabella I of Castille and King Ferdinand II of Aragon the Catholic.

Furthermore, the seventeenth certainly represents a century of genius and the temporal epicenter of the Scientific Revolution. In 1609 Johannes Kepler presented the first two laws of planetary motion. In 1614 John Napier made use of logarithms for calculation, and five years later Johannes Kepler demonstrated laws

30 From 1687 to the American Revolution

of planetary motion, and in 1638 Galileo Galilei described his laws of falling bodies. *Philosophical Transactions of the Royal Society* became the first peer-reviewed journal in 1665 (and thereafter the bane of every tenure-track professor), and in 1669 Nicholas Steno proposed that fossils are organic remains embedded in layers of sediment, which is the basis of stratigraphy. The century produced such a surplus of genius that in 1675 Gottfried William Leibniz and Isaac Newton could fight over who created calculus.[2]

The Scientific Revolution of the sixteenth and seventeenth centuries in Europe can certainly be critiqued as a concept, but it does indeed represent the science, or natural philosophy, that most affected America.[3] Intellectually it began in 1543 with Nicolaus Copernicus's *De revolutionibus orbium coelestium* (*On the Revolution of the Spheres*), which started to upset geocentricism and ended with the "grand synthesis" of Isaac Newton's 1687 *Principia Mathematica*, which mathematically described three simple physical laws that created the foundation for classical mechanics and motion as well as the fundamental force of universal gravitation.

In addition to the science that provided the means for conquest, religious impulses powered the colonization of this country. America was founded for the sake of Christianizing. But what defined Christianity diverged significantly, and two countervailing responses to the sixteenth-century Reformation powered Catholic and Protestant voyages to the New World. As is commonly known, the sixteenth-century Protestant Reformation sought to throw off the shackles of the medieval church. Martin Luther's epic protest against indulgences joined with the voice of John Calvin (though not doctrinal twins by any means) to produce the rallying cries of "scripture alone, grace alone, faith alone" (*sola scriptura, sola gratia, sola fide*), and together they presented formidable challenges to the power of the medieval Catholic Church. And the Mother Church responded by reinforcing its traditional doctrines, employing its military might in the process.

The defeat of the Spanish Armada by the Protestant English in 1588 made this a fairer fight, but for the English Puritans, this wasn't sufficient. They were convinced that the reforming of the Church hadn't gone far enough and thus sought to make their religion more "pure." For their part, the Spanish conquistadors wanted to see how quickly the Reformation could be eradicated, or at least diluted. Thus Catholics and Protestants, fueled by religious fervor, sought a footprint in the New World. Notably, even the name "America" derives from a Latinized version of Amerigo Vespucci, who sailed around the New World in 1501 under the flag of Catholic Portugal.

In addition to Christianizing non-European lands, one has to keep in mind the intellectual colonizing work of the Enlightenment, with its relentless march of rationalizing increasing amounts of cultural territory. Of course, setting its exact boundaries varies, but I date the Enlightenment intellectually between René Descartes' *First Meditations* in 1641, with its assertion of the primacy of the individual rational "thinking subject" (thus his famous *cogito ergo sum*), and Immanuel Kant's 1781 *Critique of Pure Reason*, which began to circumscribe the limits of human rationality. The Enlightenment's tentacles reach all the way into our current consciousness, despite conversations about "postmodernity," "late-modernity," and what I hear at conferences and in scholarly books, "the failure of the Enlightenment project." Though "man" was once the measure of all things, Michel Foucault could declare in 1966, "one can certainly wager that man [*l'homme*] would be erased, like a face drawn in sand at the edge of the sea."[4] Still, no one in seventeenth-century America would have written those words.

Despite what I may have implied (or learned in my undergraduate education), the Enlightenment was not principally anti-religious. In fact it had quite distinct regional variations. In its French versions one sees a stronger anti-ecclesiological bias, while in England and Germany the tone moved toward rationalizing, and thus refining, religion. America represented an outlier: we embraced the Enlightenment political value of republicanism, and even its rationalism, without jettisoning religion. To grasp this idiosyncratic American cultural union of the Reformation and the Enlightenment is to understand religion and science in America and why both are recalcitrant in our country's consciousness.

The Spanish conquest

It has been a well-worn—and in more recent decades, much maligned—tradition to date the beginning of America with Christopher Columbus's sailing his fleet in October 1492. And of course these voyages did not bring Columbus to the land we now know as the United States. Not only were there other incursions of different durations into what we now call the Americas, and particularly what we now call the United States of America, but, instead, more appropriate is to move a century and a half later to the conquests of Francisco Vázquez de Coronado and his search, among other things, for the "hills of gold." Although Jesus declared that we can't serve both God and mammon (Matthew 6:24), the conquistadors were doing their best to subvert this rule.

To make money, as the saying goes, you need to spend money. The quest certainly started with spending. Coronado and those who supported him spent lavishly in both lives and financial resources on this inauspicious undertaking. Accompanied by a handy, movable food supply of hundreds of cattle and sheep and over a 1000 mules and horses as transport, Coronado and his entourage noted the existence of several towns (or *pueblos*), but were disappointed to discover no mythical cities of gold. Nevertheless, they continued undaunted, and still further widespread expeditions found no fabulous cities anywhere in the south-west or Great Plains. Disheartened and broke, Coronado and his men headed back south, leaving a "new Mexico" behind. It is likely that some of Coronado's horses escaped and were later captured and adopted for use by Plains Indians, who, over the next 200 years, made horses the center of their nomadic cultures.

With thousands of livestock and 500 Spanish soldiers and setters, Juan de Oñate journeyed north from Mexico a half century later. On July 11, 1598, he founded the first Spanish settlement in Nuevo Mexico. The religious intent of this incursion was hardly successful—the native peoples listened attentively to the Catholic instruction but few converted, deciding this religion was not a fit with their culture. In response, Oñate became enraged and more brutal, which continued through his successors. Ultimately, on August 10, 1680, the pueblos decided they had to resist, and through an enterprising coordination involving messengers running over great distances, they successfully launched the Pueblo Revolt.[5] Obviously this did not represent the last incursion of the Spanish in the west, and on September 14, 1692, having arrived with troops, Diego de Vargas persuaded the pueblos to peace through a formal act of repossession.

I mention the south-west to note that it was not only the Pilgrims that colonized this country. Everything did not simply radiate from Pilgrim Rock. I could have added St. Augustine Florida, founded by Catholic missionaries and Spanish conquerors in 1565, or Alaska to the far north-west, "the eighteenth century birthplace of Russian Orthodox Christianity in America."[6] I'm also offering a reminder of the religious justifications for these acts, both in the south-west and the north-east. I'm still struck, as a Northern Californian, that almost every major city is named after a saint: San Jose, San Francisco, San Rafael, etc. The legacy of Father Junipero Serra endures. The western states began as the beachhead of the Catholic advance into the New World. It is also inadequate to tell the story of American religion without at least noting the spiritual and religious practice of the indigenous peoples and that this hasn't always been a "Christian America." And, of course, Native American traditions are quite diverse and they represent varied histories and beliefs of individual tribes and clans. For example, as I've mentioned above about the Pueblo Indians, there is no clear word that translates as "religion," and indeed their beliefs may be monotheistic, polytheistic, henotheistic, or animistic, and often a combination of these.

My comments on the Catholic and Native American influence in the story of science and religion will be minor themes. I'm writing a majority, and not a minority, report; although my hope is that other voices will complete what is lacking here. And while the Catholic Spaniards arrived first in the south-west, the Puritans landed in the north-east and began their march into the lands of this country and planted their cultural seeds in its intellectual soil.

The Puritans' colonizing

Even though I will soon move to the eighteenth century, a good portion of the story I'm telling has its roots in the "New England" colonial era, which could be described as largely Protestant, and more particularly Puritan.[7] In this respect I'll turn to Andrew Delbanco again, who begins his recounting of the American Dream as follows, realizing that taking recourse in New England's hyper-Protestants has its cultured despisers:

> Let me begin by proposing to do something the historian Alan Taylor has recently described as "quaint." "What could be more quaint," he asks, "than

From 1687 to the American Revolution **33**

to seek [the roots of American identity] in colonial New England, the land of Puritans, Salem witches, the *Mayflower*, and Plymouth Rock?" Of course, he is right. Anyone who has been even half-awake in the last twenty years or so knows it is no longer safe to assume, as Tocqueville did, that there is "not an opinion, not a custom, not a law" that the New England origin of American civilization does not explain. Nevertheless, that is where I shall look for some clues to understanding our culture as it was first established and as it has since evolved.[8]

Indeed, the science that we know and that has shaped American culture is largely defined by the Scientific Revolution in Europe, and so too the religion delineated by the European Reformation. Seeking to negotiate their lives between the Enlightenment and the Reformation, the Puritan experiment represents a perfect test case for the subject at hand. And Delbanco continues on the next page,

I turn first to New England not because it was the whole story of early America, but because it was the place where the purest—or, if you prefer, most virulent strain of the Christian story first took hold, and from which many variant strains disseminated.[9]

And so I begin there as well and for similar reasons because the Puritan colonies, though certainly not the only strand of the American story, tie more directly with the interplay of religion and science, partly because Puritan pastors, as some of the most educated of their era, deciphered things both scientific and religious. They were the "first public intellectuals" in our country (Delbanco).[10] And as George Marsden has commented, "New England clergy, being the best educated persons in their communities, were often the chief interpreters of the new science" (in this case Locke and Newton).[11] For this reason, since I've had time to limit myself, I hope it's a pardonable limitation to say almost nothing in my narrative about the Catholic presence, such as in the colonies of Maryland or through the French colonies in the north. In fact, the contributions of American Catholic scientists will play a limited role in this book, which I hope can be forgiven, even in the light of the fact that the first American woman to win a Nobel Prize (in 1947) was Gerty Cori (1896–1957), a Catholic.

One colossal component of the Puritan experience—in addition to their significant hardships in colonizing New England—is the certainty of mission that accompanied their arrival in America. Indeed, they represented the "city on a hill," as Jonathan Winthrop stated it in his epic phrase from 1630 aboard the Arbella, paraphrasing Jesus's words from the Sermon on the Mount in Matthew 5:14. This internalized grand destiny fuels an immense American optimism and missionary zeal. In later years it became extended into Manifest Destiny. Its scriptural warrant also signals a key to American culture that will wind its way through these pages: the dominant importance of the Bible. In no other western culture—with the

34 From 1687 to the American Revolution

possible exception of the Lutheran strain of *sola scriptura* in Germany—have high intellectual culture and Biblicism met. (This later becomes a particular crisis in how pro-slavery and abolitionist hermeneuts interpreted the Bible, and which side presented the most faithful, evangelical interpretation of the Scripture. Literalism, let it be said, favored pro-slavery forces in the church.)

In some ways these Puritan colonies pursued religious freedom. We would normally conceive this freedom along the lines of the seventeenth-century Puritan pastor Roger Williams, "The religion of every man, must be left to the conviction and conscience of every man; and it is the right of every man to exercise it as these may dictate. This right is, in its nature, an unalienable right."[12] But of course Williams was a dissenter banished to Rhode Island... more on him in a moment. But first I'll note that religious freedom meant something quite different from what Williams and today's American culture (with Oprah Winfrey, Deepak Chopra, and Joel Osteen) take to be standard usage. As noted by Robert Bellah, Richard Madsen, William Sullivan, Ann Swidler, and Steven Tipton (hereafter "the *Habits of the Heart* team"), the Puritans sought "to escape from a religious establishment with which they disagreed in order to found a new established church. They were seeking religious uniformity, not religious diversity."[13]

In 1636, however, it's no surprise that, when Anne Hutchinson decided to subvert patriarchal authority by starting to proclaim God's message, she created a furor in Boston, and the Puritan divines literally ran her out of town. In March 1638, along with 30 other families, she left for the Rhode Island territory—where Williams was located—and founded Portsmouth. The seed of individual religious spiritual experience that arrived with the Mayflower (or sometime shortly thereafter) found its way into fertile American soil. To some this growth represented weeds that needed to be pulled as soon as humanly possible; to others, beautiful wildflowers. The Puritans certainly lived in the former category, and by the time we come to twentieth-first century America (and probably much earlier) the shift from persecuting Anne Hutchinson the heretic to a country of Anne Hutchinsons gradually became the American norm. This represents a stunning development, but not a completely unnatural one. This growth, around the fertilizer of American individualism, is indeed a significant sub-theme in this book that heads from Anne Hutchinson to today's "spiritual but not religious" crowd.

For most of the seventeenth and eighteenth centuries, Puritanism defined the colonies, especially in their influence on American culture. For almost two centuries, theirs were the leading voices of our culture. Later the spirit of the American Revolution would gradually depose Puritan rule around the turn of the nineteenth century,[14] despite how these values continue to this day. And even before that decline, revivalism, which presents a consistently anti-rationalist (read: anti-scientific) strain in American culture, rocked the staid and carefully managed religious world of Puritanism.

The Great Awakening and its ongoing importance

A central component of this story of America is the sensational change that religious revivals promise. As Winthrop Hudson makes clear in his classic, *Religion in America: An Historical Account of the Development*, one effect of the various revivals was missionary zeal: "Above all, this surging tide of evangelical religion supplied a dynamic which emboldened the Protestant churches of America to undertake the enormous task of Christianizing a continent...."[15]

Our country maintains a revivalist zeal and the distinctive hope that life can begin again. To our continual human question, *Can I change?*, revivals offer a resounding unmitigated *Yes*. And for a country founded by people seeking *the New World*, definitive spiritual renewals fit beautifully. As the Romanian poet Andrei Codrescu once quipped, "The spiritual pastime of Americans [is] getting born again, over and over."[16] A radical moment of change or *conversion* indelibly marked our consciousness and hopes. Instead of continual incremental change—e.g., the notion of *kaizen,* cherished by Japanese culture—we applaud radical, dynamic disruption, with lives marked by a specific *before* and *after*. But, of course, revivals don't always deliver.

The Great Awakening then—which spanned, broadly speaking, the 1730s and 1740s—decisively marked our country's life. Among its many voices, the preaching of Anglican George Whitefield burned into the American consciousness an emotionalism, inner experience, individualism, and thus a move toward "religion" that continues to play a starring role in the drama of our American history. And partly it was the power of the oratory with Whitefield and others like him. Let it be written about Whitefield that his skills were profound enough to be praised by skeptics from Benjamin Franklin to David Hume. The latter once commented that a sermon by Whitefield "surpassed anything he ever saw or heard in any other preacher."[17] Though resisted by the religious rationalist and modernist Charles Chancey, Whitefield found an ally and defender in Jonathan Edwards, to whom I will soon turn. Ecclesiastical leaders could not contain these revivals, which sometimes happened in church buildings; other times in fields of the open air or under the cover of tent revivals; and increasingly in non-religious venues as congregations resisted this enthusiastic and unconstrained new thing.

Worth underlining here is the strain of American individualism that runs through this story. The *Habits of the Heart* team employs a striking phrase, "ontological individualism," which they define: "The individual is prior to society, which comes into existence only through the voluntary contract of individuals trying to maximize their own self-interest."[18] And though I'm still in the eighteenth century, it's not hard to look into the nineteenth and Thomas Jefferson, who declared in an 1819 letter, "I am of a sect by myself, as far as I know."[19] This persisted and morphed through the nineteenth-century Transcendentalists such as Ralph Waldo Emerson, Henry David Thoreau, and, later, Walt Whitman and Charles Eliot Norton, who determined in 1867 that religion is "the most private and personal part of the life of every man."[20] And even in the early twentieth century, specifically 1926, Alfred North Whitehead presented the following definition at King's Chapel, Boston, "Religion is what the individual does with his own solitariness,"[21] as William James described religion as the "feelings, acts and experiences of individual men in their solitude, so far as they apprehend themselves to stand in whatever they may consider the divine."[22] Critical terms and phrases for describing religion in America, such as "individual" (Whitehead) and "individual men" and "whatever they may consider" (James), represent continuation of a tradition started by revivalism. (Note, for example, the contrast with Émile Durkheim's community-focused "collective effervescence."[23]) This individualist trend started, at least here, in the eighteenth century, and we cannot let it leave our minds if we want to understand American religion.

Jonathan Edwards: a brief case study

I will take a bit more space to pause and note a unifying voice that we might overlook, perhaps America's greatest theologian, the Congregationalist Jonathan Edwards (1703–58). He merits a brief deceleration and a measure of sustained attention as a case study in the relationship of science and religion in the eighteenth-century United States and as a symbol of this period, particularly because he gloried in the findings of nature and metaphysics. (Do I need to add that I don't intend to obscure the important contributions of other denominations, such as Methodists, and particularly their founder, John Wesley, who integrated his Christian theology with the best natural science of the day and even wrote his own *Compendium of Natural Philosophy*?[24])

If one followed stereotypes of religion and science in America, one would not expect as conservative a theologian as Edwards to reconcile the antinomies of revealed and natural religion. In some ways this period—and thus this person—represents a time no longer available to us in America, in which a notably conservative Christian theology can be wedded with a robust engagement with natural philosophy (i.e., "science" in contemporary language), even if Newtonian mechanics described to many minds a mechanistic and godless universe. Many, such as the deist John Toland, "had accepted the world of Newton's mechanics of a God who worked through secondary causes, God's personal interventions could easily seem superfluous."[25]

Edwards's life falls in the early part of the story I'm telling. He not only represents a remarkable figure in American intellectual history who brought together religion and science, but also offers us insight into how the eighteenth century encouraged the fusion of these two fields. For example, later I will consider Charles Hodge (1797–1878), who in many ways offered similar insights to Edwards as a Reformed theologian well-informed on matters of science, but around whom the intellectual—and particularly scientific—world had changed so dramatically. Hodge himself commented, "the fact is painfully notorious that there is an antagonism between scientific men as a class, and religious men as a class."[26] With these

From 1687 to the American Revolution **37**

later cultural voices in the air, Hodge's integration of science and Christian doctrine all sounded entirely dissonant and dissimilar from Edwards's.

One way to underline Edwards's importance is to consider how he, though in many ways a unique intellectual, also found his voice at a time when colonial America wanted to grasp the best way "to plunder the Egyptians" and their gold from Enlightenment rationalism (Exodus 3:19–22). Here I'm following Robert Jenson's comments that Edwards and his environment fit together in an almost symbolic fashion:

> The fit between Edwards and America, to be described in this book, may be stated here with utmost schematization: Edwards knew what to make of the great eighteenth-century Enlightenment, and America and its church are the nation and the church the Enlightenment made.[27]

Despite such praise, for more than 200 years Edwards's significance was lost; an irrelevant, intolerant, fanatical Puritan. Thankfully Perry Miller's rediscovery of Edwards in the mid-twentieth century[28] helped rehabilitate him to a rightful place of importance in American intellectual thought. Here is a man who demonstrated early interest in the natural world and wrote a study of spiders as a child, entered Yale at 13 (the average age during Edwards's time was 16[29]) and graduated at 17. Indeed, here was a scholar who subsequently committed to the life of the mind and of a burning piety—a man who rose at 4am and made it a practice to study for 13 hours a day. Edwards was brilliant. So to place him as a leading American intellectual helps expunge the sole image of Edwards as simply the hateful, Puritan preacher who delivered on July 8, 1741, *Sinners in the Hands of an Angry God*, in which God suspends us sinners over the realities of hell like a spider dangles from a web (the one reading from him presented to many American high schoolers).

In Miller's hands, Edwards became a bit *too* rational.[30] We need to take in both Edwards's powers of rationality *and* his theological intensity, his meticulous metaphysics, and his defense of religious affections (or "habitual inclinations at the core of a person's being"[31]). He did in fact preach hellfire sermons. Marsden's magisterial biography of Edwards offers a useful portrayal—the "Angry God" is not exclusive, but still vital, for grasping Edwards's theology.

> In its subject, *Sinners in the Hands of an Angry God* was not unusual either for Edwards or for New England preaching. Preaching on hell was a routine part of covering the full range of Gospel topics, and others' sermons were more lurid in depicting hell's agonies.[32]

With those comments in mind, Miller's exaltation of Edwards is overblown but not entirely wrong: for him, Edwards represented "the last great American, perhaps the last great European, for whom there could be no warfare between religion and science, or between ethics and nature."[33] I appreciate Miller's appraisal of Edwards,

38 From 1687 to the American Revolution

but I cannot agree with his evaluation of where we are today (or even where Miller was in the mid-twentieth century).

Edwards sought to uphold the Great Awakening around Whitefield's preaching and yet to pursue the new lines of natural philosophy. How did Edwards achieve this? In many ways his theological engagement with science drew from his ability to find a mediating concept in the concept of beauty, a nexus for relating theology and science.[34] And this beauty extended to his ideas themselves, which were beautiful. Miller called Edwards an artist, in fact "one of America's five or six major artists, who happened to work with ideas instead of with poems or novels."[35] If leading thinkers today want to bring together these two—and not have them separated or conflicting—some mediating value is usually present.

Beauty, in fact, is one of the key motifs in Edwards's thought, and may be his greatest contribution to understanding science and religion. It remains particularly relevant to this study. First of all, Edwards self-consciously fashioned his work in the wake of Newtonian physics—especially Isaac Newton's *Principia*—and thus engaged in an ongoing dialogue with scientific insight. Edwards presented a fascinating blend of Newtonian physics wedded to sustained Puritan reading of Scripture. As *Christianity Today* wrote, "Edwards believed that God's providence was literally the binding force of atoms—that the universe would collapse and disappear unless God sustained its existence from one moment to the next. Scripture affirmed his view that Christ is 'upholding all things by his word of power' (Heb. 1:3, RSV)."[36] This engagement with science, or, more properly, natural philosophy, characterized the work of clergy in Edwards's eighteenth-century New England. As the most educated members of his society, pastors such as Edwards would naturally comment on the scientific discoveries of their day. In fact, few of his contemporaries thought of theology and natural science in conflict.[37]

Edwards steeped himself in the observation of nature that marked the seventeenth century's exuberant scientific explosion. Consequently he structures his conceptions around the beauty of the cosmos, linking what we would see today separated as "science" and "religion" but which Edwards seems to take as self-evident. He sees a world full of God's glory in a way reminiscent of earlier church writers:

> For as God is infinitely the greatest being, so he is allowed to be infinitely the most beautiful and excellent: and all the beauty to be found throughout the whole creation is but the reflection of the diffused beams of that Being who hath an infinite fullness of brightness and glory.[38]

Beauty for Edwards can be defined as proper relations and harmony, not unlike most of the philosophical and theological tradition that preceded him. Beauty exists within this semantic field for Edwards of "glory," "excellence," and "goodness," and manifests itself where and when things fit properly together; that is when they "consent," to use Edwards's language. As he sets out more succinctly: "Beauty does not consist in discord and dissent, but in consent and agreement."[39]Marsden offers

From 1687 to the American Revolution **39**

the analogy of music, not unlike the music of J.S. Bach, whose subtle and rich harmonies permeate his work. One of Edwards's "favorite terms was 'harmony,' which he often used as synonymous with 'proportion.'"[40]

Although Edwards certainly learned from Berkeley, Descartes, Malenbranche, and Locke, his emphasis contrasted with the emerging Enlightenment mechanistic worldview. Unlike many voices that surrounded him and often worked to cleave fact from value, and thus nature from ethics, Edwards counters with an important move of wedding cosmology to ethics. This is the second movement in his theory of beauty: beauty has ethical implications. To act with virtue is to follow these divine beams (which he called "Being") that shoot through creation. This view of beauty, incidentally, had other consonant voices, such as the fourth Earl of Shaftsbury, whose theory of beauty, which appeared in 1709 in *The Spectator,* and which Edwards probably first read as a student at Yale. Virtue—or a beautifully ethical life—is in line with Being or the cosmos. Therefore the most virtuous life is that which gives glory to God. Miller identifies this as an ethics of beauty: "That which is called 'virtue' is a certain kind of beautiful nature, form or quality that is observed in things."[41] In sum, beauty became an umbrella for both ethical and cosmological telos, unifying theology, science, and ethics.

Beauty encompassed for Edwards the right perception of God and God's creation, as well as living rightly. For Reformed theology following Edwards, God's glory, which includes divine beauty, constitutes the ultimate goal of creation. This was a dialogue—and, often, argument—that he carried on with Francis Hutcheson, a Scottish ex-Calvinist. Hutcheson's work reflects the "turn to the subject" endemic to the eighteenth century that also found its way in the individualism of the Great Awakening: "Let it be observed, that in the following papers, the word *beauty* is taken for *the idea raised in us.*"[42] He also tended to see the beauty of virtue as derived from a universal moral conscience, whereas Edwards emphasized the truly spiritual side of virtue as a component of redemption.[43] Consequently, when there is a realization that a virtuous life is beautiful and pierces the human soul, we are rightly related to God. And conversely Edwards describes the experience of the spiritual life as the apprehension of the beauty of God and of God's creation. Ultimately—and in consonance with the Reformed commitment to divine sovereignty—this is an act of God. Louis J. Mitchell offers this summary: "For Edwards the structure of religious experience was that of beauty. Authentic religious experience began with and was defined by an infusion of the Holy Spirit, God's beauty."[44]

What do we learn from the case of Jonathan Edwards about relating science and religion? Natural philosophy ably pierced through the phenomenal world to see this beauty. Partly, as I mentioned, this was a sociological moment in history when science was expanding and a New England pastor had the goods to interpret this knowledge theologically … or, better, to think scientifically and theologically about nature. It is worth adding that, due to a variety of historical forces as we will see in the coming chapter, this reconciliation was not to last, and therefore I would be gloriously mistaken to proclaim that all we need to do is follow Edwards and the reconciliation of science and religion in the United States would be complete.

40 From 1687 to the American Revolution

Notes

1 The Galileo Project, "The Telescope," retrieved June 20, 2019, http://galileo.rice.edu/sci/instruments/telescope.html.
2 Much of this story can be found in Lawrence Principe's fabulous concise treatment, *The Scientific Revolution: A Very Short Introduction* (Oxford: Oxford University Press, 2011).
3 See Principe, *Scientific Revolution*, 2–3.
4 Famously critiqued by Michel Foucault in *The Order of Things: An Archaeology of the Human Sciences* (New York: Vintage, 1973), 387.
5 From a visit to the Taos Pueblo in January 2017, I can affirm that the memory of this victory still lives in an innovative blend of Catholic symbols into their traditional practices, stories, and beliefs.
6 Edwin Gaustad and Leigh Schmidt, *The Religious History of America: The Heart of the American Story from Colonial Times to Today* (San Francisco: HarperCollins, 2004), 4.
7 Winthrop Hudson, *Religion in America: An Historical Account of the Development of American Religious Life*. 3rd edition. (New York: Charles Scribner's Sons, 1981), 6ff.
8 Andrew Delbanco, *The Real American Dream: A Meditation on Hope* (Cambridge, MA: Harvard, 2000),15, citing Alan Taylor, "In a Strange Way," his review of Jill Lepore, *The Name of War: King Philip's War and the Origins of American Identity, New Republic,* April 13, 1998: 37.
9 Delbanco, *Real American Dream*, 16.
10 Ibid., 34.
11 George Marsden, *Jonathan Edwards: A Life* (New Haven and London: Yale University Press, 2003), 68.
12 Cited in Herbert W. Schneider, *A History of American Philosophy*. 2nd edition (New York and London: Columbia University, 1963), 51.
13 Robert Bellah, Richard Madsen, William Sullivan, Ann Swidler, and Steven Tipton, *Habits of the Heart* (Berkeley: University of California Press, 1985), 220.
14 Delbanco, *Real American Dream*, 43.
15 Hudson, *Religion in America*, 60.
16 Cited Gaustad and Schmidt, *Religious History of America*, 427.
17 A.R. Buckland, ed., *Selected Sermons of George Whitefield,* The World's Great Sermons (London: Religious Tract Society, 1904), xiv.
18 Bellah et al., *Habits of the Heart*, 143.
19 Thomas Jefferson, letter to Ezra Stiles Ely, June 25, 1819, retrieved May 16, 2019, https://founders.archives.gov/documents/Jefferson/98-01-02-0542.
20 Charles Eliot Norton, "Religious Liberty," *North American Review* 104 (1867): 588.
21 A.N. Whitehead, *Religion in the Making* (Cambridge: Cambridge University Press, 1927), 6.
22 James, *Varieties of Religious Experience*, 42.
23 Émile Durkheim, *Emile Durkheim on Morality and Society*, ed. Robert Bellah (Chicago: University of Chicago Press, 1973), 195; cf. Bellah's preface, xliii.
24 See, for example, Mark H. Hamm, "Wesley and the Two Books" in Matthew Nelson Hill and Wm. Curtis Holzen, eds., *Connecting Faith and Science: Philosophical and Theological Inquiries*, Claremont Studies in Religion 1 (Claremont, CA: Claremont Press, 2017).
25 Marsden, *Edwards*, 71.
26 Charles Hodge, *What is Darwininism?* (Scribner, Armstrong, 1874), 126.
27 Robert W. Jenson, *America's Theologian: A Recommendation of Jonathan Edwards* (New York: Oxford University Press, 1988), 3.
28 E.g., Perry Miller, *Jonathan Edwards*, (New York: William Sloane, 1949).
29 Marsden, *Edwards*, 34.
30 Consider this quote from Miller as he analyzes the intellectual acumen of Edwards's *Original Sin*, "Instead of a dialectical demonstration out of given premises, or destruction of opponents with a logical and semantic *reduction ad absurdum*, it is a strictly empirical investigation, an induction, in the manner of Boyle and Newton, of a law for

phenomena" (Miller, *Edwards*, 266–7). Possibly ... or it might just be a theological defense of the Christian doctrine of original sin. Similarly, Marsden's critique about Miller's biography of Edwards is well-placed, "Miller's enthusiasm, mixed with some brilliant insights was of immense value in promoting appreciation and study of Edwards" (*Edwards*, 523, n. 6).

31 Mark Noll, *America's God: From Jonathan Edwards to Abraham Lincoln* (Oxford: Oxford University Press, 2005), 23.
32 Marsden, *Edwards*, 231.
33 Miller, Edwards, 72; quoted in Marsden, *Edwards*, 61.
34 Cf. my article, "How Nature and Beauty Can Bring Scientists and Theologians Together," *Theology and Science* 9, vol. 4 (2011): 379–93.
35 Perry Miller, *Jonathan Edwards* (New York: William Sloane Associates, 1949), xii.
36 *Christianity Today*, "Jonathan Edwards America's Greatest Theologian," retrieved January 25, 2019, http://www.christianitytoday.com/history/people/theologians/jonathan-edwards.html.
37 Marsden, *Edwards*, 66.
38 John E. Smith, Harry S. Stout, and Kenneth P. Minkema, eds., *A Jonathan Edwards Reader* (New Haven, CT: Yale University, 2003), 252. This slim volume provides an accessible collection of other writings by Edwards on beauty: e.g., his early essay, "Beauty in the World," which demonstrates the importance of this theme, or what the editors call "his preoccupation with beauty, excellence, and the goodness of creation" (ibid., xii).
39 Smith et al., eds., *Jonathan Edwards Reader*, 245.
40 Marsden, *Edwards*, 79.
41 Miller, *Edwards*, 290.
42 Cited in Paul Edwards, ed., *Encyclopedia of Philosophy* (New York: Macmillan, 1972), 1:265.
43 Marsden, *Edwards*, 465.
44 Louis J. Mitchell, *Jonathan Edwards and the Experience of Beauty*, Studies in Reformed Theology and History, No. 9 (Princeton: Princeton Theological Seminary, 2003), 30.

Bibliography

Bellah, Robert, Richard Madsen, William Sullivan, Ann Swidler and Steven Tipton. *Habits of the Heart*. Berkeley, CA: University of California Press, 1985.

Buckland, A.R., ed. *Selected Sermons of George Whitefield*. *The World's Greatest Sermons*. London: The Religious Tract Society, 1904.

Christianity Today. "Jonathan Edwards America's Greatest Theologian." Retrieved January 25, 2019. http://www.christianitytoday.com/history/people/theologians/jonathan-edwards.html

Cootsona, Greg. "How Nature and Beauty Can Bring Scientists and Theologians Together." *Theology and Science*, 9, Vol. 4 (2011): 379–393.

Delbanco, Andrew. *The Real American Dream: A Meditation on Hope*. Cambridge, MA: Harvard, 2000.

Durkheim, Émile. *Emile Durkheim on Morality and Society*. Edited by Robert Bellah. Chicago, IL: University of Chicago Press, 1973.

Edwards, Jonathan. *The Religious Affections*. Carlisle, PA: The Banner of Truth Trust, 1986 [1746].

Edwards, Paul, ed. *Encyclopedia of Philosophy*. New York: Macmillan, 1972.

Foucault, Michel. *The Order of Things: An Archaeology of the Human Sciences*. New York: Vintage, 1973.

42 From 1687 to the American Revolution

Galileo Project. "The Telescope." Retrieved June 20, 2019. http://galileo.rice.edu/sci/instruments/telescope.html

Gaustad, Edwin and Leigh Schmidt. *The Religious History of America: The Heart of the American Story from Colonial Times to Today*. San Francisco, CA: HarperCollins, 2004.

Hill, Matthew Nelson and Wm. Curtis Holzen, eds. *Connecting Faith and Science: Philosophical and Theological Inquiries*. Claremont Studies in Religion 1. Claremont, CA: Claremont Press, 2017.

Hodge, Charles. *What is Darwininism?* London and Edinburgh: Scribner, Armstrong, 1874.

Hudson, Winthrop. *Religion in America: An Historical Account of the Development of American Religious Life*. 3rd edition. New York: Charles Scribner's Sons, 1981.

Jefferson, Thomas. Letter to Ezra Stiles Ely. June 25, 1819. Retrieved May 16, 2019. https://founders.archives.gov/documents/Jefferson/98-01-02-0542

Jenson, Robert W. *America's Theologian: A Recommendation of Jonathan Edwards*. New York: Oxford University Press, 1988.

Marsden, George. *Jonathan Edwards: A Life*. New Haven and London: Yale University, 2003.

Miller, Perry. *Jonathan Edwards*. New York: William Sloane Associates, 1949.

Mitchell, Louis J. *Jonathan Edwards and the Experience of Beauty*. Studies in Reformed Theology and History, No. 9. Princeton, NJ: Princeton Theological Seminary, 2003.

Noll, Mark. *America's God: From Jonathan Edwards to Abraham Lincoln*. Oxford, UK: Oxford University Press, 2005.

Norton, Charles Eliot. "Religious Liberty." *North American Review*, 104 (1867): 588.

Principe, Lawrence. *The Scientific Revolution: A Very Short Introduction*. Oxford, UK: Oxford University Press, 2011.

Schneider, Herbert W. *A History of American Philosophy*. 2nd edition. New York and London: Columbia University, 1963.

Smith, John E., Harry S. Stout and Kenneth P. Minkema, eds. *A Jonathan Edwards Reader*. New Haven, CT: Yale University, 2003.

Whitehead, Alfred North. *Religion in the Making*. Cambridge, UK: Cambridge University Press, 1927.

4

THE REVOLUTIONARY PERIOD TO 1859

The deism of Thomas Paine

Jonathan Edwards, the third president of the College of New Jersey (later Princeton University), died in 1758, the victim of a deadly form of smallpox vaccine. (Though conservative theologically, he was no anti-vaxer.) It would certainly be an overstatement to say that bad science killed Edwards, but a scientific ideology was undermining the hegemony of his form of Christianity. To focus on Edwards might distort the picture of America, even in the eighteenth century, a country that has dead roots in Enlightenment "free thinking," deism, a measure of atheism, but especially rationalism. In the Revolutionary period the intellectually cultured gradually eased away from religion and toward an increased rationalism or scientific thought. This is a significant move, though of course not without its complexities.

Accordingly, I'll note a few major scientific developments to set the scene. In 1752 Benjamin Franklin proved that lightning is electrical with his famous kite experiment. In 1763 the British Presbyterian minister Thomas Bayes formulated the first version of his theorem, thus setting out Bayesian probability and further reifying the rigors of logical analysis. In 1796 George Cuvier established extinction, which dealt a blow to the traditional view of divine creation and fixity of all creatures.

As a result, scientific advance and rationalism began to wax, while the moon of religious enthusiasm waned. According to Sydney Ahlstrom, "The revolutionary era was a period of decline for American Christianity as a whole." And Mark Noll, writing with particular sensitivity to the influence of evangelicalism in colonial America, summarized well the religious climate, calling it "Evangelical Decline ca. 1750–1780."[1] To be sure, there were evangelical Christians like Sam Adams, John Jay, Patrick Henry, John Witherspoon, Elias Boudinot, and Roger Sherman, but the most influential during the founding of our country were anti-evangelical.

44 The revolutionary period to 1859

The founders who mattered most—like the Episcopalians George Washington, Thomas Jefferson, James Madison, and John Wilson; the Congregationalist John Adams; and the unattached Alexander Hamilton and Benjamin Franklin—were either so reticent about their own religious convictions or so obviously deist as to represent positive opposition to evangelicalism.[2]

The Founding Fathers engaged in spirited debates about the presence of religion in the foundation of our country—often specifically related to the First Amendment—but, as Noll writes, "the overwhelmingly this-worldly character of those debates reveals no preoccupation with explicitly Christian, much less explicitly evangelical, concerns."[3] The Declaration of Independence's phrase "Nature and Nature's God" hardly echoes the mellifluous voice of Whitefield in his revivals less than 40 years earlier, and in fact exemplifies the surging natural religion and its deism.

This is a stunning change in American religious life, one that cannot be argued as logically necessary, but contingent (as history is wont to be).

One can see a general rationalizing tendency among the religious elite. Some key religious voices in this movement are the Unitarian pastor William Ellery Channing (1780–1842) and, before him, the Congregational pastor Charles Chauncy (1705–87), who occupied the prestigious pulpit of First Church Boston for 60 years. He preached "an optimistic gospel to that effect that the 'infinitely benevolent Creator' was concerned for the happiness of each of his creatures," which melded well with his universalism, a view he first held in secret and then proclaimed in his 1784 sermon *"The Salvation of All Men; the Grand Thing Aimed at in the Scheme of God."*[4] Both men promoted a rationalizing of religious thought. Contrasted with Edwards's relationship with emotionalism, Chauncy's unmitigated rational theology was found in sermons bearing titles such as *Enthusiasm Described and Cautioned Against.*[5] Chauncy hated revivalism's emotionalism because it gave religious believers over to the vagaries of feelings. One week Christians would be excited about their newfound religious vitality, and the next they would return to life as usual. Or as Edwin Gaustad and Leigh Schmidt phrased it in their survey, *The Religious History of America*, "But revivalism is notoriously fleeting, a surge of heightened excitement inevitably followed by a decline and lull."[6]

And, of course, rationalism can head in an opposite direction. Thomas Paine (1736–1809) struck anti-ecclesiastical chords similar to Robert Ingersoll and Richard Dawkins when he grumbled about, in his *Age of Reason* (published in three parts in 1794, 1795, and 1807), "the continual persecution carried on by the Church, for several hundred years, against the sciences and against the professors of science."[7] Note the language: the church is the instrument of *persecution*. Still, Paine, like so many (but not all) Enlightenment voices, was not anti-religion *in toto*—he wanted to replace revealed, and thus irrational, religion with a deism based on the study of nature.

The revolutionary period to 1859 **45**

Roughly 33 years younger than Edwards, Paine certainly represented an anti-phonal view. Born in England in 1736, he moved to the New World in 1774 thanks in part to Benjamin Franklin (who also felt no particular fondness for organized religion) and can be numbered among the pantheon of Founding Fathers, if for no other reason because he participated in the American Revolution. He is probably most famous for his case for revolution pamphlet *Common Sense* and the pamphlet series "The American Crisis."

The Age of Reason, however, contained his most strident words against traditional, revealed religion. For the purpose of creating a foil to Edwards and the majority Puritan voice, a pastiche of his sayings will do. The first demonstrates his individualism, his resistance to organized religion, and his rationalizing faith.

> I do not believe in the creed professed by the Jewish Church, by the Roman Church, by the Greek Church, by the Turkish Church, by the Protestant Church, nor by any Church that I know of. My own mind is my own Church.[8]

This freedom of religion, and its mooring in human will, becomes a moral tirade (at least implicitly) against those who profess a religion in a church structure that they don't truly believe.

> It is necessary to the happiness of man that he be mentally faithful to himself. Infidelity does not consist in believing, or in disbelieving; it consists in professing to believe what one does not believe. It is impossible to calculate the moral mischief, if I may so express it, that mental lying has produced in society. When man has so far corrupted and prostituted the chastity of his mind, as to subscribe his professional belief to things he does not believe, he has prepared himself for the commission of every other crime.[9]

And finally, human beings receive any revelation through their minds, not through sacred texts.

> Revelation is necessarily limited to the first communication—after that it is only an account of something which that person says was a revelation made to him; and though he may find himself obliged to believe it, it can not be incumbent on me to believe it in the same manner; for it was not a revelation made to ME, and I have only his word for it that it was made to him.[10]

For the purposes of this book, Paine notably set his denunciations of the religious *status quo* within an emphasis on scientific reason in antithesis to religious belief. Or as he put it: science is the "true theology."[11] Still, he did not ultimately see a way to negotiate a peace between the two. For Paine and his rationalism it was instead an intellectual version of Sherman's March to the Sea and its scorched-earth policies, laying waste to the traditional religion that stood in his path.

46 The revolutionary period to 1859

Paine's views on rationality and religion raised the ire of many of his contemporaries, including a famous denunciation by George Washington. Paine died in 1809 in Greenwich Village, New York City, only two years after publication of *The Age of Reason*. The famous nineteenth-century antitheist Robert Ingersoll wrote a paean to Paine that's worth a long citation because it demonstrates as much about Ingersoll as Paine and reveals much about the rationalist-scientific strain in American thought.

> Thomas Paine had passed the legendary limit of life. One by one most of his old friends and acquaintances had deserted him. Maligned on every side, execrated, shunned and abhorred—his virtues denounced as vices—his services forgotten—his character blackened, he preserved the poise and balance of his soul. He was a victim of the people, but his convictions remained unshaken. He was still a soldier in the army of freedom, and still tried to enlighten and civilize those who were impatiently waiting for his death. Even those who loved their enemies hated him, their friend—the friend of the whole world—with all their hearts. On the 8th of June 1809, death came—Death, almost his only friend. At his funeral no pomp, no pageantry, no civic procession, no military display. In a carriage, a woman and her son who had lived on the bounty of the dead—on horseback, a Quaker, the humanity of whose heart dominated the creed of his head—and, following on foot, two negroes filled with gratitude—constituted the funeral cortege of Thomas Paine.[12]

Paine represents a countervailing force to traditional religion and religious revival—and even the blending of rationality and "affections" in Edwards—as well as the Revolutionary period's increase in rationalism, liberal theology, and free thought. Given the course I'm following here, this is a simultaneous leaning toward the pole of science in American thought.

Ironically, not only rationalizing deism but also enthusiastic Christianity furthered the disentanglement of religious from political life. Perhaps the most significant decision during the Revolutionary period for the history of religion in America (and thus its relation to science) was, to use Philip E. Hammond's phrase, the "first disestablishment" of religion in the Bill of Rights, which separated church and state.[13] Sidney Mead has noted, "not only had the Established Church of England been rejected, but, more importantly, the very idea of 'Establishment' had been discarded in principle by the new Constitution."[14] And with this first disestablishment, as Roger Finke commented, "The state was denied the privilege, and freed of the obligation, of regulating religion."[15] Thus the individualization of religious life and practice continued to expand.

Blending science and religion with Common Sense Realism

Adapting C.S. Lewis's caveat about periodizing and Michel Foucault's term, the *epistemes* of American culture are never entirely neat. For example, during the years

The revolutionary period to 1859 **47**

between 1790 and 1840 most historians document the Second Great Awakening,[16] a series of religious revivals that sparked remarkable growth in Protestant churches and presented a countervailing force to the growth of deism and rationalism. It could also be credited with reviving the Romantic spirit of emotionalism and enthusiasm.

More importantly, and despite thinkers that sought to divide science and religion, Scottish Common Sense Realism (which some called a key to Scotland's Enlightenment) provided a reconciling force for the two. Commenting on its influence, Herbert W. Schneider wrote, "The Scottish Enlightenment was probably the most potent single tradition in the American Enlightenment"[17] and represented "the marriage of natural science with morals and religion."[18] This realist approach to science, especially mediated through the philosophical work of Glasgow University's Thomas Reid (1710–96), allowed for direct observation as the cornerstone of science, thereby providing a more direct connection with religious belief. It provided for the "gentlemen scientist" who could study nature as a non-specialist, as an *amateur*, literally one who pursues a task out of love (*amator* in Latin) and not for profit.

The motivation behind the development of Common Sense Realism was to impugn the philosophy of another Scottish philosopher, David Hume, who to this day remains an ongoing presence, by way of a prominent statue, in the heart of Scotland's academic life in Edinburgh. Whereas Hume's skepticism in *An Enquiry Concerning Human Understanding* and *A Treatise of Human Nature* led him to replace cause and effect with "constant conjunction" and to question our ability to know the world around us, "Reid's response to Hume's epistemological skepticism featured subtle arguments concerning how ordinary human experience simply required people to take for granted the existence of an external world, real connections between cause and effects."[19] The world outside the knower really exists and can be perceived through common sense. Indeed, real causal connections in nature formed a necessary component of the growth of science—it's challenging to form a science based on Hume's "constant conjunction."

As Noll has observed in his study of American theology from colonial America up to the time of Lincoln, there was an additional element to the surprising rise of Scottish Common Sense Realism in the States in the latter half of the eighteenth century: "Also important for an age growing in its respect for science was the Hutchesonian claim that, by attending systematically to what that moral sense communicated, it was possible to construct a Baconian ethical science."[20] In other words, common sense built moral foundations more secure than Humean skepticism and ostensibly connected to rising science.

Common Sense Realism flowered profusely in American universities such as Princeton, especially under the leadership of John Witherspoon who emigrated from Scotland and imported Common Sense to his new homeland. He was the sixth president of the college (1768–94), as well as a signer of both the Declaration and the Articles of Confederation. "Witherspoon was not the first proponent of the Scottish science of morals in America, but he was soon the most influential"

48 The revolutionary period to 1859

(Noll).[21] Witherspoon's position at Princeton would also have a marked influence on Presbyterians, a prominent denomination in the seventeenth and eighteenth centuries in negotiating rationality and faith. Besides Hutcheson and Reid himself, arguably the more important player in the promulgation of Scottish Common Sense in the States was Witherspoon.

Worth noting is that the flagship training ground for Presbyterian pastors, Princeton Theological Seminary, was yet to open its doors in 1812, but eventually the debate between its leading light, Charles Hodge, and Princeton University's eleventh president, James McCosh (1811–94), would center around how to bring together science and religion after Darwin. Those particulars will re-emerge in the next chapter, though it's worth noting now that "McCosh and his Presbyterian colleagues restored to the evangelical churches a philosophical grounding for their faith which they had lost since Edwards."[22] As I mentioned above, they wedded this philosophy to Baconian induction. This theory followed the scientific work of Francis Bacon (1521–1626) that moved from direct observation to generalizable laws.

All in all, one could hardly overestimate the influence of Common Sense Realism during the period from the latter quarter of the eighteenth century through much of the nineteenth. (Darwinism represents a key force that began to erode it.) Indeed, it represented the most important stream of American intellectual history for my purposes.[23]

A few notes are in order on key early nineteenth-century scientific discoveries. In 1802 Jean-Baptiste Lamarck presented his theory of the inheritance of acquired characteristics, which could lead to a teleological form evolution; that is, natural development directed toward a goal. The famous Scottish scientist and lay theologian Michael Faraday discovered electromagnetic induction in 1831, and Lord Kelvin, another voice for the integration of Christianity and science, formulated the concept of absolute zero in 1848 (among his many scientific achievements).

The early 1800s and a brewing discontent

A conciliatory blend of religion and science emerged in the antebellum period with an accent on evangelical engagement with science, or what Theodore Bozeman called "Doxological Science."[24] For example, Benjamin Silliman (1779–1864) served as one of the first American professors of science (in his case, chemistry and natural history) at Yale College from 1802 to 1853. In 1818 he founded *The American Journal of Science*, the oldest continuously published US scientific journal. Converted to Christianity under Yale president Timothy Dwight, Silliman found that science could tell us "the thoughts of God."[25] And though Bozeman noted where the conversation headed, he also recorded the strong tie between evangelical Christianity and science:

> In the latter part of the century, under the influence of Darwinism and a strong positivist movement, science increasingly asserted itself as an

The revolutionary period to 1859   **49**

autonomous secular force indifferent or antagonistic to traditional religion. But during the antebellum era the initiative lay with evangelicalism. A much older conception of science, forged in the seventeenth century, was strongly reasserted and heavily conditioned the way in which many thinkers envisioned the ongoing scientific movement.[26]

Seen from the twenty-first century, the fabric of science and piety in early nineteenth-century America, mediated by Baconian inductivism, showed signs of fraying. For example, Pierre Simon Laplace's nebular hypothesis offered a thoroughly mechanistic approach to creation. In addition, the notable Christian thinker and Harvard scientist Louis Agassiz, though generally friendly toward traditional religion, proffered polygenesis (that the human races are of different origins). Though the consensus Christian view maintained the unity of all humankind through the first parents, Adam and Eve, Agassiz's polygenesis maintained that some races, such as Africans and Asians, could not be found in the "Table of Nations" (the genealogy of the sons of Noah) in Genesis 10. This also created a convenient scientific basis for slavery, since polygenesis allowed for the superiority of certain races.

And speaking of the Christian scripture, the rise of biblical criticism, as a cause for the decline of evangelicalism and the rise of religious liberalism, is generally set in the late nineteenth century, but the trend of debating how to understand the Holy Book emerged earlier. "The major theological crux of the period leading up to the (Civil) war was the interpretation of Scripture" (Noll).[27] The simplest, literalistic reading of the Bible broadly supports slavery, such as those passages in the New Testament epistles that offer instructions such as "Slaves, obey your earthly masters with respect and fear" (Ephesians 6:5; cf. Colossians 3:22–4, 1 Timothy 6:1–2, 1 Peter 2: 18, Titus 2:9–10). Abolitionists' arguments required a more subtle hermeneutic, and this made them sound more liberal. Similarly, the growing scientific support for an old earth further problematized a literal reading of the Bible. Some like Turner conclude (with some measure of cynicism) that in this period "The veracity of the Bible was rescued only by repudiating its total factuality."[28] Turner was working toward his thesis that the United States grew increasingly more unbelieving in the nineteenth century, which pushed his analysis in a particular direction. Others, with more subtle strokes, recognize that America was fighting over its foundational text. "On the face of it," wrote Noll, "it would be hard to imagine a nation more thoroughly biblical than the United States between the American Revolution and the Civil War."[29] Without an established set of teaching like the Roman Catholic Church magisterium, Protestants, especially in the free church tradition, quarreled over what the text meant in antebellum America.

Looming clouds gradually covered a clear cultural sky. Traditional American religion (especially Puritanism) had lost its clear hold on biblical interpretation and its former dominion on the culture. Notably it was 1833 when Massachusetts abandoned the final vestige of seeking to establish a religion. The *Habits of the Heart*

50 The revolutionary period to 1859

team noticed that, "Once religion is disestablished, it tends to become part of the 'private sphere,' and privatization is part of the story of American religion."[30] This signaled as well that no one religious tradition, in this case Puritan Christianity, held hegemony. And so the marketplace of American religion takes hold—each religious tradition and denomination competing for attention from the market of potentially interested participants and givers.

Partly this shift occurred because the Puritans had lost their ability to captivate the religious market. Part of this disestablishment was intellectual as well. The radical wing of the Enlightenment and the French Revolution, as they made their way into American intellectual life, began to put a wedge between revelation and reason. Similarly, the writings of both William Maclure and Thomas Cooper, prominent and noteworthy leaders in early nineteenth-century geology and chemistry, were intended to clear the study of nature for purely secular ends. In fact, they, as well as Gilbert Vale, Frances Wright, and Robert Dale Owen, believed the observation of nature liberated human beings from the illusions of religion.[31] This produced a number of blocks to an easy association between religion and science.

In addition, Ralph Waldo Emerson (1803–82), the American essayist, lecturer, philosopher, and poet, led the mid-nineteenth century Transcendentalist movement, which intensified an individualizing of American religion. His younger contemporary, Henry David Thoreau (1817–62), brought together work and life as an American essayist, philosopher, poet, abolitionist, yogi, and historian. With words that seem both characteristic of high intellectual culture in the early eighteenth century and remarkably naïve in light of the continuing presence of religion in America, Emerson declared that "the Puritans in England and America found in the Christ ... and in the dogmas inherited from Rome, scope for their austere piety and their longings for civil freedom. But their creed is passing away, and none arises in its room."[32] It is especially this "none" that rings discordant with subsequent history, and yet also signals a somewhat subterranean shift that gradually demonstrated cracks in the foundations of American religious culture. And, of course, today we hear it echoing in the moniker of the *nones* as those not affiliated with any particular religion.

Moreover, restorationist and millenarian movements chipped away authority from Protestant hegemony. Mormons, or the Church of Jesus Christ Latter Day Saints, began with Joseph Smith's visions, particularly the presentation of golden tablets in "reformed Egyptian" hieroglyphics in upstate New York in the 1820s and his efforts to restore the true church in the "latter days." Smith's extra-biblical scriptures, his denunciations of the various Protestant churches, and his pronouncements on polygamy, among other things, made him exceedingly controversial. After Smith's 1844 murder at the hands of a mob in Carthage, Illinois, the Mormons followed Brigham Young to what would become the Utah Territory, focused around Salt Lake City. In the 1840s William Miller, an American Baptist preacher, is credited with beginning the mid-nineteenth century North American religious movement known as Millerism, which spawned Seventh Day

The revolutionary period to 1859 **51**

Adventism. I note these two—among many other possible options—primarily as signs of religious splintering. What religion would Americans bring to science?

Key words and critical shifts

Certain key words began to change significantly in the 19th century.

In the 1830s the definition of *science* shifted and the term *scientist* was coined. As Louis Principe noted, the move from *natural philosophy* to *science* (meaning largely the natural sciences) brought a restriction that eliminated, at least to some degree, theology and metaphysics.[33] Science increasingly eschewed those realities that could not be counted or calculated. The nineteenth-century Cambridge geologist Adam Sedgwick (and teacher of Charles Darwin) defined the term *science* in 1833: "the consideration of all subjects, whether of a pure or mixed nature, capable of being reduced to measurement and calculation."[34] God, as it were, cannot be measured and began not to be invited into the conclusions of scientific scholarship.

Another key historical moment arrived in 1833 when the Rev. William Whewell (1794–1866), an English polymath—poet, astronomer, and philosopher of science, among other things—who had coined many hybrid terms, including *ion, anode,* and *cathode*—added *scientist* to the list. *Scientist* later found its way into an 1834 publication in the same paragraph in which he created *physicist*. [35] Interestingly, he wanted to avoid gender connotations of "man of science" for at least two reasons: first, because of its appearance in a positive review of Mary Somerville's *On the Connexion of the Physical Sciences*, and, second, because of "the newness of Somerville's endeavor—her attempt to connect all the physical sciences with one another."[36]

I take this new word as a signal. Among other things, the practice of what we know today as *natural science* was becoming sufficiently complicated that it needed specific practitioners and had therefore drifted away from a kind of common sense science. Science in America was indeed becoming self-aware. In 1848 the founding of the American Association for the Advancement of Science (AAAS),

> marked the emergence of a national scientific community in the United States. While science was part of the American scene from the nation's early days, its practitioners remained few in number and scattered geographically and among disciplines. AAAS was the first permanent organization formed to promote the development of science and engineering at the national level and to represent the interests of all its disciplines.[37]

In some ways this is the story of the specialization and thus splintering of knowledge. It certainly set the scene for Darwin's theory, which is not a deductive argument consistent with Baconian inductivism (as Bozeman remarked above), but something akin to an inference to the best explanation (defined much later by Peter Lipton).[38] Science now became increasingly difficult for non-

52 The revolutionary period to 1859

specialists to evaluate. For example, when Charles Hodge ran into his difficulties with criticizing Darwin, it was partly due to Hodge's role as a theologian and not as a "scientist."

The refined taxonomy of science mirrored a similar reification of religions and makes sense of what Peter Harrison has argued: the term *religion* began to focus on a distinct set of practices, narratives, and doctrines, which meant there could be new categories of world religions (although, I hasten to repeat, few scholars today define *religion* as a set of beliefs and practices.[39]) Harrison noted that, in English, "Boudhism" made it first appearance in 1801, "Hinduism" in 1829, "Taouism" in 1838, and "Confucianism" in 1862.[40] The liberal tradition, represented expertly by Friederich Schleiermacher's "feeling of absolute dependence,"[41] could see this common religious experience expressed in a variety of forms, and a conservative theology could determine that these other religions represented a variety of ways of deviating from the propositions and truths claims of Christianity.[42]

There had to be some reason for this new consciousness of other religions, and related to this taxonomy is the gradual emergence of non-Protestant religions in the United States outside of Christianity. The 1848 California gold rush subsequently brought many Chinese immigrants as laborers and with them Buddhism, Daoism, and Confucianism. Thomas Tweed, in fact, set the beginning of Buddhist influence on the United States slightly earlier, when Elizabeth Palmer Peabody published the ground-breaking text of Buddhist scripture in the Transcendentalist publication *The Dial* early in the 1840s.[43]

Some, like the historian Merle Curti, conclude that 1830–1860 was marked by "increasing secularization of life."[44] But this strikes me as premature. Turner's analysis seems to me more nuanced and accurate as he takes in the storms of biblical criticism and science that buffeted the ship of Christian orthodoxy: "Indeed, one suspects that the ordinary Christian never heard that there might be any reason to leave port. But from the 1830s onward, a small but increasing number of voyages away from Christianity led to a variety of non-Christian theisms."[45] This, as Turner and others argue, led to brewing discontent with many things, including Protestant cultural hegemony, and this also signals the rise of American agnosticism in postbellum America, which is the subject of the next chapter.

Brief notes on antebellum America, race, and slavery

I hope I can ask your indulgence as a reader if I simply offer a few miscellaneous remarks as a means of sketching the looming storm of America's internal struggle over slavery. By the middle of the nineteenth century the country found itself unable to avoid the scourge of chattel slavery—resting on a literalistic reading of the Bible and putatively scientific notion of race. (This could be extended to scientific support that was bandied about to support misogyny and women's inferiority, but, as I mentioned in my preface, because of space I've had to leave several topics aside. I can only hope someone else will pursue this thread.) Edwin Gaustad and Leigh Schmidt offered this summary statement: "Even for the most triumphalist and complacent, slavery was a fire bell ringing in the night, a dark cloud that grew ever more ominous and menacing."[46]

Churches were splitting. Schisms in the three leading Protestant denominations in antebellum America—Methodist (1844), Baptist (1845), and Presbyterian (1857)—meant that there were now southern and northern branches. And despite one political compromise after another (such as the 1820 Missouri Compromise), the country seemed inexorably moving toward civil war.

Abraham Lincoln, who would bear the violent effects of racism in his assassinated body, realized in never-published excerpts from 1854 that the notion of race was incoherent and socially constructed. Admittedly, this piece doesn't rise to the level of rhetoric in the 1865 Second Inaugural, which is worth citing first:

> With malice toward none; with charity for all; with firmness in the right, as God gives us to see the right, let us strive on to finish the work we are in; to bind up the nation's wounds; to care for him who shall have borne the battle, and for his widow, and his orphan—to do all which may achieve and cherish a just, and a lasting peace, among ourselves, and with all nations.[47]

Nonetheless, this earlier piece does reflect similar sentiments in Lincoln's later statement and included some profound ideas. Particularly relevant to science and religion is Lincoln's impugning arguments for racial supremacy (and thus negative eugenics, which I will address anon).

> If A. can prove, however conclusively, that he may, of right, enslave B.—why may not B. snatch the same argument, and prove equally, that he may enslave A?
>
> You say A. is white, and B. is black. It is *color*, then; the lighter, having the right to enslave the darker? Take care. By this rule, you are to be slave to the first man you meet, with a fairer skin than your own.
>
> You do not mean *color* exactly? You mean the whites are *intellectually* the superiors of the blacks, and, therefore have the right to enslave them? Take care again. By this rule, you are to be slave to the first man you meet, with an intellect superior to your own.
>
> But, say you, it is a question of *interest*; and, if you can make it your *interest*, you have the right to enslave another. Very well. And if he can make it his interest, he has the right to enslave you.[48]

Despite such ideas, a search for the scientific support of racial superiority accelerated, especially as the drums beat for secession and civil war. Supporters of slavery needed justification for racial discrimination, which in a few decades the science of eugenics would supply.

Lincoln, of course, pursued the topic much further. Always believing that the Declaration of Independence's pronouncement that all are equal constituted "the apple of gold within the silver frame of the Constitution,"[49] he realized slavery

54 The revolutionary period to 1859

repudiated America's commitment to freedom and equality. Moreover, the abolitionist Frederick Douglass not only deployed the Bible against slavery; in his famous July 4, 1852, speech he described powerfully the injustice of slavery and how it repudiated American values, "What to the American slave is your Fourth of July? I answer, a day that reveals to him more than all other days of the year, the gross injustice and cruelty to which he is the constant victim. To him your celebration is a sham."[50]

If these citations seem to be taking my story far afield, let me underscore that this is the context in which science and religion argued about the goods of America, about what "life, liberty, and the pursuit of happiness" meant.

There is obviously much more ground to cover in describing the history of our country during the early nineteenth century. Nonetheless, my goal has been to outline the shape of the cultural narratives and conflicts related to science and religion that we have inherited today (which represents a perhaps overly ambitious goal by itself). And thus I now turn to the most cataclysmic moment in American history, the Civil War.

Notes

1 Mark Noll, *America's God: From Jonathan Edwards to Abraham Lincoln* (Oxford: Oxford University Press, 2005), 161ff.

2 Noll, *America's God*, 163.

3 Ibid., 164.

4 Herbert W. Schneider, *A History of American Philosophy*. 2nd edition. (New York and London: Columbia University, 1963), 54.

5 Winthrop Hudson, *Religion in America: An Historical Account of the Development of American Religious Life*. 3rd edition. (New York: Charles Scribner's Sons, 1981), 72.

6 Edwin Gaustad and Leigh Schmidt, *The Religious History of America: The Heart of the American Story from Colonial Times to Today* (San Francisco: HarperCollins, 2004), 224.

7 Thomas Paine, *The Age of Reason* (Feedbooks online, 1807), 54.

8 Ibid., 4–5.

9 Ibid., 5.

10 Ibid., 6.

11 Ibid., 32.

12 Robert Ingersoll, *The Works of Robert Ingersoll*, 12 vols., C.P. Farrell, ed. (New York: Robert Ingersoll Publishers, 1900), 11: 338–9.

13 Philip E. Hammond, *Religion and Personal Autonomy: Third Disestablishment in America*, studies in Comparative Religion. (Columbia, SC: University of South Carolina Press, 1992), 167.

14 Sidney Mead, *The Old Religion in the Brave New World* (Berkeley and Los Angeles: University of California Press, 1977), 76; cited by Hammond, *Religion and Personal Autonomy*, 9. In the fuller citation, Mead actually asserts that the American Revolution "completed, let us say, with John Adams by around 1815," but that nuance isn't critical here.

15 Roger Finke, "Religious Deregulation: Origins and Consequences," *Journal of Church and State* 32 (Summer) 1990: 609; cited in Hammond, 9.

16 E.g., Sydney Ahlstrom, *A Religious History, A Religious History of the American People* (New Haven, CT: Yale University Press, 1972), 415ff.

17 Herbert W. Schneider, *A History of American Philosophy*. 2nd edition. (New York and London: Columbia University, 1963), 216.

18 Schneider, *A History*, 217.

The revolutionary period to 1859 55

19 Noll, *America's God*, 108. See also Theodore Bozeman, *Protestants in an Age of Science: The Baconian Ideal and Antebellum American Religious Thought* (Chapel Hill: University of North Carolina Press, 1977), 4–30.
20 Noll, *America's God*, 108.
21 Ibid., 104.
22 Schneider, *A History*, 219.
23 Bozeman's *Protestants in an Age of Science* is particularly insightful on this connection.
24 Ibid., chapter 4, pp. 71ff.
25 See, e.g., Leonard Gilchrist Wilson, *Benjamin Siliman and his Circle* (New York: Science History Publications, 1979), 19 and Daniel Walker Howe, *What Hath God Wrought: The Transformation of America, 1815–1848* (Oxford: Oxford University Press, 1979), 465.
26 Ibid., 77.
27 Noll, *America's God*, 368.
28 James Turner, *Without God, Without Creed: The Origins of Unbelief in America* (Baltimore and London: Johns Hopkins, 1985), 145.
29 Noll, "The Image of the United States as a Biblical Nation, 1776–1865," in Nathan O. Hatch and Mark A. Noll, eds., *The Bible in America: Essays in Cultural History* (Oxford: Oxford University Press, 1982), 39.
30 Robert Bellah, Richard Madsen, William Sullivan, Ann Swidler, and Steven Tipton, *Habits of the Heart* (Berkeley: University of California Press, 1985), 220. The ninth chapter of this book, "Religion," describes the sweep of this move from establishment to individualism.
31 Bozeman, *Protestants in an Age of Science*, 76.
32 Cited by Andrew Delbanco, *The Real American Dream: A Meditation on Hope* (Cambridge, MA: Harvard, 2000), 43.
33 See Lawrence Principe, *The Scientific Revolution: A Very Short Introduction* (Oxford: Oxford University Press, 2011), 27.
34 Quoted in Turner, *Without God*, 185.
35 See *Oxford Dictionary online*, http://www.etymonline.com/word/scientist.
36 Renée Bergland, *Maria Mitchell and the Sexing of Science: An Astronomer Among the American Romantics* (Boston: Beacon, 2008), 146. See also, ibid., xv.
37 AAAS website, "Mission and History," https://www.aaas.org/mission.
38 Here I am using Peter Lipton's term. See *Inference to the Best Explanation*, International Library of Philosophy (New York: Routledge. 2004).
39 See, for example, Clifford Geertz, *The Interpretation of Cultures* (New York: Basic Books, 1973), 90; Wilfred Cantwell Smith, *The Meaning and End of Religion* (Minneapolis, MN: Fortress, 1991), *passim*; Stephen Prothero, *God is Not One: The Eight Rival Religions That Run the World* (San Francisco: HarperOne, 2010), 324. See also, Hampton, "Rumors of War" in Hardin et al., *The Warfare Between Science and Religion: The Idea That Wouldn't Die* (Baltimore: Johns Hopkins University Press, 2018), 46ff.
40 Harrison, *Territories*, 101.
41 See Schleiermacher, *The Christian Faith, 2nd edition*, H.R. Mackintosh and J.S. Stewart, eds. (Edinburgh: T & T Clark, 1989 [1830]), e.g., 12ff., 19ff.
42 George Lindbeck describes this distinction expertly in *The Nature of Doctrine: Religion and Theology in a Postliberal Age* (Louisville, KY: Westminster John Knox, 1984), esp. chapter 2.
43 T.A. Tweed, *The American Encounter with Buddhism, 1844–1912: Victorian Culture and the Limits of Discourse* (Boston: Wisdom, 1992), xvi-xvii.
44 Curti, *The Growth of American Thought, 3rd edition.* (New Brunswick, NJ: Transaction, 1982), 299.
45 Turner, *Without God*, 163.
46 Gaustad and Schmidt, *The Religious History of America*, 184.
47 Abraham Lincoln, "Lincoln's Second Inaugural Address," retrieved June 17, 2019, https://www.loc.gov/rr/program/bib/ourdocs/lincoln2nd.html#American.
48 Abraham Lincoln, "Fragment on Slavery," retrieved June 20, 2019, http://teachingamericanhistory.org/library/document/fragments-on-slavery.

56 The revolutionary period to 1859

49 Cited by Delbanco in "Andrew Delbanco: The Real American Dream: A Meditation on Hope," video recorded at the Gilder Lehman Institute, Harvard University, retrieved June 20, 2019, https://vimeo.com/17684400.
50 Frederick Douglass, "Hypocrisy of American Slavery," July 4, 1852, retrieved June 20, 2019, http://billhowe.org/MCE/hypocrisy-of-american-slavery-by-frederick-douglass-july-4-1852.

Bibliography

Ahlstrom, Sydney. *A Religious History of the American People*. New Haven CT: Yale University Press, 1972.

Bellah, Robert, Richard Madsen, William Sullivan, Ann Swidler and Steven Tipton. *Habits of the Heart*. Berkeley, CA: University of California Press, 1985.

Bozeman, Theodore Dwight. *Protestant Thought in an Age of Science*. Chapel Hill, NC: University of North Carolina Press, 1977.

Curti, Merle. *The Growth of American Thought*. Third edition. New Brunswick, NJ: Transaction, 1982.

Delbanco, Andrew. *The Real American Dream: A Meditation on Hope*. Cambridge, MA: Harvard, 2000.

Delbanco, Andrew. "Andrew Delbanco: The Real American Dream: A Meditation on Hope." Video recorded at the Gilder Lehman Institute, Harvard University. Retrieved June 20, 2019. https://vimeo.com/17684400

Douglass, Frederick. "Hypocrisy of American Slavery." July 4, 1852. Retrieved June 20, 2019. http://billhowe.org/MCE/hypocrisy-of-american-slavery-by-frederick-douglass-july-4-1852.

Gaustad, Edwin and Leigh Schmidt. *The Religious History of America: The Heart of the American Story from Colonial Times to Today*. Revised edition. San Francisco, CA: HarperCollins, 2004.

Hammond, Philip E. *Religion and Personal Autonomy: Third Disestablishment in America*. Studies in Comparative Religion. Columbia, SC: University of South Carolina Press, 1992.

Hardin, Jeff, Ronald L. Numbers and Ronald A. Binzley, eds. *The Warfare Between Science and Religion: The Idea That Wouldn't Die*. Baltimore, MD: Johns Hopkins University Press, 2018.

Hatch, Nathan O. and Mark A. Noll, eds. *The Bible in America: Essays in Cultural History*. Oxford, UK: Oxford University Press, 1982.

Howe, Daniel Walker. *What Hath God Wrought: The Transformation of America, 1815–1848*. Oxford, UK: Oxford University Press, 1979.

Hudson, Winthrop. *Religion in America: An Historical Account of the Development of American Religious Life*. 3rd edition. New York: Charles Scribner's Sons, 1981.

Ingersoll, Robert. *The Works of Robert Ingersoll*. 12 volumes. Edited by C.P. Farrell. New York: Robert Ingersoll Publishers, 1900.

Mead, Sidney. *The Old Religion in the Brave New World*. Berkeley and Los Angeles, CA: University of California Press, 1977.

Noll, Mark. *America's God: From Jonathan Edwards to Abraham Lincoln*. Oxford, UK: Oxford University Press, 2005.

Paine, Thomas. *The Age of Reason*. Feedbooks online, 1807.

Schneider, Herbert W. *A History of American Philosophy*. 2nd edition. New York and London: Columbia University, 1963.

Turner, James. *Without God, Without Creed: The Origins of Unbelief in America*. Baltimore and London: Johns Hopkins University Press, 1985.

Wilson, Leonard Gilchrist. *Benjamin Siliman and his Circle*. New York: Science History Publications, 1979.

5

POST-DARWIN

Setting the break with Darwin's *Origin of Species*

It's alluring to identify a conclusive break of science and religion with the publication of Charles Darwin's *On the Origin of Species*. It has been done, most notably—and with rhetorical flourishes of the highest order—by Richard Dawkins: "Although atheism might have been *logically* tenable before Darwin, Darwin made it possible to be an intellectually fulfilled atheist."[1] If grasping the truth of common ancestry leads an intellectual to atheism, then a believer in a theistic God post-Darwin must be anti-intellectual, anti-scientific, and recalcitrantly medieval.

Indeed, in this chapter I *am* setting the break in religion and science in the United States with the 1859 *Origin*. But this I do primarily for the purposes of clarity, and I fully admit that every shift in history is a judgmental call. This is no different. I return to the rubric of two of my key sources: "There is nothing in history that quite corresponds to a coastline or a watershed in geography" (C.S. Lewis),[2] and "Seek simplicity and distrust it" (Whitehead).[3] At the same time, this decision is not arbitrary. As Herbert Hovecamp summarized it, "Increasingly after the 1850s there would be a feeling in the colleges and seminaries that scientific language spoke about one world, religious language about another. Intellectual freedom, academic freedom—even religious freedom—demanded it."[4] Scientists and religious leaders begin to orbit different suns. By the late nineteenth century the words *religion* and *science* have essentially the same meaning as they do today, and increasingly it was only "scientists" that could legitimately practice the latter. The disciplines had begun to splinter, and this is one battle that Charles Hodge faced when he commented on Darwinisim. In addition, as James Turner has noted, postbellum America gradually became more and more agnostic and atheist,[5] even if it did not attain the heights of the growing anti-religious sentiment of Continental Europe.

58 Post-Darwin

I intend to take more time and care than slogans and rhetorical flourishes allow. In these next three chapters, I will chart what happened in post-Darwinian America through to the modern study of science and religion in the mid-1960s with characters such as Timothy Draper, Andrew Dickson White, Hodge, and Asa Gray, as well as events like the 1925 Scopes Trial and the fundamentalist-modernist split in the 1920s, the rise and fall of eugenics, and the key scientific discoveries (especially relativity and quantum theories) that defined this 100 years or so. The United States was coming of age intellectually and culturally and continued to find an uneasy relationship with a variety of impulses. Put another way, both scientific advances and religious expansion—sometimes in alliance, sometimes in antagonism, and sometimes in coexistence mark this period.

I have mentioned that we should be careful not to overstate Darwin's immediate influence. The year 1859 hardly represents the most favorable one for science to make a decisive mark in the United States. We had other concerns. All the cultural and political forces that created the 1861–1865 Civil War were already in play. I remember reading David Herbert Donald's massive biography *Lincoln* recently and experiencing second-hand the tortuous means by which our sixteenth President sought to keep the union of our states intact.[6] In fact, though the Civil War falls directly after the division I have created for this sketch of American intellectual history, in many ways it both accelerated and slowed the engagement of religion and science.

Thus the Civil War—arguably the greatest event in US history—delayed a full reception of *On the Origin of Species*. Few had the leisure to consider the full scientific and religious implications of Darwin's monumental publication. In that sense, the war largely belongs to another, pre-Darwinian, era, a fact that returns me to my earlier concerns about the problems of clearly demarcated periods of culture and history. Nonetheless, Lincoln and the Congress found time to promote scientific progress. In February 1863—i.e., right in the midst of the war—Massachusetts Senator Henry Wilson helped draft a bill to incorporate the National Academy of Science (NAS). President Lincoln, seeing the importance of science for our country's future, signed the bill and NAS was founded on March 3, 1863. And, naturally, these scientific efforts were soon directed toward war. Its first act established uniform weights and measures, seemingly unrelated to the Civil War battles.

> But requests for advice on matters related to the war were soon to come. Very shortly after the Committee on Weights, Measures, and Coinage was brought into being, the Navy Department requested no less than three studies, two of which were addressed to subjects directly related to the capabilities of the Union fleet, and one of which concerned wind and current charts used for commercial navigation.[7]

It's even arguable that other forms of science, in generating massive carnage, affected the era of the Civil War more powerfully than Darwin's cataclysmic theory. The war demonstrated anew that science's effects through technology were fast outstripping traditional military mores. The nature of the battles had changed, and yet the armies' generals did not adjust and clung to older traditions. (This indeed we can read as a parable about the larger interaction of religion and science. Science was changing, but other cultural forms are often slow to adapt.)

Because they summarize so much so adroitly, I will cite Peter Carroll and David Noble's study of US history, *The Free and the Unfree*, at length.

> The staggering mortality of the Civil War, far greater than any American war before or since, reflected a perverse inability of the military readers to comprehend the implications of technological warfare. Experienced, if at all, in the Mexican War, a conflict characterized by dashing strategic sweeps and technological obsolescence, the Civil War generals and their political leaders remained committed to grand climactic battles that would destroy the enemy at once. In traditional warfare, such victories had come from bold frontal assaults, wave upon wave of charging soldiers overwhelming an embattled advisory. In an age of slow-loading inaccurate weapons, such bravery produced celebrated heroes and casualties remained low.
>
> The introduction of new rifled weapons, however, and the invention of expanding minié bullets revolutionized warfare. Where the old smooth-bored muskets encouraged bold rushes and close fighting, guns like the Springfield rifle could annihilate an advancing infantry across fields.[8]

Culturally, the war and the subsequent Reconstruction further exacerbated the division between the North and South, having already split denominations. This division at the Mason-Dixon line would play out with a vengeance in the 1925 Scopes "Monkey" Trial. It continues to this day. Increasingly the North's industrial, anti-traditional, and secular values were set in violent conflict with Southern traditional religion and agrarian morals. I will certainly have more to unfold on those themes below.

And, of course, the gears of scientific discoveries elsewhere, which would make their way to America, didn't suddenly grind to a halt. I have already mentioned Darwin's theory of evolution by natural selection in 1859, which—it should be noted—was paralleled in the scientific work of Alfred Russel Wallace. In 1865 a little-known Augustinian friar from Moravia, Gregor Mendel, developed his laws of inheritance, which later became the basis for genetics and a critical component of neo-Darwinism; but, because of Mendel's obscure location, his discoveries were little known for several decades. In America, little could be heard over the guns of Bull Run, Antietam, and Gettysburg.

What Darwin's theory really meant for American religion

Certainly, Darwinian evolutionary thought challenged the heretofore-reigning Christian narrative of a creation *ex nihilo* as well as the spontaneous creation of Adam and Eve and their uniqueness as animals bearing the divine image. It

60 Post-Darwin

questioned William Paley's 1802 Watchmaker Analogy in his *Natural Theology* [9] as a means to secure legitimate place for *natural theology;* that is, a way to find about God's existence and attributes without recourse to special revelation. The easy association of God's character and the natural world that had dominated the dialogue of nineteenth-century England and America through Paley and *The Bridgewater Treatises* became problematized. Science, once the friend of Christian belief, became a much more complicated companion, and began to utter quips through Darwin such as the "clumsy, wasteful, blundering, low, and horribly cruel works of nature."[10] To this extent, Edward Larson is correct,

> By replacing the divine Creator with a survival-of-the-fittest process as the immediate designer of species, Darwin's theory undermined natural theology. This carried cultural significance in the English-speaking world, where natural theology served as an organizing concept in science and an intellectual prop for Protestant Christianity.[11]

But, of course, this narrative is too easy. ("Seek simplicity and distrust it.") Darwin played a role, but he wasn't the first one on the stage. Even if Paley dominated the conversation in the Anglo-American world (Darwin had to study *Natural Theology* as a Cambridge student of divinity), David Hume had already managed to strike the tree of natural theology at its roots with a mortal blow in his 1776 *Dialogues Concerning Natural Religion,*[12] with his philosophical objections to Paley. Hume also rekindled the debate about final causation and whether God is properly a part of science, or, to quote Pierre Laplace's famous declaration to Napoleon in 1802 about whether the deity could be found in his scientific equations, "Sir, I have no need of that hypothesis."[13]

Similar challenges certainly predated Darwin. Notably, the doctrine of creation *ex nihilo* had already faced its fierce objections centuries earlier: an eternal universe fit well with Newtonian science, and Thomas Aquinas and others had argued in the thirteenth century that creation out of nothing could not be established philosophically, but only through revelation. In this view, an eternal, simple deity could create an eternal universe as its First Cause and thus the doctrine of creation *ex nihilo* might not even be that important.[14] Nonetheless, evolution through natural selection took on another aspect of Christian doctrine; human beings *ex nihilo*, or, at least, out of the dust (Genesis 2:7). Darwin himself knew his ideas threatened the core of what it meant for those living in Christian Europe and the United States to be human. He recognized that his ideas would be accused of causing the "death of Adam" and that many would quickly argue that human beings weren't "created from monkeys" (which, with even a cursory reading of Darwin, hardly represents his theory of natural selection). But then again, popularists often find truth an inconvenient detail. The famous evangelist Billy Sunday (1862–1935) can be presented as Exhibit A: "If by evolution you mean advance, I go with you, but if you mean by evolution that I came from a monkey, good night!"[15] And that indeed has stuck with popular consciousness.

I'm not denying that we see in Darwin's theory the strands of methodological naturalism, the rejection of a direct creation of Adam and Eve (or even sole progenitors of all humankind), as well as the age of the earth and universe. These themes will continue in my narrative. Nevertheless, these don't exhaust the story of how Darwin influenced the relationship of religion and science in America.

With those observations in hand, what did *Darwin* mean with the word *evolution*? Notably, *Origin* contains the term "evolved" only once because Darwin desired to avoid connotations of a conclusive unfolding. Instead he emphasized the unpredictable character of change in nature. By 1872, in *Expression of Emotions*, he clearly employed the term, and thus we associate evolution with Darwinism. Here are a few citations from *Origin* that, strung together, summarized his theory.

> Owing to the struggle for life, any variation, however slight and from whatever cause proceeding, if it be to any degree profitable to an individual of any species, in its infinitely complex relations to other organic beings and to external nature, will tend to the preservation of that individual, and will generally be inherited by its offspring.
>
> The preservation of favourable variations and the rejection of injurious variations, I call Natural Selection. Variations neither useful nor injurious would not be affected by natural selection, and would be left a fluctuating element.
>
> It follows that as each selected and favoured form increases in number, so will the less favoured forms decrease and become rare. Rarity, as geology tells us, is the precursor to extinction.
>
> According to my view, varieties are species in the process of formation, or, as I have called them, incipient species.[16]

Four words—mutation, variation, and natural selection—can summarize evolution's mechanisms (as Kenneth Miller in fact does).[17] None of these unequivocally states, "God created it this way." And that bothered many in the nineteenth century.

There is certainly some good fuel for the fires of Dawkins's atheistic conjoining of the rise of atheism and Darwin. Nonetheless, as I mentioned above, it would be tempting to conjoin these, but it is also distorting. Some religious voices did shout strong rejoinders to Darwin, but many were thoughtful and restrained, awaiting further scientific work, and others were even enthusiastic about the theory of evolution through natural selection.

Two of Darwin's earliest theological proponents were Charles Kingsley (1819–75) and Frederick Temple (1821–1905). Even if not Americans—I will note those below—they represent appreciative theological responses. Kingsley, who called himself "an orthodox priest of the Church of England,"[18] offered the noteworthy phrase that God could "make things that make themselves" through evolution and that this kind of deity was more praiseworthy than One who simply made things by fiat. He is worth citing at length:

62   Post-Darwin

If, then, that should be true which Mr. Darwin writes: "It may be metaphorically said that natural selection is daily and hourly scrutinising throughout the world, every variation, even the slightest; rejecting that which is bad, preserving and adding up that which is good, silently and incessantly working whenever and wherever opportunity offers at the improvement of every organic being"— if that, I say, were proven to be true, ought God's care and God's providence to seem less or more magnificent in our eyes? Of old it was said by Him without whom nothing is made: "My Father worketh hitherto, and I work." Shall we quarrel with Science if she should show how those words are true? What, in one word, should we have to say but this?—We knew of old that God was so wise that He could make all things; but behold, He is so much wiser than even that, that He can make all things make themselves.[19]

Similarly, John Hedley Brooke has written that Temple, who later became the archbishop of Canterbury, "welcomed the extension of natural law because it gave analogical support for belief in moral law."[20] Many of these ideas found echoes in the writings of Joseph S. Van Dyke (1832–1915), Presbyterian pastor and lecturer at the College of New Jersey (later Princeton University) who published *Theism and Evolution* in 1886, and B.B. Warfield (1851–1921) at Princeton Theological Seminary (to whom I'll turn in a page or two).

Moving back to the United States, one of the pre-eminent historians of the nineteenth century, Claude Welch[21] (and this is echoed by Ron Numbers[22]), told a more varied tale:

For three or four decades after 1859, *The Origin of Species* was both a special focus for the problem of relating the religious and scientific world views and a symbol of the changing relations of theology and culture in general. By the end of the century, except for incipient Protestant fundamentalism and Roman Catholicism, the controversy over biological evolution seemed largely resolved. Evolution even became a master image for new ways of viewing all things religious and cultural.[23]

After noting that Darwinism would eventually "destroy the tranquility of Christian academia," George Marsden commented,

The initial evangelical reactions to Darwinism, however, were not as strident nor as generally negative as might be imagined. In fact, with the exception of Harvard's Louis Agassiz, virtually every American Protestant zoologist and botanist accepted some form of evolution by the early 1870s. What they insisted on, contrary to Darwin's own view, was that evolutionary development was compatible with purposeful design.[24]

Admittedly, Bishop Ussher's famous seventeenth-century chronology of creation beginning on October 23, 4004 BCE still had some adherents. (Incidentally, lest we think of Ussher as an outlier, his date found remarkable consensus with John Lightfoot's conclusion in 1644 that 3929 BCE was the date of creation, Johannes Kepler's date of 3992 BCE, and Isaac Newton's estimate of 4000 BCE.[25]) Nevertheless, most scientists and academic theologians by the time of Darwin's *Origins* had concluded that geological time needed to be extended quite substantially, and this caused many to infer that the days of Genesis 1 had to be threateningly long—at least threatening to a literalist. For example, the Princeton University geologist and geographer Arnold Henry Guyot (1807–84) took recourse in *day-age creationism*; that is, the Hebrew word *yom* in Genesis can mean *days* and also simply *time,* and thus the six days of creation in Genesis 1–2a are not ordinary 24-hour days, but periods of time (from thousands to billions of years). Others agreed with the ancient church that the early chapters of Genesis were allegorical. Finally, the nineteenth century became philosophically and theologically more comfortable with change and process over stasis and fixity (the latter had predominated in ancient thought) through the Romantics like Gotthart Ephraim Lessing and Johann Gottfried Herder, but especially through G.W.F. Hegel.[26] All these factors provided a smooth pathway to Darwinism for many.

John William Draper, Andrew Dickson White, and the circumstances surrounding them

It wasn't simply the religious conservatives that churned the sea of American culture. Caviling against the religionists of his day, Robert Ingersoll (1833–99) demonstrated his training as a lawyer and set out his case for how believers subvert the progress of science and rationality: "They are, for the most, engaged in poisoning the minds of the young, prejudicing children against science, teaching the astronomy and geology of the Bible, and inducing all to desert the sublime standard of reason."[27] Ingersoll, the son of clergyman, demonstrated the zeal of a convert as one converted not to religious belief, but to atheism.

Another preacher's son, John William Draper, echoed the spirit of Ingersoll, though not entirely his rhetoric. Draper, the first president of the American Chemical Society, was not only a chemist, philosopher, physician, historian, and photographer, but was also the first to produce a clear photo of a female face. Donald Fleming, in his treatment of Draper, offered this assessment, "It was not Draper's own way to be fatigued with thinking; he had the remorseless fluency and dialectical zest to go to the end of all arguments."[28] Draper's 1874 *History of the Conflict between Science and Religion* made short work of any harmony between science and religion. It asserted instead—and note the capitalization of Science (perhaps an apotheosis?)—"The history of Science is not a mere record of isolated discoveries; it is a narrative of the conflict of two contending powers, the expansive force of the human intellect on the one side, and the compression arising from traditionary faith and human interests on the other."[29]

Draper outlined ancient Greek origins of science and then narrated the development of Christianity as leading to repression of science. His argument, aimed at

64 Post-Darwin

his fellow Protestants, employed anti-Catholic rhetoric, and many of these arguments were already present in his 1861 *Intellectual Development of Europe*. Fleming wrote of Draper's *Conflict*, "The emotional climax of the book is the vain effort of Roman Catholicism to hold back the universal phenomenon of the scientific spirit."[30] And Lawrence Principe added, "The *Conflict* has long been recognized as a specifically *anti-Catholic* rant."[31] It appears that Draper was angered by the rise of immigrants from Catholic countries and that his sister had become a nun.[32] Draper stated clearly, "Roman Christianity and Science are recognized by their respective adherents as being absolutely incompatible; they cannot exist together; one must yield to the other; mankind must make its choice—it cannot have both."[33] Draper nevertheless concluded that these "two rival divisions of the Christian church" could be found "in accord on one point: to tolerate no science except such as they considered agreeable to the Scriptures," and both were liable to "theological odium."[34] Worth mentioning here is Draper's reliance on Auguste Comte's Law of Three Stages, which denote progress, of theological-philosophical-scientific/positive.[35] To some degree Draper sought to produce a Comtean positivist religion.[36] But, even more, Draper created an idiosyncratic rationalist, and putatively scientifically-based, one. "In the end, his book is not so much about a conflict between 'science' and 'religion,' but rather about a conflict between Draper's religion and all others."[37]

Historians often pair William Draper (1811–82) and his *History of the Conflict between Religion and Science* (1874) with Andrew Dickson White. In considering White (1832–1918), we also cannot forget one unique challenge: he was facing the need to fundraise and thus find financial support for the first self-consciously secular college, namely Cornell (for which White was the first president). In 1865, at the founding of Cornell College, he proclaimed that it would be "an asylum for *Science*—where truth shall be sought for truth's sake, not stretched or cut exactly to fit Revealed Religion."[38] He continued to refine this thesis for three decades and issued this in his 1896, two-volume *A History of the Warfare of Science with Theology in Christendom*—a title that hardly rolls off the tongue. Though influential, it is a bloated book that offered any number of historical inaccuracies, which have reasonably been criticized by historians.[39] In it he argued "the great majority of the early fathers of the Church, and especially Lactantius, had sought to crush it [science] beneath the utterances attributed to Isaiah, David, and St. Paul."[40] Despite significant flaws, the book became an extremely influential text on the relationship between science and religion, and is largely responsible for the dissemination of the conflict thesis.

Besides the motivations in founding Cornell, it is worth noting that White was himself a church person who had grown increasingly concerned about the retrograde effect of Christianity, particularly from the Catholic church, which was fighting its own boundaries against the incursion of modernism such as Marxism, democracy, and rationalism. White saw, for example, the First Vatican Council of 1869–70 and the early 1864 Syllabus of Errors that pronounced a rejection of the assertion, "The method and principles by which the old scholastic doctors cultivated theology are no longer suitable to the demands of our times and to the progress of the sciences," and by extension repudiated much of modernism.[41] He hoped to disentangle science in its wrestling with religion, but perhaps disabled the latter in the process.

I am mentioning both Draper and White not to present a full response to their work but to describe enough to signal their profound influence on the narrative of religion and science in America. Most assuredly, it was to set these two cultural forces in direct contradiction.

Besides Darwin and the midrash of reaction around his work (both positive and negative), there are manifold other cultural forces that eroded belief in evangelical and biblical Christianity. One of those forces was the rise, especially in the late nineteenth century, of biblical higher criticism. In his novel *In the Beauty of Liles*, John Updike depicted the travails of a New Jersey Presbyterian minister, Clarence Arthur Wilmot, who loses his faith as the twentieth century begins. Having studied at Princeton Theological Seminary, Wilmot recalls the unwinding of his confidence in the biblical texts at the hands of German higher critics:

> In those student days, hungry for knowledge and fearless in his youthful sense of God's protection close at hand, he had plunged into the chilly Baltic sea of Higher Criticism—all those Germans, Semler and Eichhorn, Baur and Welhausen, who dared to pick up the Sacred Book without reverence, as one more human volume, more curious and conglomerate than most, but the work of men—of Jews in dirty sheepskins, rotten-toothed desert tribesmen with eyes rolled heavenward, men like flies on flypaper caught fast in a historic time, among myths and conceptions belonging to the childhood of mankind.[42]

Although I've noted earlier challenges to traditional views of biblical authority, the assault on the Bible as God's inerrant Word constitutes a major theme in American culture that found new vigor and wider support in late nineteenth century American life.

Reconciliation and rejection: Asa Gray, Charles Hodge, and others

Part of the problem in telling the story of religion and science with a break at Darwin's *Origin* remains the thinkers that worked hard to bring the emerging science together with a reasonably conventional religion. And so I return to the more complicated story than Draper, White, and Ingersoll (and Dawkins) are prone to tell.

I cited Jonathan Edwards above, the eighteenth-century Reformed theologian who worked intensively and brilliantly in bringing together natural philosophy and Christian faith. I turn now to Hodge (1797–1878)—the Presbyterian theologian who dominated the Princeton Theological Seminary faculty for decades and later influenced twentieth-century fundamentalism—a scholar who certainly knew scientific thought well enough to publish extensively throughout his prodigious career.

66 Post-Darwin

In the context of science and religion, Hodge is most often cited now for his resistance to Darwin's thought. One might miss, however, Hodge's serious interest and engagement with science and particularly his project to forge a scientific approach—particularly one based on Baconian induction—to theology. "The Bible is to the theologian what nature is to the man of science. It is his store-house of facts." He continues in the next paragraph with the implications, "In the second place, the duty of the Christian theologian is to ascertain, collect, and combine all the facts which God has revealed concerning himself and our relation to Him. These facts are all in the Bible."[43]

In Darwin's theory, however, Hodge simply could not countenance the lack of teleology. His famous essay addressing Darwinian evolution ends by answering the question that entitles this 1874 piece, *What is Darwinism?* Hodge looked to Asa Gray in the latter's 1872 address to the AAAS as its ex-president:

> If Mr. Darwin believes that the events which he supposes to have occurred and the results we behold around us were undirected and undesigned; or if the physicist believes that the natural forces to which he refers phenomena are uncaused and undirected, no argument is needed to show that such belief is atheistic.[44]

Then Hodge moved toward his key concern—whether there is design in nature.

> We have thus arrived at the answer to our question, What is Darwinism? It is Atheism. This does not mean, as before said, that Mr. Darwin himself and all who adopt his views are atheists; but it means that his theory is atheistic; that *the exclusion of design from nature* is, as Dr. Gray says, tantamount to atheism (italics mine).[45]

Here one should take note of Hodge's nuance. He was not accusing Darwin of being an atheist, but of removing God from the work of nature which leaves God nothing to do, thereby creating an atheistic biological theory. Naturally this distinction represents the very point of the spear that Dawkins, Coyne, and others thrust into the side of theism. If nothing else, Hodge highlighted the very central issue that endures to this day. He could not join together evolutionary thought and belief as Gray did—and thus he determined, "Dr. Asa Gray, avows himself an evolutionist; but he is not a Darwinian."[46] Hodge found the mechanistic thread in Darwin's theory untenable. Consequently, because it did not include final causation, this necessitated that Hodge reject evolution.

I noted Hodge's scientific capabilities because they were no less impressive than Edwards's. But the culture had changed around them in the intervening decades. A century or more after Edwards, science had become its own field, and it was gradually sloughing off clerical attachments. In addition, *scientist* had become a discrete profession. Consider this: Edwards's theological study at Yale was imbedded in Yale College, where theology was key (Yale was founded to train pastors) and other humanities and sciences were part of the curricula. Princeton Theological Seminary was founded in 1812 to focus specifically on ministerial training, partly to separate itself from the secularization that the divinity schools at Yale and Harvard had undergone.[47] But that mirrored a wider cultural sequestering of theology from other disciplines, an unwinding of theological study from other scholarship. And here Hodge's reach became restricted. Even Gray, who shared many theological points with Hodge as Calvinist evangelicals, could comment about Hodge, "whether right or wrong on particular points, he is not often right or wrong in a way of a man of science."[48] These and other facts meant that, though Hodge and Edwards stated some very similarly reconciling comments about science and religion—both within the Reformed tradition—the notes they sounded, once harmonious, had become discordant to the melody of "cultured despisers" (to borrow Friedrich Schleiermacher's term).

Surprisingly, Hodge's denunciation of evolution stood in contrast to Warfield, his younger colleague, who famously formulated the doctrine of biblical inerrancy, which remains to this day critical for the doctrines of later fundamentalists. And yet in 1888 Warfield commented,

> I do not think that there is any general statement in the Bible or any part of the account of creation, either as given in Genesis 1 and 2 or elsewhere alluded to, that need be opposed to evolution. [...] There is no *necessary* antagonism of Christianity to evolution, *provided that* we do not hold to too extreme a form of evolution.[49]

In fact, many relatively conservative late nineteenth-century Christian thought leaders could similarly integrate evolution into their theologies.

Hodge's rejection of Darwinism at Princeton Theological Seminary has often been contrasted with the institution just a couple of blocks away, Princeton University, an institution still under the influence of the Presbyterian church. The university's president from 1868–88, James McCosh, reconciled science and Scripture with a type of *two books* approach first presented by Francis Bacon: "Both reveal order in the world, the one appointed by God, the other discovered by man."[50] In particular, McCosh could see evolution as consonant with Christian faith and offered that, "Those who view development in the proper light see in it a form or manifestation of law."[51] Similarly, another college president and ordained minister, Martin Brewer Anderson at the University of Rochester, "pointed out in answer to Hodge that the term 'evolution' could be used in two different ways— either as God's method of development or as pure chance."[52] This differentiation still cleanly demarcates the theistic approach to Darwin from a materialistic one.[53] It still separates Dawkins and Francis Collins.

I could not help but remark on Gray above, and if Hodge represented a theologian who rejected Darwinism then Gray (1810–88), the Fisher Professor of Natural History at Harvard where he taught from 1841–73, provided the most marked contrast in accepting evolutionary thought. He was an enthusiastic

68 Post-Darwin

colleague of Darwin's as well as an evangelical Christian, and this fact alone is enough to problematize the idea that orthodox Christianity immediately rejected Darwinism. As A. Hunter Dupree wrote, "Gray, the symbol of the Darwinian theist, was now openly allied with theologians such as George Frederick Wright and openly a contrast to Huxley, to John Tyndall ... and to Darwin himself."[54] Similarly, *Christian History* wrote of Gray,

> Gray, a noted botanist, taught at Harvard alongside Louis Agassiz. He met Darwin at Kew Gardens in London in 1838 and began correspondence with him in 1855. Gray had developed similar ideas on his own and was immediately convinced by Darwin's theory. He even arranged for the American publication of Origin of Species. But Gray disagreed with his English friend on the subject of religion, repeatedly trying to convince Darwin that his system left room for God's design and occasional intervention. Darwin demurred. Nonetheless, Gray included his theistic synthesis when he promoted Darwin's ideas—efforts that greatly aided the acceptance of evolution in America.[55]

Gray was convinced that God guided the process of evolution. In fact, he told Darwin "that variation has been led along certain beneficial lines."[56] Darwin differed with Gray's assessment, but still agreed with him in certain respects:

> I had no intention to write atheistically.... I can see no reason, why a man, or other animal, may not have been aboriginally produced by other laws; and that all these laws may have been expressly designed by an omniscient Creator, who foresaw every future event and consequence.[57]

Curiously, Gray's influence on the reception of evolution is hard to overstate. He even championed Darwin's views so that the latter would receive a fair hearing. Joshua Moritz comments on what might strike many today as an irony of history, "The early support of Darwin's theory in the United States was due largely to Gray's support."[58]

The narrative of a wholesale Christian, and even evangelical, rejection of Darwin is therefore simple, far too simple. Several voices in this chapter represented a church choir of evangelicals singing harmony with evolution. There are indeed many more within a growing theological liberalism, even if not all from academic theologians, and this theme begins my next chapter.

Notes

1 Dawkins, *The Blind Watchmaker: Why the Evidence of Evolution Reveals a Universe without Design* (New York: Norton, 1986), 6.
2 C.S. Lewis, *They Asked for a Paper: Paper and Addresses* (London: Geoffrey Bles, 1962), 11.
3 Alfred North Whitehead, *The Concept of Nature* (Cambridge: Cambridge University Press, 1920), 46.

Post-Darwin **69**

4　Herbert Hovencamp, *Science and Religion in America 1800–1860* (Philadelphia: University of Pennsylvania Press, 1978), 56.

5　James Turner, *Without God, Without Creed: The Origins of Unbelief in America* (Baltimore and London: Johns Hopkins, 1985), 171ff.

6　David Herbert Donald, *Lincoln* (New York: Simon & Schuster, 1995).

7　National Academy of Sciences, "History," retrieved June 13, 2019, http://www.nasonline.org/about-nas/history/archives/founding-and-early-work.html.

8　Peter N. Carroll and David N. Noble, *The Free and the Unfree: A New History of the United States*, 2nd edition. (New York: Penguin, 1988), 215.

9　William Paley, *Natural Theology: Evidences of the Existence and Attributes of the Deity AND Evidences of Christianity* (Oxford: Benediction Classics, 2017).

10　Charles Darwin, 1856 letter to J.D. Hooker, cited in Jon H. Roberts, *Darwinism and the Divine in America: Protestant Intellectuals and Organic Evolution* (Madison: University of Wisconsin Press, 1988), 130–1.

11　Edward J. Larson, *Evolution: The Remarkable History of a Scientific* Theory (New York: Modern Library, 2006), 90.

12　David Hume, *Dialogues Concerning Natural Religion*, 2nd edition. (Indianapolis: Hackett Pub. Co. 1998).

13　See Stephen G. Brush, *A History of Modern Planetary Physics: Nebulous Earth* (Cambridge: Cambridge University Press, 1996), p. 20.

14　R.J. Russell, "Finite Creation Without a Beginning: The Doctrine of Creation in Relation to Big Bang and Quantum Cosmologies," in Robert John Russell, Nancey Murphy, C. J. Isham, eds., *Quantum Cosmology and the Laws of Nature: Scientific Perspectives on Divine Action* (Vatican City State and Berkeley, CA: Vatican Observatory and the Center for Theology and the Natural Sciences, 1993), 293–329.

15　Billy Sunday, *Boston Herald*, November 14, 1916, p. 1.

16　*Origin of Species by Means of Natural Selection or the Preservation of Favoured Races in the Struggle for Life* (London: John Murray, 1859), 115, 131, 153, 155; cited in Christopher Southgate et al., *God, Humanity, and the Cosmos: A Textbook in Science and Religion* (Harrisburg: Trinity, 1999).

17　Kenneth Miller, *Finding Darwin's God* (New York: Cliff Street, 1999), 51.

18　Charles Kingsley, "The Natural Theology of the Future," Read at Sion College, January 10th, 1871, retrieved May 22, 2019, http://www.online-literature.com/charles-kingsley/scientific/7.

19　Ibid.

20　John Hedley Brooke, in Ronald Numbers, ed., *Galileo Goes to Jail and Other Myths about Science and Religion.* (Cambridge, MA: Harvard University, 2010), 227.

21　Claude Welch, *Protestant Thought in the Nineteenth Century,* 2 volumes (New Haven and London: Yale University, 1972, 1985), especially chapter 6 from his second volume, "Evolution and Theology: Détente or Evasion?"

22　Numbers, *Galileo Goes to Jail*, 2010.

23　Welch, *Protestant Thought* II: 183.

24　Marsden in Ashley Montagu, ed., *Science and Creationism* (Oxford University Press, 1984), 101.

25　William W. Hay, *Experimenting on a Small Planet: A Scholarly Entertainment* (New York: Springer, 2013), 63.

26　See Welch, *Protestant Thought* II: 189.

27　Robert G. Ingersoll, *Some Mistakes of Moses* (Washington, DC: C.P. Farrrell, 1880), 22–3.

28　Donald Fleming, *John William Draper and the Religion of Science* (Philadelphia: University of Pennsylvania Press, 1950), 132.

29　William Draper, *History of the Conflict between Religion and Science* (Scotts Valley, CA: CreateSpace Independent Publishing Platform, 2017 [1874]), 1.

30　Fleming, *John Draper*, 76.

70 Post-Darwin

31 Principe, in Jeff Hardin et al., eds., *The Warfare Between Science and Religion: The Idea That Wouldn't Die* (Baltimore: Johns Hopkins University Press, 2018), 18.

32 Moritz, *Science and Religion: Beyond Warfare and Toward Understanding* (Winona, MN: Anselm Academic, 2016), 23.

33 Draper, *Conflict*, 10.

34 Ibid., 126.

35 Donald Fleming, *John William Draper, passim*, and especially 69, 76, 88, 104. Cf. Principe, in Hardin et al., 14–15.

36 For Draper's reliance on Comte see Fleming, *John Draper*, 76ff.

37 Principe, "The Warfare Thesis," in Hardin et al., 20.

38 David C. Lindberg, and Ronald L. Numbers, eds., *Where Science and Christianity Meet* (Chicago; University of Chicago, 2003), 2–3.

39 See, e.g., Principe, "The Warfare Thesis," in Hardin et al.

40 White, 97.

41 The Syllabus of Errors #13, *Papal Encyclicals Online*, retrieved June 24, 2019, http://www.papalencyclicals.net/pius09/p9syll.htm.

42 John Updike, *In the Beauty of the Lilies* (New York: Fawcett, 1996), 15.

43 From Charles Hodge's Introduction to his 1872 *Systematic Theology*, cited in Mark A. Noll, ed., *The Princeton Theology, 1812–1921: Scripture, Science, and Theological Method from Archibald Alexander to Benjamin Breckinridge Warfield* (Grand Rapids: Baker Book House, 1983), 125.

44 Charles Hodge, *What is Darwinism?* (New York: Scribner, Armstrong, and Company, 1874), 176.

45 Ibid., 176–7.

46 Ibid., 174.

47 And full disclosure: I'm a graduate of Princeton Theological Seminary.

48 Asa Gray, *Darwiniana: Essays and Reviews Pertaining to Darwinism*, A. Hunter Dupree, ed. (Cambridge, MA: Belknap Press of Harvard University Press, 1963), 210.

49 Taken from Warfield's 1888 "Lectures on Anthropology," which are now held at Speer Library, Princeton Theological Seminary. See Denis Alexander, *Rebuilding the Matrix: Science and faith in the 21st Century* (Oxford: Lion, 2002), 177.

50 Marsden, *Fundamentalism and American Culture*. (Oxford: Oxford University Press, 1980), 19, citing "Religious Aspects of the Doctrine of Development."

51 Ibid., 19.

52 Ibid.

53 Denis Alexander carries this discussion to its contemporary setting in *Is There Purpose in Biology?* (Oxford: Lion Hudson Limited, 2018).

54 Dupree, in Gray, *Darwiniana*, xxii.

55 Elesha Coffman et al, "What is Darwinism?" *Christian History* 107 (2013), retrieved June 24, 2019, https://christianhistoryinstitute.org/magazine/article/107-what-is-darwinism.

56 Asa Gray, quoted in Charles Darwin, *Variation of Plants and Animals under Domestication*, 2 vols. (New York: Orange Judd, 1868), 2:516; cited in Moritz, *Science and Religion*, 164.

57 John H. Brooke, "Darwin and Religion: Correcting Caricatures," *Science and Education* 19, nos. 4–5 (April-May 2010): 394; cited in Moritz, *Science and Religion*, 97.

58 Ibid.

Bibliography

Alexander, Denis. *Rebuilding the Matrix: Science and Faith in the 21st Century*. Oxford, UK: Lion Hudson Limited, 2002.

Alexander, Denis. *Is There Purpose in Biology?* Oxford, UK: Lion Hudson Limited, 2018.

Brush, Stephen G. *A History of Modern Planetary Physics: Nebulous Earth*. Cambridge, UK: Cambridge University Press, 1996.

Carroll, Peter N. and David W. Noble. *The Free and the Unfree: A New History of the United States*. 2nd edition. New York: Penguin, 1988.

Coffman, Elesha et al. "What is Darwinism?" *Christian History* 107 (2013). Retrieved June 24, 2019. https://christianhistoryinstitute.org/magazine/article/107-what-is-darwinism

Dawkins, Richard. *The Blind Watchmaker: Why the Evidence of Evolution Reveals a Universe without Design*. New York: Norton, 1986.

Donald, David Herbert. *Lincoln*. New York: Simon & Schuster, 1995.

Draper, William. *History of the Conflict between Religion and Science*. Scotts Valley, CA: CreateSpace Independent Publishing Platform, 2017 [1874].

Fleming, Donald. *John William Draper and the Religion of Science*. Philadelphia, PA: University of Pennsylvania Press, 1950.

Gray, Asa. *Darwiniana: Essays and Reviews Pertaining to Darwinism*. Edited by A. Hunter Dupree. Cambridge, MA: Belknap Press of Harvard University Press, 1963.

Hay, William W. *Experimenting on a Small Planet: A Scholarly Entertainment*. New York: Springer, 2013.

Hodge, Charles. *What is Darwininism?* New York: Scribner, Armstrong, 1874.

Hovencamp, Herbert. *Science and Religion in America, 1800–1860*. Philadelphia, PA: University of Pennsylvania Press, 1978.

Hume, David. *Dialogues Concerning Natural Religion*. 2nd Edition. Indianapolis, IN: Hackett Publishing Co., 1998.

Ingersoll, Robert G. *Some Mistakes of Moses*. Washington, DC: C.P. Farrrell, 1880.

Kingsley, Charles. "The Natural Theology of the Future. Read at Sion College, January 10, 1871." Retrieved May 22, 2019. http://www.online-literature.com/charles-kingsley/scientific/7

Larson, Edward J. *Evolution: The Remarkable History of a Scientific Theory*. New York: Modern Library, 2006.

Lewis, C.S. *They Asked for a Paper: Paper and Addresses*. London: Geoffrey Bles, 1962.

Montagu, Ashley, ed. *Science and Creationism*. Oxford, UK: Oxford University Press, 1984.

Moritz, Joshua M. *Science and Religion: Beyond Warfare and Toward Understanding*. Winona, MN: Anselm Academic, 2016.

National Academy of Sciences. "History." Retrieved June 13, 2019. http://www.nasonline.org/about-nas/history/archives/founding-and-early-work.html

Noll, Mark A., ed. *The Princeton Theology, 1812–1921: Scripture, Science, and Theological Method from Archibald Alexander to Benjamin Breckinridge Warfield*. Grand Rapids, MI: Baker Book House, 1983.

Paley, William. *Natural Theology: Evidences of the Existence and Attributes of the Deity AND Evidences of Christianity*. Oxford, UK: Benediction Classics, 2017.

Papal Encyclicals Online. "The Syllabus of Errors." Retrieved June 24, 2019. http://www.papalencyclicals.net/pius09/p9syll.htm

Roberts, Jon H. *Darwinism and the Divine in America: Protestant Intellectuals and Organic Evolution*. Madison, WI: University of Wisconsin Press, 1988.

Russell, Robert J., Nancey Murphy and Christopher J. Isham eds. *Quantum Cosmology and the Laws of Nature. Scientific Perspectives on Divine Action*: Volume 1. Berkeley, CA: Vatican Observatory Publications; Center for Theology and the Natural Sciences, 1993.

Southgate, Christopher et al. *God, Humanity, and the Cosmos: A Textbook in Science and Religion*. Harrisburg, PA: Trinity, 1999.

Sunday, Billy. *Boston Herald*, November 14, 1916, p. 1.

Turner, James. *Without God, Without Creed: The Origins of Unbelief in America*. Baltimore and London: Johns Hopkins University Press, 1985.

Updike, John. *In the Beauty of the Lilies*. New York: Fawcett, 1996.

72 Post-Darwin

Welch, Claude. *Protestant Thought in the Nineteenth Century*. Two volumes. New Haven and London: Yale University, 1985 [1972].

White, Andrew Dickson. *A History of the Warfare of Science with Theology in Christendom*. New York: Appleton, 1896.

Whitehead, Alfred North. *The Concept of Nature*. Cambridge, UK: Cambridge University Press, 1920.

6

1870–1925: FROM THE RISE OF RELIGIOUS MODERNISM AND PLURALISM TO THE SCOPES TRIAL

Modernism and pluralism in late nineteenth-century America

The fabric of science and religion added several new threads and patterns in 1870–1900, principally Protestant modernism/liberalism (terms I will use interchangeably). One key characteristic of theological modernism, as John Roberts notes, is the need to make necessary and significant changes to "apologetics, doctrine and biblical interpretation"[1] in light of scientific advances. He added, "The willingness to make such revisions in an effort to harmonize the Christian world view with the tenor of modern thought has rightly been viewed as one of the defining features of the American liberal Protestant tradition."[2] Or as the leading modernist theologian at the University of Chicago divinity school, Shailer Matthews, wrote in 1924, "In brief, the use of scientific, historical, and social methods in understanding and applying evangelical Christianity to the needs of living persons, is Modernism."[3]

Scientists, who regularly encounter new discoveries that challenge, modify, or enhance traditional belief, often find this accommodation uncontroversial, or even expected. For example, Joseph LeConte (1823–1901) presented his philosophy of creative evolution as a melding of science and religion. LeConte, educated under Louis Agassiz and Asa Gray at Harvard, had his greatest influence at the University of California, Berkeley, where a prominent and impressive science building bears his (and his brother's) name. He found no difficulty in describing himself in 1868 as "an evolutionist, thorough and enthusiastic." He continued by adopting the angelic and heavenly host's proclamation about the birth of Jesus in Luke 2, "not only because it is true, and all truth is the image of God in the human reason, but also because of all the laws of nature it is ... the most in accord with religious philosophic thought. It is, indeed, glad tidings of great joy which shall be to all peoples."[4]

74 The rise of religious modernism

Even if these conclusions led LeConte away from orthodox Christian belief, it did not lead him toward seeing the need to put science and religion in conflict. One of the most striking statements on science, in light of evolution, emerged from the mouth of Paul Carus (1852–1919), who, though educated at the University of Tübingen, had most of his impact in the US, where he became a colleague of the great pragmatist philosopher Charles Sanders Pierce. Carus proposed a "Religion of Science," which connected the two in extraordinary ways. Also appropriating biblical language—in this case from the first chapter of the gospel of John—he wrote, "Science is the embodiment of the immutable world-order of the Logos that was in the beginning, of God in revelation."[5] In this case, science had indeed replaced religion as a source of revelation and fundamental reality.

Another theological strategy was to take recourse in the inner world of human thought. Roberts described it this way, citing Newman Smyth's *The Religious Feeling* from 1877, "Some liberal apologists, finding 'external arguments for the being of God' less than compelling, chose to emphasize that the 'foundations of religion' was to be found 'in human nature, in the great primal instincts of the soul.'"[6] In Germany, Ernest Troeltsch similarly articulated the concept of this internal psychological reality in 1904 as the *religious a priori*, "an a priori element in consciousness, the grounding of religious ideas in the structure of reason,"[7] a notion that filled the pages of theological prolegomena as the new apologetic strategy. A divinely directed evolution, progressing through various stages until the emergence of human beings and their religious a priori, fit marvelously with postmillennial thought. Every day we are getting better and better.

Up to this point, nineteenth-century Christian theology possessed a common interest in the millennial reign of Christ described in the twentieth chapter of the book of Revelation, and yet believers held a variety of ideas. Would Christ's return happen before a 1,000-year reign (*premillennialism*), or after a blessed age with a gradual increase of the Christian message and its ethics throughout the world (*postmillennialism*)? The Calvinist heritage of Puritanism emphasized *amillennialism*— the 1,000-year reign of Christ was symbolic language because Christ was already reigning in heaven. This view was being displaced, or even forgotten, in light of the growing premillennialism. Also threatened was liberalism's *postmillennialism*, which meant, as interpreted by some, that, instead of having to wait for Christ to return and bring about the millennial reign, human progress could hasten the Kingdom. As Christine Rosen commented in her study of the wedding of liberal Christianity with eugenics, *Preaching Eugenics*, "Postmillennialists viewed the world as a place to change for the better to create the Kingdom of God on earth, and so reform a vital part of their Christianity"[8] ... and, I would add, the nation and thus the world.

A late nineteenth-century version of evolution emphasized the increase of diversity and complexity as a sign of progress, which did fit exquisitely with liberal postmillennialism. One may find no greater voice in the liberal

The rise of religious modernism   75

ecclesiastical realm than Henry Ward Beecher, whose 1885 *Evolution and Religion* was obviously an adaptation of evolutionary concepts for evangelical purposes. (Some question the degree to which he understood these ideas. William Schneider has evaluated this book's author: "there was scarcely even a pretext of science in him."[9]). Beecher's is certainly not nature "red with tooth and claw" (made famous by Alfred Lord Tennyson's *In Memoriam A.H.H.*, 1850). Instead human beings are gradually, day by day, getting better and better. Christ in fact preached this.

In his preface to this collection of eight of his sermons, he offers these telling comments, which addressed so many themes at once it is worthy of a lengthy citation:

> Slowly, and through a whole fifty years, I have been under the influence, first obscurely, imperfectly, of the great doctrine of Evolution. In my earliest preaching I discerned that the kingdom of heaven is a leaven, not only in the individual soul, but in the world; the kingdom is as a grain of mustard-seed; I was accustomed to call my crude notion a seminal theory of the kingdom of God in this world. Later I began to feel that science had struck a larger view, and that this unfolding of seed and blade and ear in spiritual things was but one application of a great cosmic doctrine, which underlay God's methods in universal creation, and was notably to be seen in the whole development of human society and human thought. That great truth—through patient accumulations of fact, and marvelous intuitions of reason, and luminous expositions of philosophic relation, by men trained in observation, in thinking, and in expression—has now become accepted throughout the scientific world. Certain parts of it yet are in dispute, but substantially it is the doctrine of the scientific world. And that it will furnish—nay, is already bringing—to the aid of religious truth as set forth in the life and teachings of Jesus Christ a new and powerful aid, fully in line with other marked developments of God's providence in this His world, I fervently believe.[10]

Later Beecher considered the core teaching for Christian life, and indeed for most Americans, in light of this new theory: "The Bible is thus a grand evolution of the nature of God. It is the unfolding of his progress, that is to say, of the progress of the human mind respecting him."[11] (As I mentioned above, progressive, directed evolution is the dominant emphasis from religious thought leaders.)

I'll note one final thinker in this growing diversity of religious life in America because of his ongoing influence on the study of religion and his use of scientific methods, particularly the new insights of the science of psychology: the Harvard psychologist William James. In the Gifford Lectures at the University of Edinburgh in 1901–02 he analyzed the human experience of religion, and his penetrating insights were published shortly thereafter as *The Varieties of Religious Experience.*[12] It is a classic study of religion, even if James's examples are almost entirely drawn not from religion generally but from Christianity. It could even be

76 The rise of religious modernism

argued to represent a *scientific* study of religion. Jacque Barzan, in his foreword to the 1958 edition of *The Varieties,* notes James's early training as a chemist and a physician who didn't use this training to explain away religious life. "The reader of *The Varieties*, however, will not find James a conventional 'scientist' who uses the facts of physiology or psychology to explain away the facts of religious life."[13] In fact, in a phrase that will echo in the halls of the Gifford Lectures almost a century later through the voice of John Polkinghorne, James argues against a materialistic conception where "other people criticise our own more exalted soul-flights by calling them *'nothing but'* expressions of organic dispositions."[14] Later James himself directly addresses the "science of religions,"[15] noting "the conclusions of the science of religion are as likely to be adverse as they are to be favorable to the claim that the essence of religion is true."[16] In his view, science seeks to be free from dogma.

My hope is that these voices are sufficient to demonstrate further that Darwin could be appropriated in a variety of ways and purposes. I will return to evolution (I couldn't entirely leave the topic if I wanted), but first need to note further alterations in the way religion appeared in America during the late nineteenth and early twentieth centuries.

With the expansion of migration from non-European countries in the latter decades of the nineteenth century, America began to witness a growing religious diversity, especially from Jewish and Catholic immigration. In 1860 the US population numbered 31 million; by 1890 ten million new immigrants had arrived, followed by 15 million between 1890 and 1914.[17] This emergence of new cultures and their religious traditions brought along with it a reaction and a resistance—an undeniable thread in American culture—enshrined in the 1880 Chinese Exclusion Act, which banned most immigration from China, and in the Immigration Act of 1924, which I'll discuss shortly.

Additionally there were new Christian voices, and those derived from Christianity and its nineteenth-century millennialism, such as the Jehovah's Witnesses, organized by Charles Taze Russell in 1872, which grew out of the disappointments that William Miller's prophecies did not materialize in the 1840s. And, second, the religious options available to Americans expanded, exemplified in the 1893 World Parliament of Religions mounted by the city of Chicago, which was also playing host to the World Columbian Exposition (really an early world's fair). With people arriving from all over the world, smaller conferences were held at the same time (such as the World Parliament), which Charles C. Bonney, a judge and Swedenborgian layman, organized. The Christian clergyman John Henry Barrows was appointed the first chair of the General Committee (and later became a leader in the study of comparative religion at the University of Chicago). In many ways the Parliament marked the first organized gathering in America of leaders from eastern and western religions. It took shape later in the establishment of the International Association for Religious Freedom in 1900, the World Congress of Faiths in 1936, and the World Council of Churches, which was first incorporated in 1937 and established formally in 1948.

Fundamentalism

Fundamentalism finds its roots deep in American religious soil, especially in the older, broader evangelicalism, and leads all the way back to essential elements of American Christianity; Biblicism, revivalism, the nineteenth-century Princeton Theology, and premillennialism. I will outline each of these briefly. As with many terms, the particular story began perhaps half a century earlier—in the 1870s, as Christian leaders tussled over how to integrate, or to reject, new learning—but the word *fundamentalist* wasn't coined until 1920, when a newspaper editor, Curtis Lee Law, described this theological shock troop as ready "to do battle royal for the Fundamentals."[18] In the midst of its struggles, the 1910 Presbyterian General Assembly affirmed a list that became the five marks of the fundamentalist movement: the inspiration and inerrancy of the Bible; the Virgin birth of Christ (or, more accurately, the Virginal Conception of Christ); Christ's substitutionary atonement; the bodily resurrection of Christ; and the historicity of the biblical miracles.[19] (Some also look to the 1895 Niagara Bible Conference, which presented, more or less, the same list, substituting Christ's imminent return for biblical miracles.)

I noted above the strands that led to fundamentalism. Biblicism is certainly rooted in the religious practice of the Puritans, as well as being embedded in the root of *evangelical*, "related to the *evangel*, or gospel." Here it became wedded to a doctrine of inerrancy, presented by the venerable and highly influential tradition of the old Princeton Theology that set out an intellectually rigorous basis for a resistance to modernizing trends in theology, particularly in the doctrine of the inerrancy of original autographa (or manuscripts) of the Bible via B.B. Warfield.[20] Revivalism, as I've noted above, wound its way throughout American history and is particularly important in relation to the late nineteenth-century evangelistic sensation, Dwight L. Moody (1837–99). And, finally, the teachings of Charles Darby, which found their way into the popular 1909 *Scofield Reference Bible*, hastened the advance of dispensationalism and solidified premillennialism.

Of course, we still have not arrived at 1920 and the first usage of *fundamentalist*, but I would be remiss not to note that, between 1910 and 1915, the Testimony Publishing Company of Chicago published *The Fundamentals*, meant to be "A Testimony To The Truth," a set of 90 essays, first presented quarterly in 12 volumes and then republished by the Bible Institute of Los Angeles (later known as Biola College). Its foreword declared that the Fundamentals were intended to be "a new statement of the fundamentals of Christianity." And thus the moniker "fundamentalist" fit easily just a few years later. The contents focused on theological innovations of liberal Christianity, particularly biblical criticism. Oddly enough—and the history of ideas can be very odd indeed—many of the signers of the Fundamentals did not reject evolution or at least a long history to the earth. This period followed decades of growing theological pluralism in the United States, exemplified partly in the response to the cacophony of voices interpreting the Bible around slavery.[21] This is also a period of responding to modernist inroads

78 The rise of religious modernism

into new biblical scholarship, often arriving at the hands of German academics via higher criticism (which challenged traditional biblical interpretation) as opposed to lower or textual criticism (which analyzed the transmission, and thus preservation, of the biblical texts). At any rate, these European academics began a process of trying to discern in what ways the Bible is a human book with equally human flaws. As a response, the fundamentalists focused on five key doctrines (which bear repeating): the divine inspiration of scripture; the Virgin birth; individual salvation solely through Christ's sacrifice; the bodily resurrection of Jesus and his followers; and the authenticity of miracles.[22]

The fundamentalist-modernist split

With any move to integrate a wider variety of voices—and even to synchronize their insights and seek unity—there's a backlash that creates further division. And, certainly, one key component of the story I'm telling is the split over how Christians, and particularly Protestants, interacted with culture. The modernists generally welcomed culture and its contributions to their beliefs, while the fundamentalists perceived in the world evidence for the Fall. And that becomes apparent in two major events: the fundamentalist-modernist split and the Scopes Trial. Let me take them in that order.

But first, in contrast to this rising fundamentalism, a new understanding of the Gospel was arising that has some specific characteristics that could also be described as modernist but that did not correlate entirely with other liberal theologians. Walter Rauschenbusch, minister at the Second German Baptist Church in close proximity to New York City's Hell's Kitchen (now renamed "Clinton"), observed human suffering and proclaimed the Christian church's responsibility to respond. He had already come to national attention with his 1907 *Christianity and Social Crisis*, but his most profound and enduring contribution remains his 1917 *A Theology of the Social Gospel*. Though late in the progressive era, it articulated well its characteristic concepts with clearly Christian notes. As Claude Welch commented, "The social gospel has recovered the authentic message of the Hebrew prophets' demand for justice and Jesus' proclamation of the kingdom of God as a call to new righteousness under the law of love."[23] In that light Rauschenbusch formulated the "social gospel" clearly and brilliantly ... and therefore controversially: "The social gospel is the old message of salvation, but enlarged and intensified." An individualistic message of salvation may have its place, but "it has not evoked faith in the will and power of God to redeem the permanent institutions of human society from their inherited guild of oppression and extortion."[24] The progressive era had found its theological voice.

In his early 1912 book *Christianizing the Social Order*, Rauschenbusch also transformed evolutionary discourse into a religious zeal that would change society: "We now have such scientific knowledge of social laws and forces, of economics, of history that we can intelligently mold and guide the evolution in which we take part."[25] Lest we put Rauschenbusch on the side of the angels, he combined this

The rise of religious modernism **79**

zeal for a kind of democratic socialism with a racially based Aryanism. Thomas Leonard commented on this "mishmash of the social gospel, economic reform, Darwinism and anti-Catholicism" with this summary: according to Rauschenbusch, "Cooperation and common property were 'dyed into the fiber of our breed' innate to the Anglo-Saxon."[26]

I will focus on eugenics in a moment, but it's important to mention that, around this time, most modernists, whether theological or not, adopted eugenics as the vanguard of science. (We have returned to the theme of the modernists' embrace of culture and its contributions.)

One marker of this movement was the famous 1922 sermon by the iconic liberal pastor Harry Emerson Fosdick whose radio show, National Vespers Hour, reached an estimated two to three million people. His sermon, *"Shall the Fundamentalists Win?"*[27] sought to bring together faith and science as a defining mark of liberals and a distinguishing factor (at least in their eyes) from fundamentalists, and called for an open-minded and intellectually engaged Christian fellowship. (Interestingly, Fosdick also joined the American Eugenics Society Advisory Council, although it's not entirely clear what his views on eugenics were.[28]) This sermon and his long-standing liberal views cost him his post at New York's First Presbyterian Church. Having been removed from its pulpit for his liberal theology, John D. Rockefeller built for him the glorious Riverside Church in New York City where Fosdick enjoyed a long tenure. (Incidentally, to this day, one of the marks of Riverside is the stained-glass window celebrating Albert Einstein.)

Fosdick ends a rousing call to keep free of stains of fundamentalism with this,

> I do not even know in this congregation whether anybody has been tempted to be a Fundamentalist. Never in this church have I caught one accent of intolerance. God keep us always so and ever increasing areas of the Christian fellowship; intellectually hospitable, open-minded, liberty-loving, fair, tolerant, not with the tolerance of indifference, as though we did not care about the faith, but because always our major emphasis is upon the weightier matters of the law.[29]

The fight between these two poles of Christendom would in fact carry forward to this day, especially in negotiating sacred, traditional sources (such as the Bible) in light of scientific discoveries and trends. The Bible or science? Modernists affirm both *if* we update the Bible and its interpretation. Conservatives, most notably fundamentalists, hold to the Bible above science, and science as it coheres to their biblical interpretation. And, naturally, those in between often couldn't compete with the cacophony of the conservatives versus the modernists.

Another strain of theology arrived directly from Europe, which tended to sidestep the issue of science as an irrelevancy for hearing God's Word. With Karl Barth's cataclysmic 1922 second edition of *Epistle to the Romans*, European theological liberalism was dying and a new generation of "dialectical theologians" was ascending. Though removed from American fundamentalism by thousands of

80 The rise of religious modernism

literal miles—and even more theological ones—they shared a profound sense of disruption. For Barth it was the horrors of World War I that "inflicted serious damage on optimistic fusions of human evolution with divine providence" (to cite John Hedley Brooke).[30] Apropos to the relationship of science and religion, Barth resisted natural theology—especially his 1930 *Nein!* to a "point of contact" and his 1945 eschewing of all scientific insights in formulating his doctrine of creation. In these convictions Barth reflected the views of the late nineteenth-century liberal theological giant, Wilhelm Hermann, who offered this deep trench between science and religion,

> It is just as clear to the believer as it is to those who are acquainted with science, that science has not part or lot in the content of these thoughts ... the believer breaks down every bridge between his own conviction, and all that science can acknowledge to be real, simply because these thoughts have grown out of the faith awakened by God's historical revelation.[31]

The influence of Barth, who though Swiss was arguably the most influential theologian of the twentieth century even in the United States, not only through such theological training grounds as Princeton Theological Seminary, but also among like-minded theologians Reinhold Niebuhr, who taught for many years at New York City's Union Theological Seminary, and his brother, H. Richard Niebuhr, who spent decades at Yale Divinity School 75 miles north of his elder sibling. In sum, almost all sides of the American theological ledger failed to build an early twentieth-century legacy of integration with modern science.

Scientists like Robert A. Millikan, a Nobel Laureate in physics, came to similar conclusions about the independence of science and religion. Jon H. Roberts summarized Milken's views:

> In 1923, he succeeded in securing the signatures of more than thirty well-known scientists, theologians, and clergy to a "Joint Statement upon the Relations of Science and Religion" that affirmed that these enterprises "meet distinct needs" and thus "supplement rather than displace or oppose each other." Millikan's statement held that whereas scientific investigation sought "to develop, without prejudice or preconception of any kind, a knowledge of the facts, the laws, and the processes of nature," it was the role of religion "to develop the consciences, the ideals, and the aspirations" of humankind.[32]

Stephen Jay Gould and his Non-Overlapping Magisterial Authority certainly has its precursors.

Finally, Ronald Fisher (1890–1962) produced a 1918 paper that many consider the beginning of the modern evolutionary synthesis, by itself a notable scientific achievement. Fisher also dedicated himself to "working out an expressly *Darwinian* Christianity, a faith that would triumph in history through struggle and toil."[33] Moreover, he believed that evolution revealed a progress where "humans are right

The rise of religious modernism **81**

at the top."[34] An optimism in human improvement, the supremacy of Christian civilization, and evolutionary thought became bound together. These also could provide support for the growing eugenics movement.

The expansion of eugenics in America

I left the thread of evolution and religion, and particularly the various ways that Darwin could be appropriated. And now I return to some subthemes: eugenics, as well as social Darwinism, subjects certainly significant enough to deserve their own subsection. Beginning in the 1880s, America saw the rise of *eugenics*, which derives from two Greek words meaning "good creation" and is not unrelated to my previous comments on racial superiority (also called "scientific racism," or "race biology").[35] Defined by the *Oxford Dictionary of Biology,* eugenics is "the study of methods of improving the quality of human populations by the application of genetic principles. Positive eugenics would seek to do this by selective breeding programmes, a strategy that is generally deemed reprehensible. Negative eugenics aims to eliminate harmful genes (e.g. those causing haemophilia and colour blindness) by counselling any prospective parents who are likely to be carriers."[36] A related term, *social Darwinism*, represents the theory that "sociocultural advance is the product of intergroup conflict and competition and the socially elite classes (such as those possessing wealth and power) possess biological superiority in the struggle for existence."[37]

For most Americans today it's hard to fathom that eugenics was seen as good *science*; in fact, the cutting edge for about 50 years. And then it disappeared like a rock dropped into the ocean by the end of the 1930s. (I'll leave for the final chapters the topic of whether it will reappear in the near future, or perhaps already has.) Most historians begin with Francis Galton (1822–1911), who was an English anthropologist, explorer, half cousin of Charles Darwin, and, most importantly for this book, a eugenicist known for his pioneering studies of human intelligence. Galton was knighted in 1909. In fact, he coined the term eugenics and sought to hone the practices of intention breeding and selective parenthood that would improve the genetic quality—the physical and mental composition—of human populations or "races." Imbedded in eugenics was certainly the superiority of the white race as well as male superiority. Galton, it's worth noting, determined that women in all their capacities tended to be inferior to men.[38] To pursue his project of eugenics, Galton opened the Anthropometric Laboratory at London's Health Exhibition in 1884.

Evolutionary thought, in the minds of its promoters, offered scientific support for eugenics (and social Darwinism). In the United States the eugenics movement took root in the early 1900s, guided by Harry Laughlin (1880–1943)—a former teacher and principal who had particular curiosity in the science of breeding and eventually became superintendent of the Eugenics Record Office (ERO) from its origin in 1910 to its closing in 1939—and especially the leading biologist Charles Davenport (1866–1944). In his record of eugenics in America, Edwin Black has written, "The real father of eugenics was of course Charles Benedict Davenport. Galton was merely the grandfather."[39] In 1904 Davenport became director of Cold Spring Laboratory where in 1910 he founded the ERO with the explicit intention "to improve the natural, physical, mental, and temperamental qualities of the human family."[40] Cold Spring has enduring legacy in its promotion of eugenics, which, as Black aptly commented, "was nothing less than America's legalized campaign to breed a super race—and not just any super race. Eugenicists wanted a purely Germanic and Nordic super race, enjoying biological dominion over all others."[41]

Galton died in 1911, but the idea had spread to the United States. In a less literary and more chilling rhetorical manner, Irving Fischer (interestingly the son of a Congregationalist pastor) preached what Thomas Leonard calls "the gospel of eugenics," and that Americans "must make of eugenics a religion."[42] Famously, John Harvey Kellogg, the corn flake titan, organized the Race Betterment Foundation in 1911 and established a "pedigree registry," which held national eugenics conferences in 1914, 1915, and 1928. At the 1915 edition of this gathering Fischer presented a talk entitled, with language clearly appropriated from Christianity, "Eugenics—Foremost Plan of Human Redemption."[43] Fischer was even willing to carry this further—and in the process responds to Whitehead's Challenge: when America makes "eugenics the pillar of the church," then science and religion, "these two great human interests, will be marching together, hand in hand."[44]

In the early twentieth century a widespread social Darwinism began to pervade much of American thought. And here any easy association of conservative Christianity with all things backward becomes problematic. For their part the fundamentalists resisted the growing tide of eugenics, which began to sweep through the US in the first three decades of the twentieth century and had sought to give itself legitimacy based on Darwin's theories and "the survival of the fittest." D.H. Lawrence provided the most grotesque expression of this form of thought in his 1908 fantasy (and, to some extent, prophecy) of extermination:

> If I had my way, I would build a lethal chamber as big as the Crystal Palace, with a military band playing softly, and a Cinematograph working brightly, and then I'd go out in back streets and main streets and bring them all in, all the sick, the halt, and the maimed; I would lead them gently, and they would smile at me.[45]

Indeed, some of this found its way into the racial superiority language of the Ku Klux Klan and its rise in the 1910s. As Joshua Moritz writes, "During the years leading to the Scopes Trial, a scientific-sounding form of such social teaching aimed at culling the 'evolutionarily unfit' gained widespread public attention under the name eugenics."[46] In this case, "culling" meant being absolutely sure the unfit could not procreate. Edward Davis notes that, by 1925, "24 states had passed laws permitting eugenic sterilizations, and about 12,000 sterilizations had been performed."[47]

And our highest court was similarly captivated: in 1927 the US Supreme Court ruled that forced sterilization of the handicapped did not violate the Constitution. Justice Oliver Wendall Holmes offered these six cynical words, "three generations of imbeciles are enough." The ruling was overturned in 1942, but by then thousands had been forced to submit to this procedure. And Congress did its part. For example, in 1924 it enacted the Immigration Act which was signed by President Calvin Coolidge and which limited the number of immigrants to the US through quotas. And here's the curious part: immigration visas were provided to 2% of particular nationalities already in the country based on the census, but instead of a recent census (e.g., 1920 or 1910), *the 1890 national census was the standard*, which reflected a time before the influx of southern Europeans (Italians, Greeks) as well as Jews. This act limited and directed our immigration for decades before it was revised in the Immigration and Nationality Act of 1952 and, more significantly, when President Lyndon Johnson replaced it with the Immigration and Nationality Act of 1965. Although it may not technically fit the category of eugenics, I find it hard not to include the Tuskegee Study of Untreated Syphilis in the African American, the unethical and infamous clinical study conducted without the knowledge of the hundreds of participants and which began in 1932 and ran for 40 years.

The 1920s and 1930s were the heyday for the American eugenics movement, but by the 1940s the American movement began to lose cultural heft and became discredited by the horrific way Nazi Germany used eugenic principles to exterminate Jews, "gypsies," homosexuals, and others they found undesirable for their creation of an Aryan race. Black writes that two factors converged to lead America's retreat from eugenics: "Hitler's ascent in Germany and the climatic exit of the pseudoscience's founding fathers from Cold Spring Harbor."[48] In 1934 Davenport left Cold Spring for the Carnegie Institution at age 68. And as a result of swirling controversies, especially with the rise of Nazism and increasing scrutiny of the Carnegie Institution, Laughlin officially retired on December 31, 1939. The next day, ERO was shuttered. There is more to say, of course, [49] but for the purposes of this book I only need to note the cultural sway of eugenics was greatly diminished by the end of the 1930s.

However, in 1925 eugenics was still in fashion. When later conservative Christian resistance to evolution was channeled at the Scopes Trial through William Jennings Bryan, eugenics played a key role (which I will describe shortly). But first an explanation for why I believe eugenics, as an outgrowth of Darwinian theory, is worth mentioning at such length. Although it became discredited, I am concerned for a resurgence today. The rise of racism and especially white nationalism in the United States may lead to uses of genetic engineering and transhumanism to support eugenics as well as racial superiority. I will return to these themes briefly later.

84 The rise of religious modernism

The 1925 Scopes Trial

A major iconic moment for science and religion in America remains the July 1925 Scopes "Monkey" Trial in Dayton, Tennessee, a small town of 1,500 inhabitants. In fact, when compared with the 1633 trial of Galileo or the 1860 Oxford evolution debate between William Wilberforce and T.H. Huxley, this is the only iconic religion versus science event (if it is indeed that) on American soil. (The 2005 Dover case, which I'll discuss later, deserves a more minor status.) Formally known as *The State of Tennessee v. John Thomas Scopes*, the trial was deliberately staged in order to attract publicity; the town leaders wanted some publicity and to put Dayton on the map.[50] According to the leading historian of this event, "media-savvy participants billed [this] as 'a battle-royale between science and religion.'"[51]

The trial brought forth a substitute high school teacher, John T. Scopes, as a *cause célèbre*, accused of violating Tennessee's 1925 Butler Act, which had made it unlawful to teach human evolution in a state-funded, public school. The American Civil Liberties Union opposed the statute because it violated free speech and invited the town leaders to test it in court. William Jennings Bryan, former Secretary of State and three-time Democratic Party presidential nominee, offered his assistance to the prosecution. He was no mean orator (known as the Boy Orator of the Platte) who combined conservative religious opinions with liberal politics. Facing off against Bryan, ardent secularist and famous/infamous lawyer Clarence Darrow took a lead role on the defense. Two titans, themselves representing epic cultural forces, were set to clash in this small town, all around a misdemeanor trial.

This was not the first time Bryan had demonstrated either his antagonism for evolution or his interest in science. On December 30, 1924, he paid five dollars for membership of the American Association for the Advancement for Science (AAAS) since it had already demonstrated its interest in promoting Darwinian evolution.[52] Bryan had made it clear where this clash of religion with evolution needed to take place. As Edward Larson commented,

> The taxpayers, to use the crassest formulation of the argument, had the democratic right to determine what was taught in their schools. If the information contradicted the knowledge of the Bible and the custom of their culture, it was clearly the right and duty of citizens to reject it as false. Bryan did not demand a specifically Christian education, he cautioned, only the exclusion of any non-Christian science, of the teaching of notions that would shake the Christian pillars of society.[53]

It's impossible for me not to hear echoes in Philip Johnson's diatribe against Darwin in the 1990s—that evolutionary science is inherently anti-Christian and therefore contrary to American values.

Bryan had a deep antagonism to evolutionary science, but not only for reasons contemporary readers might reject. Certainly, biblical literalism and basic ignorance

The rise of religious modernism   **85**

of evolution played its part, but so did the morality of eugenics. Bryan's Christian faith led him to resist both what he perceived as the undermining of conservative biblical hermeneutics and the rise of social Darwinism (which for him was synonymous with evolution). As Christine Rosen commented in *Preaching Eugenics: Religious Leaders and the American Eugenics Movement,*

> Religious leaders pursued eugenics precisely when they moved away from traditional religious tenets. The liberals and modernists in their respective faiths—those who challenged their churches to conform to modern circumstances—became the eugenics movement's most enthusiastic supporters.[54]

If God is working through culture—as many liberal theological leaders advocated—then there is nothing to critique culture. Bryan, however, would be Exhibit A for Rosen's assertion: he stuck with traditional theology.

And clearly the textbook that Scopes taught, *Civil Biology* by George William Hunter, had imbedded eugenics along with evolutionary thought. It "featured a section on eugenics that identified mental deficiency, alcoholism, sexual immorality, and criminality as hereditary, offered 'the remedy' of sexual segregation and sterilization for these disabilities; and urged students to select eugenically 'healthy mates.'"[55] And as Hunter himself wrote in the textbook, "if the stock of domesticated animals can be improved, it is not unfair to ask if the health and vigor of future generations of men and women on the earth might not be improved by applying to them the law of selection."[56] We could, it appears, apply the teachings of evolution to making a better human species. But when Hunter considered the mentally ill, epileptics, and habitual criminals, he lamented, "If such people were lower animals, we would probably kill them off to prevent them from spreading."[57] Mark Noll has commented that Bryan resisted Darwinian evolution because he "saw clearly the great problem with evolution was not the practice of science but the metaphysical naturalism and consequent social Darwinism that scientific evolution was often called to justify."[58]

Bryan's stance wasn't about an entirely narrow reading of the Bible, at least by contemporary creationist standards. His resistance to evolution was also not about the age of the earth. In fact Bryan, like many fundamentalists, was an old earth creationist, which his stringent biblical hermeneutic could countenance.[59] As one exhibit, the interchange between Darrow and Bryan is noteworthy. In it Darrow challenged Bryan to take the stand, and the latter rashly became a witness for the prosecution and was interrogated by Darrow.

CLARENCE DARROW [D]: Mr Bryan, could you tell me how old the earth is?
WILLIAM JENNINGS BRYAN [B]: No, sir, I couldn't.
[D]: Could you come anywhere near it?
[B]: I wouldn't attempt to. I could possibly come as near as the scientists do, but I had rather be more accurate before I give a guess.

86 The rise of religious modernism

|D|: Does the statement, "The morning and the evening were the first day," and "The morning and the evening were the second day," mean anything to you?

|B|: I do not think it necessarily means a twenty-four-hour day.

|D|: You do not?

|B|: No.

|D|: Then, when the Bible said, for instance, "and God called the firmament heaven. And the evening and the morning were the second day," that does not necessarily mean twenty-four hours?

|B|: I do not think it necessarily does. I think it would be just as easy for the kind of God we believe in to make the earth in six days as in six years or in six million years or in 600 million years. I do not think it important whether we believe one or the other.

|D|: And they had the evening and the morning before that time for three days or three periods. All right, that settles it. Now, if you call those periods, they may have been a very long time.

|B|: They might have been.

|D|: The creation might have been going on for a very long time?

|B|: It might have continued for millions of years.[60]

And yet, it is important to clarify that Bryan defended several aspects of conservative biblical interpretation in this same interchange, such as "the whale" who swallowed Jonah. (Of course, in the Hebrew Bible, it isn't particularly a whale.) "I believe," affirmed Bryan, "in a God who can make a whale and make a man and make both of them do what he pleases...."[61]

Bryan's hermeneutic had loose ends, and Darrow was happy to have him tied in knots with them. One famous interchange demonstrates the brilliance of Darrow's approach and why, to his critics (but certainly not to most assembled that day in Dayton), Bryan appeared confused and irrational:

|D|: You believe the story of the flood to be a literal interpretation?

|B|: Yes, sir.

|D|: When was that flood?

|B|: I would not attempt to fix the date. The date is fixed, as suggested this morning.

|D|: About 4004 BC?

|B|: That has been the estimate of a man that is accepted today. I would not say it is accurate.

|D|: That estimate is printed in the Bible?

|B|: Everybody knows, at least, I think most of the people know, that was the estimate given.

|D|: But what do you think that the Bible itself says? Don't you know how it was arrived at?

|B|: I never made a calculation.

|D|: A calculation from what?

The rise of religious modernism **87**

[B]: I could not say.
[D]: From the generations of man?
[B]: I would not want to say that.
[D]: What do you think?
[B]: I do not think about things I don't think about.
[D]: Do you think about things you do think about?
[B]: Well, sometimes.[62]

As for the broader implications for science and religion, oddly Scopes was unsure whether he had ever actually taught evolution—he purposely incriminated himself so that the case brought by the ACLU could have a defendant. Despite the glorious interrogation by Clarence Darrow—and the less glorious responses by Bryan—the court found Scopes guilty and fined him $100 (or about $1,500 today). Later a higher court overturned the verdict on a technicality. Moritz presented this conclusion:

> To summarize, then, a closer look at the historical and social context of the Scopes Monkey Trial shows that the main conflict was not between "science and religion" as such. Rather, the debate was chiefly between those who, like Darrow, utilized science to attack religion, a view called scientism, and those who, like Bryan, accepted scientific geology and even many scientific components of evolutionary theory, but, in the name of the values of Christian religion, object to the social application of Darwin's theory in eugenics.[63]

Even more, the Scopes Trial most Americans know is much larger than, and quite different from, the actual legal event in the summer of 1925. Perhaps it began with Bryan's death just a week after the trial—to some a martyr for the truth of old-time religion and to others a relic of a tired and irrelevant "old-time religion." Writers and pundits quickly began to offer their spin. As Larson wrote, "Media accounts at the time suggested that the trial mainly served to intensify positions on both sides of the public controversy over the teaching of evolution."[64] And so the Scopes Trial was equally ambiguous for determining which side won. In 1941 Irving Stone concluded that the trial "dealt a deathblow to Fundamentalism."[65] And the 1955 Broadway play, five years later made into a film, *Inherit the Wind*, extended the mythology of this event, framing it as the triumph of reason over religious dogmatism and stupidity. It added, for example, that Scopes (or Bertram Cates) is arrested in class, thrown in jail, denounced by a fundamentalist preacher (whose daughter is in love with Cates), and burned in effigy, all of which is entirely fictional. And in some ways, following the Scopes Trial and, even more, a well-publicized scandal involving wildly popular and flamboyant evangelist Aimee Semple McPherson and a mysterious lover, fundamentalists began to lose the cultural influence they enjoyed in the 1920s.

88 The rise of religious modernism

A response to the rising contributions and challenges of science certainly has its place in the split of fundamentalist and modernist in various denominations, especially the Northern Baptists, the Disciples of Christ, and the Presbyterians. Fundamentalists soon lost battles against modernists (or liberals) in two major denominations. But the loss didn't stem from a response to science or the Bible, but sociology. It's possible to divide the Presbyterians, for example, of the 1920s into three camps, those who were fundamentalists and sought a purer form of Christianity, those who were modernists and wanted an updated faith, and, the most important group, those who essentially agreed with the fundamentalists doctrinally but did not want to create schism.[66] "From 1922 to 1925," George Marsden has written, "fundamentalists were close to gaining control of the Northern Presbyterian and Northern Baptist groups. Suddenly in 1926 they were much weakened minorities."[67] One of the most famous and accomplished minds of theological conservatism was J. Gresham Machen, author of the trenchant attack on modernist Christianity, *Christianity and Liberalism.*[68] After years of trying to extinguish modernists (in his view) at Princeton Theological Seminary, he emerged on the wrong side of the power struggle and left in theological disgust to form Westminster Theological Seminary in Philadelphia in 1929. He later created a new branch of his denomination, the Orthodox Presbyterian Church, in 1936. Similarly, the fundamentalists were unable to wrest institutional control in several other contexts.

And so it would seem that the modernists had won. For the next three decades at least—and perhaps all the way into the mid-1960s, mainline Protestantism would be ascendant. And yet this is far too simplistic: twentieth-century fundamentalism found a martyr in Bryan and a cause for which to fight, even if that strife had to occur outside of the courts and American politics. They created 26 new institutions of learning in the 1930s, while the Depression ravaged the United States. Wheaton College and Dallas Theological Seminary gained in vibrancy. The Southern Baptist Convention gained a million and a half members in the 1920s and 1930s.[69] Most importantly, fundamentalists would later re-emerge as liberal Christianity declined. In post-Trump America—and this comment borders on the patently obvious—Christian fundamentalists (though now within the tribe of "white evangelicals") persist as a formidable social, cultural, political force in American life. They continue to have resounding influence on the relationship of science and religion in America.

Notes

1 John Roberts in Hardin et al., eds., *The Warfare Between Science and Religion: The Idea That Wouldn't Die* (Baltimore: Johns Hopkins University Press, 2018), 144.
2 Ibid.
3 Matthews, "Modernism as Evangelical Christianity," in Mark A. Noll, ed., *Eerdmans' Handbook of Christianity in America* (Grand Rapids, MI: Eerdmans Publishing, 1983), 379.
4 Cited in Elesha Coffman et al., "What is Darwinism?" *Christian History* 107 (2013), retrieved June 24, 2019, https://christianhistoryinstitute.org/magazine/article/107-what-is-darwinism.

The rise of religious modernism **89**

5 Quoted in Herbert W. Schneider, A History of American Philosophy (New York and London: Columbia University, 1963), 290. For a fuller treatment of his ideas, see LeConte, *Evolution: Its Nature, Its Evidences, and Its Relation to Religious Thought*, 2nd edition. (New York: D. Appleton and Company, 1897).
6 Roberts in Hardin et al., 147.
7 Claude Welch, *Protestant Thought in the Nineteenth Century*, 2 vols., (New Haven and London: Yale University, 1972, 1985), II: 273.
8 Christine Rosen, *Preaching Eugenics: Religious Leaders and the American Eugenics Movement* (Oxford: Oxford University Press, 2004), 17
9 Schneider, *A History*, 335.
10 Henry Ward Beecher, *Evolution and Religion*, vol. 1 (Cambridge: Cambridge University Press, 2009), 3–4.
11 Ibid., 36.
12 William James, *The Varieties of Religious Experience: A Study of Human Nature* (New York: Signet), 1958.
13 Jacque Barzun, in his foreword to James, *Varieties*, vi.
14 James, *Varieties*, 29; italics mine.
15 Ibid., 369–71.
16 Ibid., 371.
17 Edwin Gaustad and Leigh Schmidt, *The Religious History of America: The Heart of the American Story from Colonial Times to Today* (San Francisco: HarperCollins, 2004), 209.
18 George Marsden, *Understanding Fundamentalism and Evangelicalism* (Grand Rapids, MI: Eerdmans, 1991), 57,
19 Edwin Gaustad, Edwin and Leigh Schmidt, *The Religious History of America: The Heart of the American Story from Colonial Times to Today* (San Francisco: HarperCollins, 2004), 293.
20 Noll's summary of the Princeton Theology is excellent. See particularly Warfield's 1893, "The Inerrancy of the Original Autographa," in Mark Noll, ed., *The Princeton Theology, 1812–1921: Scripture, Science, and Theological Method from Archibald Alexander to Benjamin Breckinridge Warfield*. (Grand Rapids, MI: Baker Book House, 1983), 268–74.
21 Mark Noll, *America's God: From Jonathan Edwards to Abraham Lincoln* (Oxford: Oxford University Press, 2005), 389ff.
22 See George Marsden, *Fundamentalism and American Culture* (Oxford: Oxford University Press, 1980), 118–23; Edward Larson, *Summer for the Gods: The Scopes Trial and America's Continuing Debate Over Science and Religion* (New York: Basic Books, 2006), 33.
23 Welch, *Protestant Thought* II: 263.
24 Walter Rauschenbusch, *A Theology for the Social Gospel* (Nashville: Abingdon, 1978), 5.
25 Walter Rauschenbusch, *Christianizing the Social Order* (New York: Macmillan, 1912), 40–1.
26 Thomas C. Leonard, *Illiberal Reformers: Race, Eugenics, and American Economics in the Progressive Era* (Princeton and Oxford: Princeton University Press, 2016), citing *Christianizing the Social Order* (New York: Macmillan, 1914 [1912]), 178.
27 See Gaustad and Schmidt, *Religious History of America*, 296.
28 Rosen, *Preaching Eugenics*, 116.
29 Henry Emerson Fosdick, "Shall the Fundamentalists Win?" retrieved May 24, 2019, http://historymatters.gmu.edu/d/5070.
30 John Hedley Brooke, in Brooke and Numbers, eds., *Science and Religion Around the World* (Oxford: Oxford University Press, 2011), 111.
31 Hermann, *The Communion of the Christian with God*, trans. Robert Voelkl (Philadelphia, 1971), 354; cited in Welch *Protestant Thought* II; 48.
32 Roberts in Hardin et al., 156; citing Millikan, "Science and Religion," June 1923; italics in the original citation.
33 James Moore, "R.A. Fisher: A Faith Fit for Eugenics," *Studies in History and Philosophy of Science Part C* 38, no. 1 (2007): 118. Cited in Joshua M. Moritz, *Science and Religion: Beyond Warfare and Toward Understanding* (Winona, MN: Anselm Academic, 2016), 165.

34 Michael Ruse, *From Monad to Man: The Concept of Progress in Evolutionary Biology* (Cambridge: Harvard University Press, 2009), 296. Cited in Moritz, *Science and Religion*, 165.

35 Eric D. Weitz, *A Century of Genocide: Utopias of Race and Nation* (Princeton: Princeton University Press, 2015).

36 Elizabeth Martin and Robert Hine eds., *A Dictionary of Biology*, 7th edition. (Oxford: Oxford University Press, 2016).

37 Merriam-Webster's Dictionary, "Social Darwinism," retrieved June 20, 2019, https://www.merriam-webster.com/dictionary/social%20Darwinism.

38 See Miriam Lewis and Cheryl Wild, "The Impact of the Feminist Critique on Tests, Assessments, and Methodology," *Psychology of Women Quarterly* 15 (1991): 581–96.

39 Edwin Black, *War Against the Weak: Eugenics and America's Campaign to Create a Master Race* (United Kingdom: Basic Books, 2004), 243.

40 Karen Norrgard, "Human testing, the Eugenics Movement, and IRBs," *Nature Education* 1 vol. 1 (2008): 170, retrieved June 24, 2019, https://www.nature.com/scitable/topic-page/human-testing-the-eugenics-movement-and-irbs-724.

41 Black, *War Against the Weak*, 7.

42 Leonard, *Illiberal Reformers*, 112.

43 Irwing Fischer, "Eugenics—Foremost Plan of Human Redemption," *Proceedings of Second National Congress on Race Betterment*, August 4–8, 1915, Battle Creek, MI, pp. 63–6; cited in Leonard, *Illiberal Reformers*, 112.

44 Leonard, *Illiberal Reformers*, 113, citing Fischer in 1913, "Eugenics," *Good Health Magazine* 48 (11): 583–4.

45 Quoted by Leonard, *Illiberal Reformers*, 114.

46 Moritz, *Science and Religion*, 33.

47 Edward Davis, "Science and Religious Fundamentalism in the 1920s," *American Scientist* 93 (May-June 2005): 254–5.

48 Black, *War Against the Weak*, 385.

49 See, for example, Black's elaboration, ibid., 385–409.

50 Larson in *Galileo Goes to Jail*, 178–86. See also Larson, *Summer of the Gods*, and the Tokens Show, "Dichotomies in Dayton," recorded July 17, 2014, retrieved June 24, 2019, https://www.youtube.com/playlist?list=PL2Rk2D2fHz5mkNCCpm6gDTwOViOUjnJoZ.

51 Larson, in *Galileo Goes to Jail*, 178.

52 Gilbert, *Redeeming Culture*, 25–7.

53 Ibid., 31.

54 Rosen, *Preaching Eugenics*, 184.

55 Larson, *Evolution: The Remarkable History of a Scientific Theory* (New York: Modern Library, 2006), 195.

56 George William Hunter, *A Civic Biology: Presented in Problems* (New York: American Book Company, 1914), 261.

57 Hunter, *Civic Biology*, 263.

58 Mark A. Noll, *The Scandal of the Evangelical Mind* (Grand Rapids, MI: Eerdmans, 1994), 189; cited in Evans, *Morals Not Knowledge*, 79.

59 This is similar (though not identical) to Hugh Ross's position today and the organization he heads, Reasons to Believe, retrieved June 24, 2019, https://reasons.org.

60 GeoChristian, "William Jennings Bryan and the age of the Earth," retrieved June 24, 2019, https://geochristian.com/2009/09/21/william-jennings-bryan-and-the-age-of-the-earth.

61 Larson, "That the Scopes Trial," 182.

62 This section I obtained through Digital History, "The Scopes Trial: Examination of William Jennings Bryan by Clarence Darrow," retrieved July 24, 2019, http://www.digitalhistory.uh.edu/disp_textbook.cfm?smtID=3&psid=1160.

63 Moritz, *Science and Religion*, 35.

64 Larson, "That the Scopes Trial," 179.

The rise of religious modernism **91**

65 Larson, *Summer for the Gods*, 229, citing Stone's *Clarence Darrow for the Defense* (Garden City: Doubleday, 1941), 437.
66 Cf. Gaustad and Schmidt, 292–3. See also, Winthrop Hudson, *Religion in America: An Historical Account of the Development of American Religious Life,* 3rd edition. (New York: Charles Scribner's Sons, 1981), 365–73, esp. 371–2.
67 Marsden, *Fundamentalism in American Culture,* 191.
68 J. Gresham Machen, *Christianity and Liberalism* (Grand Rapids, MI: Eerdmans, 1923).
69 Marsden, *Fundamentalism in American Culture,* 194.

Bibliography

Beecher, Henry Ward. *Evolution and Religion*. Volume 1. Cambridge, UK: Cambridge University Press, 2009.
Coffman, Elesha et al. "What is Darwinism?" *Christian History*, 107 (2013). Retrieved June 24, 2019. https://christianhistoryinstitute.org/magazine/article/107-what-is-darwinism
Davis, Edward. "Science and Religious Fundamentalism in the 1920s." *American Scientist*, 93 (May-June 2005): 253–260.
Digital History. "The Scopes Trial: Examination of William Jennings Bryan by Clarence Darrow." Retrieved July 24, 2019. http://www.digitalhistory.uh.edu/disp_textbook.cfm?smtID=3&psid=1160
Evans, John H. *Morals Not Knowledge: Recasting the Contemporary U.S. Conflict Between Science and Religion*. Oakland, CA: University of California Press, 2018.
Fosdick, Henry Emerson. "Shall the Fundamentalists Win?" Retrieved May 24, 2019, http://historymatters.gmu.edu/d/5070
Gaustad, Edwin and Leigh Schmidt. *The Religious History of America: The Heart of the American Story from Colonial Times to Today*. San Francisco, CA: HarperCollins, 2004.
GeoChristian. "William Jennings Bryan and the age of the Earth." Retrieved June 24, 2019. https://geochristian.com/2009/09/21/william-jennings-bryan-and-the-age-of-the-earth
Hardin, Jeff, Ronald L. Numbers and Ronald A. Binzley, eds. *The Warfare Between Science and Religion: The Idea That Wouldn't Die*. Baltimore, MD: Johns Hopkins University Press, 2018.
Hatch, Nathan O. and Mark A. Noll. *The Bible in America: Essays in Cultural History*. Oxford, UK: Oxford University Press, 1982.
Hudson, Winthrop. *Religion in America: An Historical Account of the Development of American Religious Life*. 3rd edition. New York: Charles Scribner's Sons, 1981.
Hunter, George William. *A Civic Biology: Presented in Problems*. New York: American Book Company, 1914.
James, William. *The Varieties of Religious Experience: A Study of Human Nature*. New York: Signet, 1958.
Larson, Edward J. *Evolution: The Remarkable History of a Scientific Theory*. New York: Modern Library, 2006.
Larson, Edward J. *Summer for the Gods: The Scopes Trial and America's Continuing Debate Over Science and Religion*. New York: Basic Books, 2006.
LeConte, Joseph. *Evolution: Its Nature, Its Evidences, and Its Relation to Religious Thought*. 2nd edition. New York: D. Appleton and Company, 1897.
Leonard, Thomas C. *Illiberal Reformers: Race, Eugenics, and American Economics in the Progressive Era*. Princeton and Oxford: Princeton University Press, 2016.
Lewis, Miriam and Cheryl Wild. "The Impact of the Feminist Critique on Tests, Assessments, and Methodology." *Psychology of Women Quarterly*, 15 (1991): 581–596.

92 The rise of religious modernism

Lienesch, Michael. *In the Beginning: Fundamentalism, the Scopes Trial, And the Making of the Antievolution Movement*. Chapel Hill, NC: University of North Carolina Press, 2007.

Machen, J. Gresham. *Christianity and Liberalism*. Grand Rapids, MI: Eerdmans, 1923.

Marsden, George. *Fundamentalism and American Culture*. Oxford, UK: Oxford University Press, 1980.

Marsden, George. *Reforming Fundamentalism: Fuller Seminary and the New Evangelicalism*. Grand Rapids, MI: Eerdmans, 1987.

Marsden, George. *Understanding Fundamentalism and Evangelicalism*. Grand Rapids, MI: Eerdmans, 1991.

Martin, Elizabeth and Robert Hine, eds. *A Dictionary of Biology*, 7th edition. Oxford, UK: Oxford University Press, 2016.

Merriam-Webster's Dictionary. "Social Darwinism." Retrieved June 20, 2019. https://www.merriam-webster.com/dictionary/social%20Darwinism

Moritz, Joshua M. *Science and Religion: Beyond Warfare and Toward Understanding*. Winona, MN: Anselm Academic, 2016.

Noll, Mark A. ed. *Eerdmans' Handbook of Christianity in America*. Grand Rapids, MI: Eerdmans Publishing, 1983.

Noll, Mark A. ed. *The Princeton Theology, 1812–1921: Scripture, Science, and Theological Method from Archibald Alexander to Benjamin Breckinridge Warfield*. Grand Rapids, MI: Baker Book House, 1983.

Noll, Mark A. *America's God: From Jonathan Edwards to Abraham Lincoln*. Oxford, UK: Oxford University Press, 2005.

Norrgard, Karen. "Human testing, the Eugenics Movement, and IRBs." *Nature Education*, 1 (2008): 170. Retrieved June 24, 2019. https://www.nature.com/scitable/topicpage/human-testing-the-eugenics-movement-and-irbs-724

Rauschenbusch, Walter. *Christianizing the Social Order*. New York: Macmillan, 1912.

Rauschenbusch, Walter. *A Theology for the Social Gospel*. Nashville, TN: Abingdon, 1978.

Reasons to Believe. Retrieved June 24, 2019. https://reasons.org

Rosen, Christine. *Preaching Eugenics: Religious Leaders and the American Eugenics Movement*. Oxford, UK: Oxford University Press, 2004.

Schneider, Herbert W. *A History of American Philosophy*. 2nd edition. New York and London: Columbia University, 1963.

Tokens Show. "Dichotomies in Dayton." Recorded July 17, 2014. Retrieved June 24, 2019. https://www.youtube.com/playlist?list=PL2Rk2D2fHz5mkNCCpm6gDTwOViOUjnJoZ

Welch, Claude. *Protestant Thought in the Nineteenth Century*. Two volumes. New Haven and London: Yale University, 1985 [1972].

7

FROM SCOPES TO 1966

Major scientific discoveries: relativity and the quantum revolution[1]

In this book it is painfully obvious to me that I am constantly limited as to which philosophy, theological declaration, or scientific and technological discovery I discuss. My rubric continues to be this: *Only that which sets up the story of science and religion in the present and that has had an ongoing cultural impact in our country*. Therefore, I haven't paid significant attention to pure science. Nonetheless, as we arrive at the early twentieth century, I need to concentrate on a few major scientific discoveries, especially in the discipline of physics, which would both change and expand our view of the universe.

Here is a brief list of the major scientific discoveries from 1900–60. In 1905, the *annus mirabilis*, Albert Einstein formulated the theory of special relativity and explained Brownian motion, as well as the photoelectric effect. In 1911 Ernest Rutherford described the atomic nucleus, and two years later Henry Moseley defined the atomic number, while Niels Bohr presented his model of the atom. In 1915 Einstein produced the theory of general relativity (along with David Hilbert). In 1924 Wolfgang Pauli conceived the quantum world through the Pauli exclusion principle, and in 1925 Erwin Schrödinger developed the Schrödinger equation, which forms the basis of much of quantum mechanics. Two years later, in 1927, Werner Heisenberg framed his uncertainty principle, the same year Georges Lemaître offered his mathematical support for the Big Bang theory, thus complementing Einstein's general relativity. Paul Dirac presented the Dirac equation and Neils Bohr his concept of complementarity in 1928, both key elements of quantum theory. Edwin Hubble also introduced his law of the expanding universe in 1929, which offered further proof of general relativity and especially Big Bang cosmology.

The Nuclear Age also began to dawn with Ernest Walton and John Cockcroft's work to create nuclear fission by proton bombardment in 1932, Enrico Fermi's nuclear fission by neutron irradiation in 1934, which was complemented by Otto Hahn, Lise Meitner, and Fritz Strassmann's work in nuclear fission of heavy nuclei in 1938. In 1943 Oswald Avery proved that DNA represents the genetic material of the chromosome, while in 1953 James Watson, Francis Crick, Maurice Wilkins, and Rosalind Franklin discovered the structure of the double helix in DNA. (This is an extremely significant development for confirming evolution and for the development of genetics. I will comment on the implications in successive chapters.) In 1964 Murray Gell-Mann and George Zweig postulated quarks, leading to the standard model of physics, and in that year Arno Penzias and Robert Woodrow Wilson detected cosmic background radiation as experimental evidence for the Big Bang.

In sum, these key scientific breakthroughs set the context for relativity and quantum theories—especially Einstein's 1905 theory of special relativity and his 1915 theory of general relativity—and the development of quantum theory from about 1900–30 by titanic thinkers such as Max Planck, Schrödinger, Bohr and Heisenberg. Relativity and quantum mechanics have continuing cultural impact and affect the history of American culture and thus religion.

Special relativity led to a world in which light doesn't travel in a straight line, but bends, and in which time could also bend if forced to by the speed of the observer. Put another way, the velocity of light (symbolized by the letter c) represents the great constant of the universe. Because of this aspect of the theory, Einstein preferred *Invarianztheorie*—to highlight the invariance of the velocity of light (or c)—but *relativity* stuck. It does not mean that all is relative, but that even our most constant universal realities, like time, are relative to the great c. This theory had two critical implications. First of all, the velocity of light represents the absolute limit for how fast information can travel. Second, instead of three dimensions of space and a dimension of time, Einstein's theory depicts a universe of four-dimensional *spacetime*. The religious implications are vast, and here I'll simply mention one. Thomas Torrance connected the concept of light as a description of Christ in the New Testament and early Christian thought with the invariance of the velocity of light in special relativity, thereby finding common themes in modern science and orthodox Christianity.[2] Nevertheless, the religious payoff is found with general relativity because it leads to Big Bang cosmology.

Through much of religious and scientific history, human beings have assumed that the world has stayed the same. I mentioned above that Thomas Aquinas found this view so persuasive that he was unwilling to decide philosophically whether the universe has a beginning or not. (Thomas ultimately decided that we know the world had a beginning because of revelation.) Similarly, the theory of general relativity described something other than a steady state universe, which represented what Einstein, convinced by Baruch Spinoza's metaphysics, clearly preferred. Instead it implied that our universe is expanding. If it is expanding today, then in the past there had to be a beginning point when time began, the "day without yesterday." At t = 0 (or the beginning of time), space was infinitely curved and all energy and all matter were concentrated into a single quantum.[3] We can imagine the universe as an expanding cone of the universe with a point, and that point is the Big Bang.

Thus Einstein was no outlier with his preference for a static universe, and it took Lemaître, the Belgian Jesuit priest and mathematician, and the astronomer Edwin Hubble, the virtuoso at observing the universe and crunching astronomical data, to convince Einstein he was right. Einstein, however, was not the only scientist in need of persuasion. Fred Hoyle, the superb Cambridge University astronomer, and his two colleagues, Herman Bondi and Thomas Gold, proposed *steady state* cosmology in 1948; that the universe was virtually unchanging and of infinite age. Hoyle disparaged the alternative with a slight, naming it the "Big Bang." For decades these two theories contended for scientific approval, but, as I noted above, Wilson and Penzias of Bell Laboratories detected background static radiation in the cosmos and in 1989 the COBE satellite probed outer space and confirmed this background radiation.

I have taken some space for the Big Bang because it seems to have consonance—or in some minds, even proved—with God's creation *ex nihilo,* or, to use Paul's words in Romans 4:17, there is the God who "calls into being things that were not." The late Robert Jastrow, astronomer, planetary physicist, and self-described agnostic, thought so:

> A sound explanation may exist for the explosive birth of our Universe; but if it does, science cannot find out what the explanation is. The scientist's pursuit of the past ends in the moment of creation.... This is an exceedingly strange development, unexpected by all but the theologians. They have always accepted the word of the Bible: In the beginning God created heaven and earth.[4]

The quote is a godsend because it states, with rhetorical flair, a common conception about Big Bang and God's creation. But is this the case? It's not clear that to have a beginning means to be created,[5] whether t = 0 is really the initial act of divine creation or whether perhaps it's the natural coming together out of nothing that many, such as Stephen Hawking and James Hartle have hypothesized.

Quantum theory has a more resounding effect and, for some commentators, reaches into the truths of eastern religion (more below). As the twentieth century dawned—literally in 1900—the very bastion of the Enlightenment, science, and particularly physics, began to exhibit a need both to break with and enlarge on Newtonian mechanics. Planck discovered that light was actually organized in packets, which he called *quanta.* What was once thought to be a wave demonstrated the qualities of particles. And Heisenberg, while recuperating from a bout with hayfever in 1925 on the small North Sea archipelago of Heligoland, created matrix mechanics, which—along with Schrödinger's wave mechanics—led to a maturing understanding of the quantum world.[6] In Heisenberg's later reflections

96 From Scopes to 1966

on this period he notes that by the spring of 1927 a consistent interpretation of quantum theory was developed (by him and Niels Bohr). Named after the site of Bohr's famed center for the scientific study of quantum mechanics, this came to be known as the "Copenhagen interpretation." In order to grasp the significance of the quantum revolution, I must note the two primary theoretical linchpins of the Copenhagen interpretation, Heisenberg's uncertainty principle and Bohr's concept of complementarity, to which I'll add quantum entanglement, which emerged a few decades later.[7]

These discoveries problematized recourse to a naïve realism and a world that science could described unproblematically. Physics, the hardest of hard sciences, discovered a world that seems to be profoundly malleable. Such implications led Bohr to comment that there are "two sorts of truth: trivialities, where opposites are obviously absurd, and profound truths, recognized by the fact that the opposite is also a profound truth."[8] When quantum revolution in physics landed, few could miss the emergence of a metaphysical shift and the elements of a scientific view of the world that have implications for relating science and religion. Quantum theory offered profound insights into the nature of the world, and thus implications for how God or the divine relate to the world, the nature of reality at its deepest, and thus science and religion. Put simply, religious thinkers have had to contend with the revolution in twentieth-century science that finally unwound the Newtonian worldview. I mention the impact of quantum theory if for no other reason than the books it has spawned—which I'll return to in the next chapter—such as Fritjof Capra's *The Tao of Physics* in the 1970s.

Science and shifting worldviews

In order to grasp this revolution it is important to step back and to see the larger picture of the world that had been transformed. What was the preceding Newtonian *worldview*?[9] And here I am drawing a distinction between scientific discoveries and the worldview they inform. Almost always it is the worldview that has cultural and religious significance. How did new physics present a radically different way of seeing the world from classical, Newtonian physics?

Ian Barbour described the Newtonian worldview with three terms: *realistic* (the theories describe the world as it is, without reference to the observer), *deterministic* (as Laplace described, the present state determines any future action and is therefore entirely predictable in principle), and *reductionistic* (behavior of the smallest parts determines the behavior of the whole).[10] The quantum worldview alters all three.

First of all the quantum world changes from *naïve* to *critical realism*. When dealing with quantum realities, an objective world does not exist entirely independently without reference to an observer. Specifically, one must take into account the act of observation and the interaction between the observer and the phenomena.[11] Photons, for example, can be understood as either a particle or a wave—but not both simultaneously—depending on the intention of the person doing the experiment.[12] This is enshrined in the concept of complementarity, which is, according to Max Jammer, "the logical relation between two descriptions or sets of concepts which, though mutually exclusive, are nevertheless both necessary for an exhaustive description of the situation."[13]Heisenberg's description expands on Jammer's.

> Bohr advocated the use of both pictures [the wave and the particle], which he called "complementary" to each other. The two pictures are of course mutually exclusive, because a certain thing cannot at the same time be a particle (i.e., a substance confined to a very small volume) and a wave (i.e., a field spread out over a large space), but the two complement each other. By playing with both pictures, by going from one picture to the other and back again, we finally get the right impression of the strange kind of reality behind our atomic experiments.[14]

Second, there is a shift from *determinism* to *indeterminacy* (without, in my opinion, letting go of the concept of causality). Heisenberg's uncertainty principle exemplifies this shift. Employing the idea of "observables," or "a quantity associated with a physical system which can be measured experimentally," John Polkinghorne offers this definition: "The quantum mechanical result, discovered by Heisenberg, which asserts that certain pairs of *observables* cannot both be known to a greater degree of accuracy than is specified by a limit expressed in terms of Planck's constant." [15] This does not mean "everything's up for grabs." Indeed, Planck's constant constrains the degree of mutual uncertainty. Still—though not impossible to define comprehensibly—the uncertainty principle results in what Polkinghorne describes as "more-or-less knowledge."[16] Since determinism has a recalcitrant presence in the minds of many scientists, this is worth a pause. Laplace, perfectly representing an eighteenth-century closed-box worldview, wrote about an "intellect," later named Laplace's Demon:

> We may regard the present state of the universe as the effect of its past and the cause of its future. An intellect which at a certain moment would know all forces that set nature in motion, and all positions of all items of which nature is composed, if this intellect were also vast enough to submit these data to analysis, it would embrace in a single formula the movements of the greatest bodies of the universe and those of the tiniest atom; for such an intellect nothing would be uncertain and the future just like the past would be present before its eyes.[17]

Even if Laplace and his Demon could perfectly predict the future—which became entirely debatable in the twentieth century—the future cannot be predicted from what is known about the present, since we don't even absolutely know the present state! "More-or-less" knowledge shifted science from the precise measurement of classical physics and its attendant determinism, and I'm not sure many in science and religion have caught up.

98 From Scopes to 1966

Third, *an interrelated, wholistic, and entangled universe replaced Newtonian reductionism.* The confirmation of this shift happened in the latter half of the twentieth century when Alain Aspect gave experimental proof in 1983 to John Bell's 1965 theorem. He demonstrated that entangled photons can communicate more rapidly and over greater distances than they should, given the constraints of special relativity (which, as I noted above, limits any communication to the velocity of light). Robert John Russell has assessed this change: "Nature reveals a highly non-local and wholistic character at the quantum level, which is strikingly different from the separability of nature of our ordinary experiences."[18]Polkinghorne commented similarly on the global nature of quantum reality, "Quantum systems exhibit an unexpected degree of togetherness. Mere spatial separation does not divide them from one another." He then adds, "I do not think that we have yet succeeded in taking in fully what quantum mechanical non-locality implies about the nature of the world."[19] The world exhibits a complex interdependent relationality that is more profound than common sense would lead one to believe, and we will return to this quantum reality below.[20]

I have taken some space for this revolution because of its importance. Sometimes scientific changes contribute a shift in worldview to the relationship of science and religion. This shift, of course, didn't just happen in the 1920s. We will see how, later in the century, quantum theory affected the dialogue of science and religion.

1930–1966: the Great Depression, WWII, the Nuclear Age, and the Eisenhower Revival

The Scopes Trial and the fundamentalist-modernist controversy thrust the liberal mainline Protestants into the center of power. The conservatives retreated culturally, though they would return. Science, and especially physics, emerged in the twentieth century with glorious discoveries. World War I (which I've failed to mention as yet) and the Roaring Twenties promoted America to its status as a world power, all of which was slowed by the 1929 stock market crash. The 1930s brought the Great Depression and a time of retrenchment. And as I bring the story of science and religion in America to "the present" (namely, from 1966 to today), I will choose just a few surprises and highlights in the intervening three decades or so.

National Socialism and its hideous policies toward the Jews affected science and religion in America by increasing the presence—and enormous impact of—Jewish scientists in this country. This is an obvious irony for the Nazis, but also for the US, which tried to restrict the immigration of Jews in 1924. (Admittedly this is a particular angle on science and religion, but it certainly had an impact on the relationship of Judaism with science.) Clifton Parker commented on the research of economist Petra Moser, who highlighted that after 1933 the number of US patents increased by 31%:

The decision by many Jews to leave Germany is perhaps best understood in light of a Nazi Germany law passed on April 7, 1933 – just 67 days after Adolf

Hitler was appointed chancellor – that forced so-called non-Aryan civil servants out of their jobs. By 1944, more than 133,000 German Jewish émigrés had moved to America – many of them highly skilled and educated. Some were even Nobel Prize winners and renowned intellectuals like Albert Einstein in physics, and Otto Loewi and Max Bergmann in chemistry.[21]

All in all, this meant that Judaism and its influence on the development of science in this country is profound. Twelve Nobel laureate scientists emigrated to America because of Nazi threats, seven of them Jews, including biologists Otto Meyerhof, Otto Loewi, and Otto Stern, as well as physicists James Franck, Eugene Wigner, Bohr, and Einstein.[22] Three non-Jewish scientists received their Nobel Prizes in physics: Enrico Fermi, Wolfgang Pauli, and Viktor Hess, along with the chemist Peter Debye and the biologist C.P. Henrik Dam. Eric Weiss commented, "Of this group of immigrant Nobelists, Pauli, Stern, Dam, and Wigner would win their prizes after coming to the United States."[23]Weiss highlighted the irony of fascist leaders causing this immigration:

> Thus it can be seen that the migration of scientists due to fascist oppression had multiple impacts on the United States and Germany. For the United States the effects were overwhelmingly positive, with immigrant Nobelists aiding in the construction of the first atomic bomb, serving as mentors for other U.S. Nobelists, and fostering a new attitude in the biological sciences.[24]

And so science—and many of the Jewish scientists at that—produced the Bomb that ended the war Hitler initiated. And for most of the 1940s the attention of the United States naturally remained poised first on the war effort and then the Cold War. It was much more practical and deadly, as the mushroom clouds over Hiroshima and Nagasaki in August 1945 proved. Humanity unleashed the fury of the atom. As Robert Oppenheimer declared, using the words of the Hindu god Shiva, "Now I am become Death, the destroyer of worlds" (perhaps demonstrating a growing religious pluralism in America). Americans could not forget the massive impact of science in this case, for perhaps justifiable, but still horrifying, results.

Not everyone took the standard liberal-modernist line in interpreting religion and science. In 1941 the founding of the American Scientific Affiliation signaled a move toward reconciling evangelical Christian faith with contemporary science, often addressing how to interpret evolution. Similarly, lest it appear that I'm selling the canard that science, and especially evolutionary science, always presents the vanguard of progressive and liberalizing ethics, consider the discovery by W.E.B. Du Bois writing in 1940,

> At Harvard, on the other hand, I began to face scientific race dogma: first of all, evolution and the "Survival of the Fittest." It was continually stressed in the community and in classes that there was a vast difference in the development of the whites and the "lower" races; that this could be seen in the

100 From Scopes to 1966

physical development of the Negro. I remember once in a museum, coming face to face with a demonstration: a series of skeletons arranged from a little monkey to a tall well developed white man, with the Negro barely out-ranking a chimpanzee. Eventually in my classes stress was quietly transferred to brain weight and brain capacity, and at last to the "cephalic index."[25]

Du Bois's comments remind me of an exhibit I saw in Germany in 1992 that looked back to the National Socialist era's treatment of the Sinti and Roma, often disparagingly called "Gypsy"—as in "the people from Egypt," which they weren't. The exhibit included photographs of cranial size measurements as grounds for the Nazis killing tens of thousands of them between 1933 and 1945.[26]

In some ways the 1950s might have started religiously in 1949, when the young Billy Graham had his breakout Los Angeles Crusade and the newspaper titan William Randolf Hearst promoted the young evangelist in his newspapers (whether or not Hearst delivered his two-word directive "puff Graham"). Graham was an instant celebrity nationwide. Thus the Fifties and their religious movement, later termed the Eisenhower Revival, had begun, and this makes it easy to think of this as the era of calm, both religiously and culturally, in America. To do that act of generalization, of course, one has to forget the segregation of our country as well as our massive racial inequalities. I for one do not find that easy to do. Nonetheless, it was an era of sufficient religious calm so that President Dwight Eisenhower could declare, "Our form of government has no sense unless it is founded in a deeply felt religious faith, and I don't care what it is. With us of course it is the Judeo-Christian concept, but it must be a religion with all men created equal."[27] In 1954 the phrase *under God* was inserted into the pledge of allegiance, and two years later President Eisenhower signed the law declaring *In God We Trust* to be the nation's official motto.

In addition, titanic religious voices broadly in the neo-orthodox tradition, Paul Tillich and Reinhold Niebuhr, were prominent public intellectuals. This was the heyday of the influence of mainline Protestantism, unmoored from fundamentalism in the latter's retreat from the wider culture. It was a time when the stated clerk of the United Presbyterian church in the USA, Eugene Carson Blake, regularly telephoned the President to offer counsel and advice. (Compare that picture with President Donald Trump's cozy relationship today with *Fox News* personality Sean Hannity.) And for what it's worth, C.S. Lewis, whom America seems to want to make our own, had already appeared on the cover of the September 8, 1947, edition of *Time* (owned by the son of a Christian missionary to China, Henry Luce) with the caption, "Oxford's C.S. Lewis. His Heresy: Christianity."

Mainline Protestant power in America had reached its twentieth-century apex—and my focus lies there. Nonetheless, I must register Pope Pius XII's significant conciliatory statements in his 1950 encyclical, *Humani Generis*. Even if he may have hoped that evolution would prove to be a passing scientific fad, the encyclical attacked those persons who "imprudently and indiscreetly hold that evolution ...

explains the origin of all things."[28] Nonetheless, Pius XII maintained that Catholic doctrine is not contradicted by a theory that suggests one species might evolve into another:

> The Teaching Authority of the Church does not forbid that, in conformity with the present state of human sciences and sacred theology, research and discussions, on the part of men experienced in both fields, take place with regard to the doctrine of evolution, in as far as it inquires into the origin of the human body as coming from pre-existent and living matter—for the Catholic faith obliges us to hold that souls are immediately created by God.[29]

In short, as long as God could specially create the human soul, or "ensoul" humankind, evolution could be endorsed, or at least tolerated.

In addition, the culture of the Fifties, fueled by the Cold War and the vast implications of the atomic bomb, also provided for the era of big science funded by public taxpayers—a "scientific revival" perhaps. Science was exploding (pun intended), in nuclear energy, biological evolution, and beyond. As James Gilbert noted, "This epoch of 'big science' was sustained not merely by awe and accomplishment, but by large and growing public subvention of laboratories and experimental and technological applications, particularly in defense industries."[30]

In addition, the Soviet Union launched Sputnik in 1957, the first artificial earth satellite, during the height of the Cold War. *They* had beat *us* in achieving superiority in space. This startled American sensibilities and elicited alarm by heightening fears that the Soviets might be achieving technological and strategic superiority and prodded the US government to fund science education systematically and intentionally. One major effort, the Biological Sciences Curriculum Study program, founded in 1958 and housed in Boulder, Colorado, with a National Science Foundation grant, "made Darwinism, and evolution more generally, the cornerstone of biology education in America" (John Evans).[31] Of course, with public funding comes public scrutiny. This move raised again the moral implications of evolution and set the stage for what happened in the 1960s with the rise of aggressive and defiant creationism. It's easy to imagine a cry emanating from a wide expanse of evangelical and fundamentalist churches: "They're teaching immoral and godless evolution to our kids!"

As I make a turn toward what I am calling "the present"—i.e., from 1966 to today—I now have a bit of housekeeping to do. Several significant elements occurred in the early 1960s, which I note in no particular order (with more in the next chapter on the radical disruption of American society that is *The Sixties*): the disenfranchisement of the church in the 1960s (which contrasts markedly with the 1950s Eisenhower Revival); the teaching of creationism in public schools (and thus the emergence of the evangelical voice in the public square); the explosion of new moves in sexuality (which will play a bigger part in the discussion of science and religion today than it did in the 1960s); and the Vietnam War and the crisis of trust in the government, as well as in older generations passing on its wisdom.

102 From Scopes to 1966

I will have more on that in the next chapter, but worthy of note is that the pre-eminently evangelical voice with roots back to the Puritan era (i.e., evangelicalism in its original form, not the desiccated version we see today) gradually lost its influence in the late nineteenth century through most of the first half of the twentieth century. The "Christian Century" embodied in the periodical of the same name essentially described the liberal Protestant century until the rise of the Moral Majority with Ronald Reagan's election in 1980. A story of a simple shift from the ascendency of the evangelicals to liberals and then back might be distorting. In some ways, as we review these rises and falls in light of the prominence in the twenty-first century of the evangelical voice (which now, in popular media, is synonymous with fundamentalism), we need to remember Ross Douthat's comments on liberal mainline churches,

> Some of what those congregations offer is already embodied in liberal politics and culture. As the sociologist N.J. Demerath argued in the 1990s, liberal churches have suffered institutional decline, but also enjoy a sort of cultural triumph, losing members even as their most distinctive commitments — ecumenical spirituality and a progressive social Gospel — permeate academia, the media, pop culture, the Democratic Party.[32]

The victory of mainline Protestants meant their disappearance because their values became those of the wider culture, including an embrace of science.

With these comments in mind—suggestive, but by no means exhaustive—we are now ready to analyze the present state of religion and science in the United States, from to 1966 to the early decades of the new millennium.

Notes

1 I have previously worked with some of this material in *God and the World: A Study in the Thought of Alfred North Whitehead and Karl Barth* (Frankfurt: Peter Lang, 2001), chapter 7.
2 Thomas Torrance, "The Theology of Light," in *Christian Theology and Scientific Culture* (Eugene, OR: Wipf and Stock, 1998), 75–108.
3 See Timothy Ferris, *Coming of Age in the Milky Way* (New York: HarperCollins, 1988), 211.
4 Robert Jastrow, *God and the Astronomers* (New York: W.W. Norton, 1992), 125.
5 Alister McGrath, *Science and Religion: A New Introduction*, 2nd edition. (Malden, MA: Wiley Blackwell, 2010), 152.
6 John Polkinghorne, *The Quantum World* (Princeton: Princeton University, 1984), 14.
7 For an *introduction* to quantum physics and its implications, see Heinz Pagels, *The Cosmic Code: Quantum Physics as the Language of Nature* (New York: Bantam, 1982); Robert H. March's somewhat deceptively titled *Physics for Poets*, 4th edition (New York: McGraw-Hill, 1996); and Nick Herbert, *Quantum Reality: Beyond the New Physics* (New York: Doubleday, 1985).
8 Cited by James E. Loder and W. Jim Neidhardt, *The Knight's Move: The Relational Logic of the Spirit in Theology and Science* (Colorado Springs: Helmers and Howard, 1992), 35
9 I have adapted a more complete treatment of this material in *God and the World*, chapter 7.
10 Ian Barbour, *Religion in an Age of Science: The Gifford Lectures, Vol. 1* (New York: HarperCollins, 1990) 95–6. Of course, one can ask whether this scientific shift has any importance.

11 I find Henry Folse persuasive in interpreting Bohr as advocating not instrumentalism but critical realism. See *The Philosophy of Niels Bohr: The Framework of Complementarity* (New York: North Holland, 1985), e.g., chapter 8.

12 Cf. Heinz Pagels' description (*Quantum World*, 117–22). The paradigmatic case of the wave-particle duality remains the "two-slit" experiment. See Robert Russell in Russell et al., eds., *Quantum Cosmology and the Laws of Nature, Quantum Cosmology and the Laws of Nature*, Scientific Perspectives on Divine Action: Volume 1 (Berkeley, CA: Vatican Observatory Publications; Center for Theology and the Natural Sciences, 1993), 344.

13 Max Jammer, *Quantum Mechanics* (New York: Wiley, 1970), 348; cited by Loder and Neidhardt, *The Knight's Move*, 73.

14 Werner Heisenberg, *Physics and Philosophy: The Revolution in Modern Science* (New York: Harper & Row, 1958), 49. Loder and Neidhardt further outline what they call "The Inner Nature of Complementarity" and its "five asymmetric couplets": (1) coexhaustiveness and mutual exclusiveness, (2) common and conjugate properties, (3) coinherence and reciprocity, (4) completeness and equal necessity, (5) asymmetry and pointing (*The Knight's Move*, 78ff).

15 Polkinghorne, *Quantum World*, 96.

16 Ibid., chapter 5.

17 Pierre Simon Laplace, *A Philosophical Essay on Probabilities*, 6th edition, trans. F.W. Truscott and F. L. Emory (New York: Dover Publications, 1951), 4.

18 Robert Russell in Russell et al., eds., *Quantum Cosmology*, 348.

19 Polkinghorne, *Quantum World*, 76.

20 Kirk Wegter-McNally has done some of the most significant work in this area in *The Entangled God: Divine Relationality and Quantum Physics*, Routledge Studies in Religion (Abingdon: Routledge, 2011).

21 Clifton Parker, "Jewish Émigrés who Fled Nazi Germany Revolutionized U.S. Science and Technology, Stanford Economist Says," *Stanford News,* August 11, 2014, retrieved June 24, 2019, https://news.stanford.edu/news/2014/august/german-jewish-inventors-081114.html.

22 Eric Weiss, "The Impact of the Intellectual Migration on the United States and Eastern Europe," retrieved June 24, 2019, https://www.vanderbilt.edu/AnS/physics/brau/H182/Term%20Papers/Eric%20Weiss.html, cf. B.S. Schlessinger and J. H. Schlessinger, eds., *The Who's Who of Nobel Prize Winners, 1901–1995* (Phoenix, AZ: Oryx Press, 1996), and Harriet Zuckerman, *Scientific Elite* (New York: The Free Press, 1977).

23 Weiss, ibid.

24 Ibid.

25 Du Bois, "Dusk of Dawn: An Essay Toward an Autobiography of a Race Concept," Henry Louis Gates, Jr., ed., (Oxford: Oxford University Press, 2007), 49.

26 See, for example, the United States Holocaust Museum's website, "Sinti and Roma: Victims of the Nazi Era," retrieved June 19, 2019, https://www.ushmm.org/learn/students/learning-materials-and-resources/sinti-and-roma-victims-of-the-nazi-era.

27 Patrick Henry, "'And I Don't Care What It Is': The Tradition-History of A Civil Religion Proof-Text," *Journal of the American Academy of Religion* 49, issue 1 (1981): 41.

28 Pius XII, "Encyclical *Humani Generis* of the Holy Father Pius XII," retrieved June 24, 2019, http://w2.vatican.va/content/pius-xii/en/encyclicals/documents/hf_p-xii_enc_12081950_humani-generis.html.

29 Ibid.

30 James Gilbert, *Redeeming Culture: American Religion in an Age of Science* (Chicago: University of Chicago, 1997), 5.

31 John Evans, *Morals Not Knowledge: Recasting the Contemporary U.S. Conflict Between Science and Religion* (Oakland: University of California Press, 2018), 81.

32 Ross Douthat, "Save the Mainline," *New York Times,* April 17, 2017, retrieved June 20, 2019, https://www.nytimes.com/2017/04/15/opinion/sunday/save-the-mainline.html.

Bibliography

See also bibliography for previous chapter.Barbour, Ian. *Religion in an Age of Science: The Gifford Lectures, Volume 1.* New York: HarperCollins, 1990.

Cootsona, Gregory S. *God and the World: A Study in the Thought of Alfred North Whitehead and Karl Barth.* Frankfurt: Peter Lang, 2001.

Douthat, Ross. "Save the Mainline." *New York Times*, April 17, 2017. Retrieved June 20, 2019.https://www.nytimes.com/2017/04/15/opinion/sunday/save-the-mainline.html

Du Bois, W.E.B. *Dusk of Dawn: An Essay Toward an Autobiography of a Race Concept.* Edited by Henry Louis Gates, Jr. Oxford, UK: Oxford University Press, 2007.

Evans, John H. *Morals Not Knowledge: Recasting the Contemporary U.S. Conflict Between Science and Religion.* Oakland, CA: University of California Press, 2018.

Ferris, Timothy. *Coming of Age in the Milky Way.* New York: HarperCollins, 1988.

Folse, Henry. *The Philosophy of Niels Bohr: The Framework of Complementarity.* New York: North Holland, 1985.

Gilbert, James. *Redeeming Culture: American Religion in an Age of Science.* Chicago, IL: University of Chicago, 1997.

Heisenberg, Werner. *Physics and Philosophy: The Revolution in Modern Science.* New York: Harper & Row, 1958.

Henry, Patrick. "'And I Don't Care What It Is': The Tradition-History of A Civil Religion Proof-Text". *Journal of the American Academy of Religion*, 49 (1981): 41.

Herbert, Nick. *Quantum Reality: Beyond the New Physics.* New York: Doubleday, 1985.

Jastrow, Robert. *God and the Astronomers.* New York: W.W. Norton, 1992.

Laplace, Pierre Simon. *A Philosophical Essay on Probabilities*, 6th edition, trans. F.W. Truscott and F.L. Emory. New York: Dover Publications, 1951.

Loder, James E. and W. Jim Neidhardt. *The Knight's Move: The Relational Logic of the Spirit in Theology and Science.* Colorado Springs, CO: Helmers and Howard, 1992.

McGrath, Alister. *Science and Religion: A New Introduction.* 2nd edition. Malden, MA: Wiley Blackwell, 2010.

March, Robert H. *Physics for Poets.* 4th edition. New York: McGraw-Hill, 1996.

Merriam-Webster's Dictionary. "Social Darwinism." Retrieved June 20, 2019. https://www.merriam-webster.com/dictionary/social%20Darwinism

Pagels, Heinz. *The Cosmic Code: Quantum Physics as the Language of Nature.* New York: Bantam, 1982.

Parker, Clifton. "Jewish Émigrés who Fled Nazi Germany Revolutionized U.S. Science and Technology, Stanford Economist Says." *Stanford News*, August 11, 2014. Retrieved June 24, 2019. https://news.stanford.edu/news/2014/august/german-jewish-inventors-081114.html

Pius XII. "Encyclical Humani Generis of the Holy Father Pius XII." Retrieved June 24, 2019. http://w2.vatican.va/content/pius-xii/en/encyclicals/documents/hf_p-xii_enc_12081950_humani-generis.html

Polkinghorne, John. *The Quantum World.* Princeton, NJ: Princeton University, 1984.

Russell, Robert J., Nancey Murphy and Christopher J. Isham, eds. *Quantum Cosmology and the Laws of Nature.* Scientific Perspectives on Divine Action: Volume 1. Berkeley, CA: Vatican Observatory Publications; Center for Theology and the Natural Sciences, 1993.

Schlessinger, B.S. and J. H. Schlessinger, eds. *The Who's Who of Nobel Prize Winners, 1901–1995.* Phoenix, AZ: Oryx Press, 1996.

Torrance, Thomas. *Christian Theology and Scientific Culture.* Eugene, OR: Wipf and Stock, 1998.

United States Holocaust Museum's website. "Sinti and Roma: Victims of the Nazi Era." Retrieved June 19, 2019. https://www.ushmm.org/learn/students/learning-materials-and-resources/sinti-and-roma-victims-of-the-nazi-era

Wegter-McNally, Kirk. *The Entangled God: Divine Relationality and Quantum Physics*, Routledge Studies in Religion. Abingdon, UK: Routledge, 2011.

Weiss, Eric. "The Impact of the Intellectual Migration on the United States and Eastern Europe." Retrieved June 24, 2019. https://www.vanderbilt.edu/AnS/physics/brau/H182/Term%20Papers/Eric%20Weiss.html

Zuckerman, Harriet. *Scientific Elite*. New York: The Free Press, 1977.

8

THE PRESENT: 1966 TO 2000 (MORE OR LESS)

Slowing down the narrative

In this part I decelerate. In these pages I cover about 50 years, whereas in the previous chapters I recounted about 350 years. On the way there I must mention that, for the purposes of this book, I am defining *the present* as roughly 50 plus years since the publication of Ian Barbour's ground-breaking 1966 classic, *Issues in Science and Religion,* [1] more or less to the present day.

I can imagine any number of critiques and challenges to this delineation. Nevertheless, following Robert John Russell and Alister McGrath, [2] I argue that the contemporary field of science and religion began with the publication of Barbour's book. His enduring (and criticized) four-part typology challenged the prevailing view among many that science and religion were either at war or, at best, indifferent to each other. Instead, he demonstrated that it was possible both (a) to be a good theologian and scientist (in his case, a physicist), and (b) that science and theology could in fact substantially, creatively, and beneficially interact with one another.

Gary Dorrien, in a perceptive speech on the legacy of Karl Barth and A.N. Whitehead, noted one other element of Barbour's achievement and why writing *Issues* was a countercultural act.

> For 150 years theologians clung to the Kantian bargain with science, assuring that theology and science were entirely different kinds of discourse that should never conflict. They only collided if somebody overstepped her boundary. As long as theologians were careful not to conflict with science, they were free to ignore it, and of course, everyone was free to ignore theology. [3]

I have not mentioned this earlier, but for many religious thinkers Immanuel Kant's 1781 *Critique of Pure Reason* effectively separated religious insight from knowledge about the external world. The latter constituted the realm of the sciences. Freidrich Schleiermacher fully embraced and imbibed this "Kantian bargain," taking a rearguard move in his 1830 *The Christian Faith* when he proclaimed that, "The controversy over the temporal or eternal creation of the world ... has no bearing on the content of the feeling of absolute dependence, and it is therefore a matter of indifference how it is decided."[4] Dorrien chocked up Barbour's new approach to his leanings toward process theology, which is partly accurate since Whitehead's process philosophy particularly sought to integrate developments in early twentieth-century science. I also take Barbour's interests as much more personal (and, admittedly, I might be veering into *ad hominem* analysis)—he was a physicist who cared deeply about theology and believed they could talk to one another (despite perhaps what Kant had declared). And thus he created a new era of science and religion.

Barbour's book signaled his maturity in the conversation in traveling beyond the conflict narrative that had energized both the fundamentalist revolt against modernism and atheistic voices critical of all things religious. At the same time it brought a liberal theological view that had the resources to engage the sciences, along with the acumen to grasp the subtleties of the sciences, especially his professional interest of physics, but also others, such as biology. It signified a fresh approach, and when I talk to theologians or scientists that are old enough to remember reading Barbour's work for the first time the experience sounds largely unexpected and therefore stunning—"like lightning from a clear sky" (to borrow the phrase C.S. Lewis employed on the occasion of publication of J.R.R. Tolkien's *The Lord of the Rings* [5]).

Still, despite Barbour's formidable accomplishment, it's time for a substantial caveat, which repeats what I wrote in the Introduction: his approach is fundamentally intellectual—that science and religion represent two systems of knowledge. It is therefore worth nothing, and citing at length, Joshua Reeves' analysis, in which he connects *Issues* with Thomas Kuhn's influential *The Structure of Scientific Revolutions*, published only four years earlier.

> Ian Barbour's *Issues in Science and Religion*, an important catalyst for the academic field of science and religion, appeared shortly after Kuhn's work and interacted heavily with it. In that work, Barbour set out many of the specific themes that would come to characterize the field over the next half century. He, in particular, drew upon post-Kuhnian philosophy of science to argue for a position called critical realism, which argued that both science and religion make cognitive claims about the world expressed through metaphors and models. Barbour's work also helped to start a large body of scholarship on the methodological relationship between science and religion over the next half century.[6]

108 The present: 1966 to 2000

First of all, Reeves noted that Barbour, even if he rejected the Kantian bargain, nevertheless adopted Kant's conclusion that the subject cannot describe the noumenal world without metaphors or models, but—and this he added—*neither can science.* [7] In addition, Reeves noted Barbour's influence over this field of science and religion for the past half century and set some boundaries on how it influenced the field—directing it toward the cognitive claims that religion and science present.

In assigning the publication of this book as the demarcation line between the past, the present, and the future, I am also asserting (or perhaps iterating) that right now we are experiencing a change. Despite the fruitful contributions of Barbour's work, the current *Sitz im Leben* represents something much more complicated than his well-worn four categories of conflict, independence, dialogue, and integration for relating science and religion.[8]

I will return to these assertions in my next chapters on the contours of the future interaction between science and religion, but there is one major lacuna in Barbour which limits his effectiveness today. One obvious change in the second half of the twentieth century is that science and *religion* has become more visibly pluralized, so that we should talk about science and *religions* (and concerns of space have limited my ability to address this topic more fully). Of historical note (and worth repeating) is the Immigration Act of 1965 that lifted most of the racially motivated immigration laws restricting Asian immigration, with the byproduct of expanding the presence of eastern religions in the US. (And as I indicated above, we might want to talk about *sciences and religions*, but I'll leave that aside until the next chapter.) All this makes this statement from Barbour sound quaint and provincial as he set the course of *Issues*, "We will consider *religion in the West*, primarily various forms of *Christianity*—and not, except incidentally, the religions of Asia."[9] (And what about, for example, Judaism in the US, where almost half of all Jews live, and the extraordinary influence of Jewish scientists in America?)

Naturally we can look back to the 1893 World Parliament of Religions as a significant sign, but we may overplay our hand. If the pluralizing of religious rings like a truism today, we need to look back not too many decades ago when a consciousness of religious diversity was just beginning to bloom. In 1963 Martin Luther King, Jr., could speak in his "I Have a Dream" speech of "all God's children, black men and white men, Jews and Gentiles, Protestants and Catholics" as a summary of religious diversity. Despite the profundity of King's vision, this three-party phrase strikes a sensitive reader of American religious life as quaint. It sounds like a period piece, something like defining pop music as Sixties rock to those who have heard hip hop and reggaeton their whole lives. We are far more than Protestants and Catholics, Jews and Gentiles. In their standard treatment of US religion, Edwin Gaustad and Leigh Schmidt, commented accordingly:

> The tripartite formula of "Protestant-Catholic-Jew" was always inadequate to name American religious pluralism, such a unifying construct was rendered intelligible only by overlooking a multitude of sects, seekers, immigrant minorities, and indigenous traditions. After 1965 any narrowly Christian and

Jewish story line about religious pluralism became utterly outworn as the United States emerged, by scholar Diana Eck's accounting, as "the world's most religiously diverse nation."[10]

We are more pluralized and secularized than in King's day and probably more than many Americans are willing to admit. Religious diversity began to emerge more clearly in Malcolm X's famous conversion at first to the Nation of Islam and then—following his 1964 *hajj* to Mecca—to mainstream Islam. Malcolm X's vision was captured in his famous *Autobiography*[11] (a book that emerged from conversations with the writer Alex Haley), which was published in 1965, the same year as his assassination. And, as I will present in Chapter Ten, the United States is increasingly more a culture of digital-streaming spirituality than of a vinyl 12-inch LP religion.

The best way to proceed—or at least the method I'm using here—is to walk through the decades and see how they carry us into the present world.

The Sixties: turbulence

The Sixties has an iconic status in American life. (In fact, since *The Sixties* is a kind of moniker, *the 1960s* just didn't look right for this subsection.) It is no surprise that Sydney Ahlstrom, the eminent historian of religion, in his tome *Religion in America* could name this decade—an unbelievably tumultuous change in American life— "The Turbulent Sixties." To mention the Sixties is to begin with a presidential election of religious significance—the United States had its first Roman Catholic chief executive in John F. Kennedy, which signaled the breaking of Protestant hegemony. It is also to mark a time of the Vietnam War, the Civil Rights protests, as well as the assassinations of President Kennedy in 1963, Malcolm X in 1965, and Martin Luther King in 1968. To mention the Sixties is also to recall the counter-culture youth who rejected the cultural standards of their parents and their religious mores, but especially its racial segregation, the Vietnam conflict, sexual standards, women's rights, and materialism. It found expression in Jack Weinberg, an activist best known for his role in the Free Speech Movement at the University of California, Berkeley, in 1964—a movement with a marked lack of self-awareness so that even though its leaders would of course someday age, it made declarations later sloganized as "Don't trust anyone over 30." The Sixties also reached its cultural manifestation in the music of rock and roll and the iconic Woodstock festival in August 1969, which attracted over 400,000.

The Sixties ended with a momentous scientific achievement: the landing of Apollo 11 on the Moon on July, 20, 1969. It is the most significant cultural symbol, after the explosions of the atomic bombs in 1945, of American science. Neil Armstrong's iconic first words, just after touching his space boot on the dusty surface of the Moon, has scientific merit: "That's one small step for man, one giant leap for mankind."[12] Science had pluralized—or at least doubled—the bodies in space where human footprints could be found.

110 The present: 1966 to 2000

Some of these cultural changes had scientific roots or causes. Stanley Kubrick's epic 1968 film *2001: A Space Odyssey* imagined what space travel might look like in the next century and introduced an artificial intelligence computer, HAL (probably a play on the computer company IBM's name), who ultimately had only a modicum of concern for human life and even less empathy. The first oral contraceptives were approved for use in 1960. A backlash in the infamous Catholic encyclical *Humanae Vitae* by Pope Paul VI in 1968 rejected most forms of artificial birth control. But it wasn't simply what science was doing to change our bodies and our babies; it had also changed our global-political relations. The ongoing Cold War, based at its core on nuclear arms, grew terrifyingly close to American shores in the Cuban Missile Crisis of 1962. We learned anew that the power of science could terrify.

The influence of the mainline was beginning to crumble as the Church became further disestablished from the centers of power. The Sixties also saw the rise of "creation science," which had its first major success in the publication of *The Genesis Flood: The Biblical Record and its Scientific Implications* in 1961. As I mentioned in the previous chapter, this movement represented a response to the rise of the public teaching of evolution. In 1963 Henry Morris founded the Creation Research Society and then in 1970 the Institute for Creation Research. Counternarratives and movements were appearing. Of specific interest are the cases of teaching creationism in public schools as heirs of the Scopes Trial and subsequently their rejection by the United States Supreme Court.[13] For example, the 1965 case *United States v. Seeger*—though not about creationism—recognized that "the nation was manifestly pluralistic in its forms of 'religious training and belief.'"[14] This recognition by the highest US court demonstrates that something in American culture had changed. The 1968 *Epperson v. Arkansas* decision "rendered anti-evolution laws unconstitutional."[15] This did not end the controversies over evolution, which will thread through this chapter.

Naturally I need to emphasize again that there is no monolithic cultural Idea, no singular *Zeitgeist*. During these years, profound antiphonal voices to conservative Christianity arose, such as Rachel Carson's significant scientific and naturalist reflection on the coming ecological crisis, her 1962 *Silent Spring*, which later found a corresponding voice, accusing Christianity of creating a deleterious relationship with nature, in Lynn White's famous 1967 *Science* essay, "The Historical Roots of Our Ecologic Crisis."[16] In addition there was a return to a pre-technological world in the communal living movement. For example, in 1968 a community that originated in the Haight-Ashbury area of San Francisco settled Black Bear Ranch in the Siskiyou Mountains and incorporated the slogan "free land for free people." I'm including it here as an example of the nature movement's flourishing in the Sixties and 1970s. The concept was to move away from the industrialized world overcome by technology to reach a deeper connection with nature. These represent cultural signs that our country's Protestant foundations were cracking.

Beyond these specific and identifiable alterations in the American religious landscape lay a diversity of new religious movements, fostered not only on the US

The present: 1966 to 2000 **111**

Constitution's First Amendment and its freedom of religion but also American individualism and free market economy. "Such movements, which for so long had found America's voluntaristic and democratized milieu a fertile seedbed, only grew more visible and variegated after the 1960s" (Gaustad and Schimdt).[17] Generally speaking, as religion becomes more individualized and more private, it atrophies in its ability to engage with science, which is fundamentally a public enterprise. This has led some commentators, like Philip Hammond, to describe a disestablishment of religion. As Mark Sibley wrote,

> Hammond shows how social changes in the 1960s accelerated fundamental change in the religion-culture relationship in the United States. Moral authority is shifting, Hammond argues, from churches to autonomous individuals. Therefore, while church membership and attendance remain relatively high in the United States, the social meaning of religious participation has changed.[18]

Hammond leaned on Wade Clark Roof and William McKinney, who commented that religion had lost its "integrative force."[19] During this disestablishment of the 1960s,

> Religion, they say, was no less visible in American life, but now it is more likely to divide than to integrate. In other words, religion since the 1960s, to the degree it is important, is more likely to be *individually* important and less likely to be *collectively* important.[20]

That last phrase demonstrates the acceleration of religious individualism, to which I'll return in the final part of this book. It is, however, worth noting that the United States is moving toward post-Christendom,[21] becoming more like Europe had already done in the nineteenth century, as C.S. Lewis noted in 1954 (and he was one of the first to do so).[22] Hammond reflected on this transformation as the "third disestablishment" of religion, which arrived after the first in the Revolutionary period and the second between the world wars, when "churches found themselves popular but less powerful."[23] (This second disestablishment I'm not as convinced of—I see a more gradual process—but that's a question I don't need to pursue for my purposes here.) He wrote, "The social revolution of the 1960s and '70s wrought a major change: a near absolute free choice in the religious marketplace. This change we have been calling the third disestablishment, and it has taken place primarily because of the greatly increased personal autonomy Americans now experience."[24] Religion has not so much been rationalized, à la Weber, but individualized.[25]

At the same time, less popularly announced changes occurred in American culture, certainly in the sphere of academic life. As I am arguing, the contemporary field of science and religion—i.e., the field as we know it today—began in this decade. The Stanford Encyclopedia of Philosophy summarizes it well:

112 The present: 1966 to 2000

Since the 1960s, scholars in theology, philosophy, history, and the sciences have studied the relationship between science and religion. Science and religion is a recognized field of study with dedicated journals (e.g., *Zygon: Journal of Religion and Science*), academic chairs (e.g., the Andreas Idreos Professor of Science and Religion at Oxford University), scholarly societies (e.g., the Science and Religion Forum), and recurring conferences (e.g., the European Society for the Study of Science and Theology holds meetings every two years).[26]

In addition to the general cultural turbulence, science and religion was becoming consolidated. In fact, as Thomas Dixon summarizes the field and concludes, "From the 1960s onwards 'science and religion' took on a more distinct existence as an academic discipline."[27] And so today we are in a cultural world in which science and religion can interact fruitfully. This has roots in this era of change. And today there exist continuing centers, journals, and academic chairs to be sure that this dialogue and integration (to use Barbour's categories) continue.

Barbour would welcome this situation. Christian theology was also undergoing its own alterations. The hold that neo-orthodox theologians had on American religious thought had begun to wane.[28] Neo-orthodox thinkers like Reinhold and Richard Niebuhr, as well as Langdon Gilkey, had taken the Kantian bargain. (For what it's worth, I don't include Paul Tillich in neo-orthodoxy.) And however much one associates Karl Barth with this theological circle, and although he lived until 1968, Barth's statements at the outset of his doctrine of creation in *Church Dogmatics* III/1 two decades earlier are particularly significant: "There can be no scientific problems, objections or aids in relation to what Holy Scripture and the Christian Church understand by the divine work of creation."[29] This hardly represents a propitious beginning to a collaborative engagement between the leading theologian of the twentieth century with natural science. (And yet one of Barth's disciples, Thomas Torrance, wrote a stirring reconciliation of science, especially its methods, with Reformed Christian theology, *Theological Science*. Indeed the world is never entirely simple.)

Thus it's reasonably uncomplicated to discern the antagonists' position in Barbour's *Issues in Science and Religion*. It arrived in the second paragraph of the Introduction: "Concerning methods, most writers today see science and religion as *strongly contrasting enterprises* which have essentially nothing to do with each other."[30] And this contrast view hasn't simply taken residence among scientists. Barbour argues that these theologians (undoubtedly neo-orthodox or "Barthian") see God's work clearly distinguishable from scientific work. And Barbour obviously wanted to change that and move toward integration.

This positive integration with mainstream science is mirrored in statements by mainline Protestant denominations. Consider the PCUS (now the Presbyterian Church, PCUSA), which has long taken a stand in support of evolution. In 1969 it concluded that "neither Scripture, our Confession of Faith, nor our Catechisms,

The present: 1966 to 2000 **113**

teach the Creation of man by the direct and immediate acts of God so as to exclude the possibility of evolution as a scientific theory."[31]

A variety of voices had emerged, none of which soloed, some of which harmonized, and others that struck discordant notes.

The 1970s: broadening the dialogue

The dialogue of religion with science becomes broader in integrating other religious traditions more clearly in the 1970s. It is also the era of political change. There are the cultural moments of Richard Nixon's second election in 1972 and his ignominious downfall in the Watergate scandal, which ultimately forced Nixon to resign his presidency on August 9, 1974; Gerald Ford's pardon of Nixon just one month later; the unexpected election two years later of a largely unknown peanut farmer and governor of Georgia, Jimmy Carter. Carter's presidency would be marked by many things, one of which arose from OPEC's oil embargo, which led to a gradual move toward energy conservation—albeit, in retrospect, we see the way in which this movement was contravened in the following decades. And the Iranian Revolution of 1979 and the capture of 52 US diplomats for 444 days, finally released in 1981, brought Islamic fundamentalism and radicalism into American consciousness.

On particularly scientific fronts, Edwin Black has noted, "Today's headline is tomorrow's footnote. In 1978 Louise Brown became the world's first test-tube baby and a braver new world shuddered. Since then *in vitro* fertilization has become common reproductive therapy."[32] Previously, in 1971, scientists successfully transferred genetic information from one animal cell to another in order to correct a genetic deficiency, and six years later Frederick Sanger had sequenced the first DNA genome of an organism. Significantly, genetic technology means that, instead of simply altering the world outside, human beings can now change ourselves. But there's more. Many other key scientific discoveries from the 1970s have particular implications for science and religion. In the early '70s Frank Drake, an American astronomer, conducted the first SETI experiment, Project Ozma, and thus extended the boundaries of science spatially in the search for extraterrestrial life. Machine computing began to make its way into our lives through "personal computers"—a term coined by Ed Roberts in 1975 and given marketing flair by Steve Jobs and Steve Wozniak the next year with their introduction of the Apple I. Also in 1975, Donald Johanson and his team discovered a partial skeleton of a female hominin, *Australopithecus afarensis*, our three-million-year-old ancestor, which they named "Lucy." The links between human beings and other animals became more apparent, and in 1978 Koko, sometimes called a "talking gorilla," was reported to have a sign language of almost 400 words. In 1977 Leon Lederman and his colleagues found evidence of the "bottom quark" at Fermilab. And, in 1979, the Three Mile Island nuclear power plant had a catastrophic meltdown, demonstrating the potential perils of nuclear power.

114 The present: 1966 to 2000

The conversation of religion generally, and thus its relationship with science, was further pluralized. Consider a few important voices that emerged in this decade. A wider environmental consciousness emerged with the first Earth Day on April 22, 1970, and in this decade Lynn Margulis and James Lovelock proposed the Gaia hypothesis in which the earth is seen as a complex and self-regulating system of the atmosphere, biosphere, hydrosphere, and pedosphere, all interlocking in an evolving system.[33] Lovelock called this system as a whole *Gaia*, after the Greek goddess who personified the earth. Gaia seeks what is optimal for life. And though Lovelock later clarified that this is not a sentient entity and instead is an "emergent property,"[34] not an organism, neopagan, naturalistic spirituality movements took up this image with religious appreciation. Nonetheless, the Gaia hypothesis found enthusiastic reception among the growing nature religions; spiritualistic naturalism, or humanistic paganism, or simply neopaganism.

Some fled science and technology and created alternative spiritual communities.[35] For example, Stephen Gaskin, who began his work as a religious leader in San Francisco in the 1960s, syncretized Christianity with eastern religions such as Buddhism, along with copious amounts of cannabis (the latter landed him, and three followers, in the Tennessee State Penitentiary in 1974).[36] Before that, and before moving to Tennessee, he had already amalgamated a variety of teachings in his "Monday Night Class," which presented ideas from Alan Watts and Aldous Huxley with more mainstream Christian and Jewish doctrines, as well as eastern religious concepts such as karma, the cause and effect of our actions. "Under the influence of psychedelics, karma could be felt instantaneously," wrote Douglas Stephenson a bit wryly, and I'll note that psychedelics represent a scientifically based means of achieving religious experience. Stephenson then added, "In short, life was a trip, and the journey was guided by taking personal responsibility for one's actions, attitude, and energy. This was the essence of Stephen's message."[37] In 1971 Gaskin along with 300 spiritual seekers from Haight-Ashbury, founded the Farm in Lewis County, near the town of Summertown, Tennessee, based on principles of this shared spirituality, respect for the earth, and non-violence. The Farm, as the website proudly demonstrates,[38] continues to this day, despite Gaskin's death in 2014 at age 79.

At least as fascinating as these communal living initiatives are the scientific voices that amalgamated their work with religious insights. Fritjof Capra's *The Tao of Physics*, first published in 1975, argued that perfect harmony found in the complementarity of particle and wave, mind and matter, and the interchangeability of energy and matter had striking similarities to eastern mysticism. Notably the accent falls on *mysticism*. Capra tied this insight to a mystical vision in the early 1970s on an unnamed beach, "watching the waves rolling in and feeling the rhythm of my breathing, when I suddenly became aware of my whole environment as being engaged in a gigantic cosmic dance."[39] It should not have surprised me to read his descriptions of eastern religious traditions or philosophies (depending on how these are viewed) and be struck by how the five chapters on The Way of Eastern Mysticism—Hinduism, Buddhism, Chinese Thought, Taoism, and Zen—are all

The present: 1966 to 2000   115

directed toward a common goal—his project. (Incidentally, one of the weaknesses of his approach is that Capra "conflates many of the 'Eastern' traditions."[40]) Even the word "Mysticism" in the section title offers a glimpse of where he's headed. Not to be missed is the connection between insights into physics and its religious and social implications—i.e., (to cite Brooke) "the conceptual shift in physics has profound social implications. To reflect the harmonious interrelatedness observed in nature, a cultural revolution is required."[41] Or as Capra himself sets it, "I see science and mysticism as two complementary manifestations of the human mind; of its rational and intuitive faculties."[42] (Notice here the similarity with Whitehead's categories of "the force of our religious intuitions, and the force of our impulse to accurate observation and logical deduction."[43])

As Capra continued in this passage, one can appreciate why, given his clear and compelling style, *The Tao of Physics* sold millions of copies.

> The two approaches are entirely different and involve far more than a certain view of the physical world. However, they are complementary, as we have learned to say in physics. Neither is comprehended in the other, nor can either of them be reduced to the other; but both of them are necessary, supplementing one another for a fuller understanding of the world [hints here of Neils Bohr's Copenhagen Interpretation].... Science does not need mysticism and mysticism does not need science, but men and women need both.[44]

In addition to Capra's contributions to pluralizing the conversation between science and religion, Amit Goswami later wrote *Self-Aware Universe* in 1995. Though two decades after Capra, I mention it now to demonstrate a common theme. In it Goswami proposed the unification of all of physics (four fundamental forces) as part of *Ātman* (single source of all). Similarly, scholars have explored the connection of Buddhism, and especially the Madhyamaka school's emphasis on *sunya* or emptiness, with modern quantum physics.[45] At any rate, Capra, as well as Goswami, encouraged America to look away from the west toward eastern religious views. In 1995 Capra founded the Berkeley-based Center for Ecoliterary, (according to his website) "dedicated to advancing ecology and systems thinking in primary and secondary education."[46]

This emergence of an amalgamation of eastern religious thought and science was predicated on the weirdness of quantum physics, where things are both something and not something—an electron can be both a wave and a particle, but not both at the same time. This, of course, is well captured in the comment by the Nobel Laureate physicist Frank Wilczek, "Niels Bohr distinguished two kinds of truths. An ordinary truth is a statement whose opposite is a falsehood. A profound truth is a statement whose opposite is also a profound truth."[47] Whether this combination between eastern religious perspectives and quantum theory is straightforward remains a contended task. Similarly, neopagans found in these texts from Margulis, Lovelock, and Capra a re-enchantment of the world, which had been disenchanted by much of modern science. It also implied for some that scientific

116 The present: 1966 to 2000

endeavors can become spiritual. As James Gilbert observed, "One of the most creative impulses of American culture is the continuing presence of religion at the heart of scientific civilization"[48]

On other fronts, Vine Deloria, in books such as *God is Red: A Native View of Religion* (1973), did not address science and religion *per se* but argued for a renewed appreciation of Native American spirituality as well as offering a criticism of traditional western views of both science and the cosmos.[49] He also made a countermove, a harsh criticism of Christianity as the problem behind our religious intolerance. As the preface by Leslie Marmon Silko sets out, "In *God is Red*, Deloria explains how Christianity is the root cause of this great weakness of the United States—the inability to respect or tolerate those who are different."[50] And this hints at some of the reasons the United States has found it difficult to embrace its putative acceptance of a variety of religions in general and, more specifically, in placing them in conversation with the sciences. It also represents a critique of Diana Eck's comment above that we are "the world's most religiously diverse nation." America may possess many religious traditions within its borders, but we don't always like that truth. Deloria (and others like him) made us more aware of this fact.

The 1980s: growth and collaboration

As I have argued throughout this book, the United States presents a testing ground for the negotiation of science and religion. If we understand how our country has negotiated the two, then we grasp American culture as a whole. In the 1980s it is hard to miss the further growth in the collaboration of science and religion and not to sense that something new was happening; in many ways a partial fulfillment of Barbour's vision.

I will again note a few scientific discoveries with particularly important religious implications. The 1980s brought the first permanent artificial heart (1982), evidence for possible exoplanets with the detection of solid matter around the star Vega (1983), and the horrific, and televised, explosion of the space shuttle Challenger on January 28, 1986, in which all seven crew members were killed, including Christa McAuliffe, a high school teacher, which made the tragedy more poignant for the average American.

In 1981 Robert John Russell founded the Center for Theology and the Natural Sciences (CTNS). Around this time there was a new focus academically on methodological issues, the development of contextual approaches, and a greater degree of detailed historical examination of the relationship between science and religion that, of course, problematized, if not largely undermined, the conflict thesis.[51] Russell particularly began to engage in the *content* of the dialogue, most notably in the collaborative venture with the Vatican Observatory. "The series actually began in 1979 with a call from Pope John Paul II for 'fruitful concord between science and faith, between the Church and the world,'"[52] and eventually produced the first book in an extensive collaboration between CTNS and the Vatican, *Physics, Philosophy and Theology: A Common Quest for Understanding*, in 1988.

In 1987, the John Templeton Foundation (JTF) began. JTF's founding, if nothing else, has radically affected the development of the field of science and religion. In fact Barbour, whose book frames "the present," received the prestigious Templeton Prize in 1999. Speaking of Barbour, who leaned in 1987 to a revisioning of God along Whiteheadian process lines, Sallie McFague published *Models of God: Theology for an Ecological, Nuclear Age*, which challenged Christians' traditional speech about God as a kind of monarch. She was convinced that the problems of ecology and the reality of nuclear holocaust necessitated Christian theology probing instead three other possible metaphors for God as mother, lover, and friend.

Naturally I cannot only mention the voice of theological liberals and their interaction with science. In this decade, creation science presented challenges to an integration of mainstream science with religious belief by impugning mainstream science and offering an alternative version of what constitutes science. Ask any of the undergraduates in my science and religion classes to name what comes to mind when you pronounce the phrase "science and religion" and the most prominent answer will be "evolution and creation." Many associate the latter (i.e., religion) with creationism (or, perhaps, Intelligent Design), and may have even heard some of the legal wrangling. In 1987 Henry Morris's book *What is Creation Science?* set the agenda for many anti-evolution forces and continues as a widely read source. Nonetheless, in that same year creation science suffered a momentous defeat when the US Supreme Court in *Edwards v. Aguillard* struck down Louisiana's Creationism Act and declared that it was unconstitutional to require the teaching of it as science. Creationism is religion, not science, the court stated, and cannot be advocated in public-school classrooms. One could see this as the death of any "equal time" law, although it would be replayed in many ways in 2005 with the famous Dover case over Intelligent Design.

Ronald Reagan's surprising election in 1980 represented the re-emergence of the fundamentalists and conservative evangelicals in the resurgent religious right. This wing of evangelical Christianity emerged from the shadows of American culture and took political power, uniting various leading voices such as Jerry Falwell, Ralph Reed, and James Dobson. "They united in promoting prayer in public schools, in opposing abortion, in condemning homosexuality, in despairing over the growth of 'secular humanism,' *in supporting at least equal time for teaching 'creationism,'* and in promoting in whatever way possible a 'return' to a Christian America" (Gaustad and Schmidt, italics mine).[53] Their anti-evolution work meant an association of evolution with communism, humanism, "dirty books," terrorism, abortion, socialism, crime, and inflation.[54]

Soon after *Edwards v. Aguillard*, Intelligent Design (or ID) took up the cause of resisting Darwinian theory. As Michael Ruse made clear in his reflection on some of the myths (meaning, in this case, untruths) about science and religion, "The phrase *intelligent design* began circulating after the US Supreme Court ruled in 1987 that it was unconstitutional to require the teaching of 'creation science' but allowed for the possibility of voluntarily teaching alternatives to evolution—if done

118 The present: 1966 to 2000

for secular reasons."[55] According to Ruse, a small Christian organization in Texas brought out the anti-evolution textbook, *Of Pandas and People: The Central Question of Origins* (1991), originally entitled *Biology and Creation* (and so, incidentally, this topic straddles the '80s and '90s). The authors, Dean Kenyon, a biologist at San Francisco State, and Percival Davis, a biology teacher in Florida "replaced the words 'creation' and 'creationists' with 'intelligent design' and 'design proponents.'"[56]

Intelligent Design needed a champion to broaden its appeal, which came from an unlikely source for a self-proclaimed scientific paradigm—the Boalt Hall constitutional law professor Philip E. Johnson, who wrote the surprisingly popular *Darwin on Trial* in 1991.[57] It mirrored the concerns of another key publication from this period (at first internal to the Discovery Institute and later leaked), the 1988 Wedge Document. This manifesto undergirded ID and noted a particular connection between Darwinism, its materialism with ethical responsibility. It argued that materialism had replaced the foundational conviction of western civilization—our creation in the image of God—and that the cultural consequences were vast. These materialists, such as Charles Darwin, Karl Marx, and Sigmund Freud, denied objective moral standards, and the social sciences, and really most of current intellectual culture, uncritically adopted this moral relativism. This undermines personal responsibility since biology and environment solely dictate human behavior and thought. In the words of the Wedge Document, "Discovery Institute's Center for the Renewal of Science and Culture seeks nothing less than the overthrow of materialism and its cultural legacies."[58] ID represents a much more sophisticated and well-educated cadre than creation science (e.g., one of its intellectual leaders, Stephen Meyer, holds a Ph.D in the philosophy of science from Cambridge University). Still, ID is no less horrified by the implications it sees in mainstream science.

The 1990s: consolidation and counter-narratives

I begin this subsection by nothing a few scientific discoveries with particularly important religious implications. In 1992 cosmologists identified temperature fluctuations in the cosmic background, further confirming the Big Bang, and two years later astronomers reported evidence for the existence of a black hole at the center of galaxy M87, 50 million light years from earth. In 1996 measurements of carbon isotope from Greenland rocks pushed back the origin of life on earth to 3.85 billion years ago. By 1998 the Supernova Cosmology Project and the High-Z Supernova Search Team discovered an accelerated expansion of the universe and hypothesized a mysterious "dark energy." Human embryos were cloned for the first time in 1992, and scientists at the Roslin Institute cloned the first mammal, "Dolly the Sheep," in 1996. The next year biologists were able to isolate human embryonic stem cells. Finally, in 1995, the Intergovernmental Panel on Climate Change found evidence of anthropogenic climate change. In these discoveries we can tick off new insights into the cosmos, means to alter animal and human

The present: 1966 to 2000   **119**

genetics, and the ethical issue that will dominate much of the contemporary discussion of science and religion, climate change.

In the 1990s some profound consolidation of this integration between science and religion, as well as an intersection of their values, took place. In 1995 the AAAS established the program of Dialogue on Science, Ethics, and Religion (DoSER) to facilitate communication between scientific and religious communities.[59] Earlier I mentioned the collaboration between the Vatican Observatory at Castel Gandolfo, Italy, and CTNS in Berkeley. In the 1990s they co-sponsored a series of conferences on divine action. It had contributors from philosophy and theology (such Tom Tracy, Ted Peters, and Nancey Murphy) and the sciences (George Ellis and Bill Stoeger). These conferences set out to understand divine action in the light of contemporary sciences. The first of these conferences papers were published in 1993 as *Quantum Cosmology and the Laws of Nature.* [60] Each of these, and the edited volumes that arose from them, was devoted to an area of natural science and its interaction with religion, including quantum cosmology (as noted above, conference in 1992 and publication in 1993), chaos and complexity (conference 1994, with publication 1995), evolutionary and molecular biology (conference 1996, with publication 1998), neuroscience and the person (conference 1998, with publication 2000), and the last, which Russell and a team authored in 2002, was entitled *Quantum Mechanics: Scientific Perspectives on Divine Action Vol. 5.* [61]

At the same time, various church leaders issued public statements on evolutionary theory that expressed hopeful integration. In 1996 Pope John Paul II affirmed evolutionary theory in his message to the Pontifical Academy of Sciences.

> Today, more than a half-century after the appearance of that encyclical [from Pope Pius XII], some new findings lead us toward the recognition of evolution as more than an hypothesis. In fact it is remarkable that this theory has had progressively greater influence on the spirit of researchers, following a series of discoveries in different scholarly disciplines. The convergence in the results of these independent studies—which was neither planned nor sought—constitutes in itself a significant argument in favor of the theory.[62]

At the same time, like Pius before him, the Pope stated the need for God to specially create the human soul and rejected its emergence as a part of evolution.

> It is by virtue of his eternal soul that the whole person, including his body, possesses such great dignity. Pius XII underlined the essential point: if the origin of the human body comes through living matter which existed previously, the spiritual soul is created directly by God.[63]

And so the Vatican embraced evolutionary science, albeit with certain adjustments based on their doctrinal standards. The liberal wing of Protestants certainly joined, and one should note that, despite the voices of creation science and ID, not

120 The present: 1966 to 2000

all conservative Christians are creationists. For example, in 1997, on the *David Frost Show*, Bill Graham commented:

> I don't think that there's any conflict at all between science today and the Scriptures. I think that we have misinterpreted the Scriptures many times, and we've tried to make the Scriptures say things they weren't meant to say. I think that we have made a mistake by thinking the Bible is a scientific book. The Bible is not a book of science. The Bible is a book of Redemption, and of course I accept the creation story. I believe that God did create the universe. I believe that God created man, and whether it came by an evolutionary process and at a certain point He took this person or being and made him a living soul or not, does not change the fact that God did create man ... whichever way God did it makes no difference as to what man is and man's relationship to God.[64]

The 1990s saw the rise of further counter-narratives with a greater degree of sophistication. In 1990 the Discovery Institute was founded as a non-profit educational foundation and think tank and moved within a few years to promote ID as a specific scientific proposal. Nevertheless, ID has not been well received by mainstream science. In 1996 Michael Behe's bestselling *Darwin's Black Box* came out, offering challenges to evolution based on "specified" and "irreducible" complexity, which, he asserted, cannot be explained by Darwinian evolution. Many conservative Christians applauded his work, but the AAAS highlighted ID's "significant conceptual flaws in its formulation, a lack of credible scientific evidence, and misrepresentations of scientific facts."[65] To add to its decline, the *Kitzmiller v. Dover* trial in 2005 saw ID go down in legal flames. Judge John E. Jones III concluded that Intelligent Design is not science and "cannot uncouple itself from its creationist, and thus religious, antecedents."[66]

This case, of course, already moves the narrative into the next decade, century, and millennium, while simultaneously suggesting to many in the listening public that religion and science conflict.

Notes

1 Ian Barbour, *Issues in Science and Religion* (New York: HarperCollins, 1971 [1966]).
2 Personal conversations with Robert J. Russell; Alister McGrath, *Religion and Science: A New Introduction,* 2nd edition. (Oxford: Wiley-Blackwell, 2010), 205.
3 Gary Dorrien, "Dialectics of Difference: Barth, Whitehead, Modern Theology and the Uses of Worldview," *American Journal of Theology & Philosophy* 30, no. 3 (2009): 267.
4 Friedrich Schleiermacher, *The Christian Faith*, H.R. Mackintosh and J.S. Stewart, eds. (Edinburgh: T&T Clark, 1989), 155.
5 C.S. Lewis, "Tolkien's *The Lord of the Rings*," in *On Stories and Other Essays and Literature,* ed. Walter Hooper (New York: Harvest Book, 1982), 83.
6 Joshua Reeves, *Against Methodology in Science and Religion: Recent Debates on Rationality and Theology*, Routledge Science and Religion Series (Oxfordshire: Routledge, 2018), 17.

The present: 1966 to 2000   121

7 See Barbour, *Issues*, chs. 18, 25. Cf. Janet Martin Soskice, *Metaphor and Religious Language* (Oxford: Clarendon, 1987).

8 For example, see my article, "Some Ways Emerging Adults Are Shaping the Future of Religion and Science." *Zygon: Journal of Religion and Science* 51, no. 3 (2016): 557–72.

9 Ian Barbour, *Issues in Science and Religion* (New York: HarperCollins, 1971 [1966]), 9.

10 Edwin Gaustad and Leigh Schmidt, *The Religious History of America: The Heart of the American Story from Colonial Times to Today* (San Francisco: HarperCollins, 2004), 412.

11 Malcolm X and Alex Haley, *Autobiography of Malcolm X* (New York: Grove Press, 1965).

12 Apparently, he meant to say "a man"—and thus him as an individual—but I think the sense is largely the same.

13 See Gaustad & Schmidt, *The Religious History of America,* 361ff.

14 Ibid., 354.

15 John H. Evans, *Morals Not Knowledge: Recasting the Contemporary U.S. Conflict Between Science and Religion* (Oakland: University of California Press, 2018), 82.

16 Lynn White, "The Historical Roots of Our Ecological Crisis," *Science* 155 (1967): 1203–7.

17 Gaustad and Schmidt, *Religious History*, 398.

18 Mark Shibley, "Hammond, Phillip E." Hartford Institute for Religion Research website, retrieved June 19, 2019, http://hirr.hartsem.edu/ency/Hammond.htm.

19 Roof and McKinney, *American Mainline Religion* (New Brunswick: Rutgers University Press, 1987), 1997, 33–9.

20 Hammond, *Religion and Personal Autonomy*, 10, citing Wade Clark Roof and William McKinney, *American Mainline Religion*, 33–9.

21 See, for example, Hammond, 15–16.

22 C.S. Lewis, "*De Descriptione Temporum*," *They Asked for a Paper: Paper and Addresses* (London: Geoffrey Bles, 1962), 20.

23 Philip E. Hammond, *Religion and Personal Autonomy: Third Disestablishment in America,* Studies in Comparative Religion (Columbia, SC: University of South Carolina Press, 1992), 10.

24 Hammond, *American Mainline Religion*, 168.

25 See also, ibid., 171.

26 Stanford Encyclopedia of Philosophy, "Religion and Science," retrieved June 24, 2019, https://plato.stanford.edu/entries/religion-science.

27 Thomas Dixon, *Science and Religion: A Very Short Introduction* (Oxford: Oxford University Press, 2008), 14.

28 Both Ian Barbour and John Dillenberger emphasize this point. E.g., respectively, Barbour *Religion in An Age of Science* (San Francisco: HarperOne, 1990), 249–50; and Dillenberger, *Protestant Thought and Natural Science: A Historical Study* (Nashville: Abingdon, 1960), 259ff.

29 Karl Barth, *Church Dogmatics III: The Doctrine of Creation, Part One,* trans. J. W. Edwards, O. Bussey, Harold Knight (Edinburgh: T&T Clark, 1958 [1945]), ix.

30 Barbour, *Issues*, 1.

31 See Kruse Kronicle, "Presbyterian Church (USA) On Evolution," retrieved June 19, 2019, https://www.krusekronicle.com/kruse_kronicle/2005/09/presbyterian_ch.html#.XQpbpS2ZMWo.

32 Edwin Black, *War Against the Weak: Eugenics and America's Campaign to Create a Master Race* (United Kingdom: Basic Books, 2004), 427.

33 Lovelock, *Gaia: A New Look at Life on Earth*, Oxford Landmark Science, reprint edition (Oxford: Oxford University Press, 2016). I've adapted many of these insights from Sarah Pike's lecture, "Nature Religions and the Spiritualization of Science," Chico State Science and Religions conference April 8, 2017, retrieved June 19, 2019, https://media.csuchico.edu/media/Nature+Religions+and+the+Spiritualization+of+Science/0_6qv681b3/66948482.

34 Lovelock, *Gaia 2*, 30.

35 See Douglas Stephenson, *Out to Change the World: The Evolution of The Farm Community* (Summertown, TN: Book Publishing Co. 2014); Tim Miller, *The 60s Communes: The*

122 The present: 1966 to 2000

Hippies and Beyond, Syracuse Studies on Peace and Conflict Resolution (Syracuse: Syracuse University Press, 1999).

36 See Douglas Martin, "Stephen Gaskin, Hippie Who Founded an Enduring Commune, Dies at 79," retrieved June 24, 2019, https://www.nytimes.com/2014/07/03/us/stephen-gaskin-hippie-who-founded-an-enduring-commune-dies-at-79.html.

37 Stephenson, *Out to Change the World*, 8.

38 The Farm Community, retrieved June 24, 2019, http://thefarmcommunity.com.

39 Fritjof Capra, *The Tao of Physics: An Exploration of the Parallels Between Modern Physics and Eastern* Mysticism, 3rd edition. (Berkeley: Shambhala, 1991 [1975]), 11.

40 Cabezón, in Alan B. Wallace, *Buddhism and Science: Breaking New* Ground (New York: Columbia University Press, 2003), 51.

41 John Hedley Brooke, *Science and Religion: Some Historical Perspectives* (Cambridge: Cambridge University, 1991), 335.

42 Capra, *The Tao of Physics*, 306.

43 A.N. Whitehead, *Science and the Modern World* (New York: Free Press, 1925), 181.

44 Capra, *The Tao of Physics*, 306.

45 E.g., Wallace, *Buddhism and Science*, part 3.

46 Fritjof Capra website, retrieved June 24, 2019, https://www.fritjofcapra.net.

47 Frank Wilczek, *The Lightness of Being: Mass, Ether, and the Unification of Forces* (New York: Basic, 2008), 11.

48 James Gilbert, *Redeeming Culture: American Religion in the Age of Science* (Chicago, IL: University of Chicago, 1997), 323.

49 See, for example, his chapter on "The Problem of Creation," Vine Deloria, *God is Red: A Native View of Religion*, 30th anniversary ed. (Golden, CO: Fulcrum, 1973), 77ff.

50 Leslie Marmon Silko in the Foreword to Deloria, *God is Red*, viii.

51 E.g., John Hedley Brooke, *Science and Religion*, 1991.

52 See the CTNS website, retrieved May 25, 2019, http://www.ctns.org/research.html#project.

53 Gaustad and Schmidt, *The Religious History of America*, 402.

54 Christopher P. Toumey, *God's Own Scientists: Creationists in a Secular World* (New Brunswick: Rutgers University Press, 1994), 96, who included an image of Richard Elmendorf's "The Evolution Tree."

55 Michael Ruse in *Darwin Goes to Jail*, 207.

56 Ibid. Cf. my comments in *Mere Science: Bridging the Divide with Emerging Adults* (Downers Grove, IL: InterVarsity, 2018), 99–102.

57 Philip Johnson, *Darwin on Trial*, 20th anniversary edition. (Downers Grove, IL: IVP Books, 2010), 1991.

58 The Wedge Document can be found here on the National Center for Science, retrieved June 25, 2019, https://ncse.com/creationism/general/wedge-document.

59 American Association for the Advancement of Science (AAAS), "About DoSER," retrieved June 19, 2019, https://www.aaas.org/programs/dialogue-science-ethics-and-religion/about. Full disclosure: I have participated on various projects for DoSER.

60 Robert J. Russell, Nancey Murphy, Christopher J. Isham, eds., *Quantum Cosmology and the Laws of Nature*, Scientific Perspectives on Divine Action, vol. 1 (Berkeley, CA: Vatican Observatory Publications; Center for Theology and the Natural Sciences, 1993).

61 Robert J. Russell, Philip Clayton, Kirk Wegter-McNelly, John Polkinghorne eds., *Quantum Mechanics*, Scientific Perspectives on Divine Action: vol. 5. (Berkeley, CA: Vatican Observatory Publications; Center for Theology and the Natural Sciences, 2002).

62 Pope John Paul II, "Message to the Pontifical Academy of Sciences," 22 October 1996, retrieved June 25, 2019, https://www.ewtn.com/library/papaldoc/jp961022.htm.

63 Pope John Paul II, ibid. The final phrase in Latin is *animas enim a Deo immediate creari catholica fides non retimere iubet.*

64 David Frost and Fred Bauer, *Billy Graham: Personal Thoughts of a Public Man.* (Colorado Springs: Chariot Victor Publishing, 1997), 72.

65 AAAS, "AAAS Board Resolution on Intelligent Design Theory." July 1, 2013, retrieved June 24, 2019, https://www.aaas.org/news/aaas-board-resolution-intelligent-design-theory.
66 *Kitzmiller v. Dover Area School District*, conclusion, retrieved June 25, 2019, https://law.justia.com/cases/federal/district-courts/FSupp2/400/707/2414073.

Bibliography

Alabanese, Catherine. *A Republic of Mind and Spirit: A Cultural History of American Metaphysical Religion*. New Haven, CT: Yale University Press, 2008.

American Association for the Advancement of Science. "AAAS Board Resolution on Intelligent Design Theory." July 1, 2013. Retrieved June 24, 2019. https://www.aaas.org/news/aaas-board-resolution-intelligent-design-theory

American Association for the Advancement of Science. "About DoSER." Accessed June 19, 2019. https://www.aaas.org/programs/dialogue-science-ethics-and-religion/about

Barbour, Ian. *Issues in Science and Religion*. New York: HarperCollins, 1971 [1966].

Barbour, Ian. *Religion in An Age of Science. The Gifford Lectures: Volume One*. San Fransisco: HarperOne, 1990.

Barth, Karl. *Church Dogmatics III: The Doctrine of Creation, Part One*. Translated by J.W. Edwards, O. Bussey and Harold Knight. Edinburgh, UK: T&T Clark, 1958 [1945].

Bellah, Robert N. et al. *Habits of the Heart*. Berkeley, CA: University of California Press, 1985.

Brooke, John Hedley. *Science and Religion: Some Historical Perspectives*. Cambridge, UK: Cambridge University, 1991.

Capra, Fritjof. *The Tao of Physics: An Exploration of the Parallels Between Modern Physics and Eastern Mysticism*. 3rd edition. Berkeley, CA: Shambhala, 1991. [First edition: 1975].

Capra, Fritjof website. Retrieved June 24, 2019. https://www.fritjofcapra.net

Center for Theology and the Natural Sciences (CTNS) website. Retrieved May 25, 2019. http://www.ctns.org/research.html#project

Collins, Francis. *The Language of God*. New York: Free Press, 2006.

Cootsona, Greg. "Some Ways Emerging Adults Are Shaping the Future of Religion and Science." *Zygon: Journal of Religion and Science*, 51, no. 3 (2016): 557–572.

Cootsona, Greg. *Mere Science: Bridging the Divide with Emerging Adults*. Downers Grove, IL: InterVarsity, 2018.

Dawkins, Richard. *The Blind Watchmaker: Why the Evidence of Evolution Reveals a Universe without Design*. New York: Norton, 1986.

Dawkins, Richard. *The Selfish Gene*, 2nd edition. Oxford, UK: Oxford University Press, 1989.

Dawkins, Richard. *The God Delusion*. New York: Mariner, 2008.

Deloria, Vine. *God is Red: A Native View of Religion*. 30th anniversary edition. Golden, CO: Fulcrum, 1973.

Dillenberger, John. *Protestant Thought and Natural Science: A Historical Study*. Nashville TN: Abingdon, 1960.

Dixon, Thomas. *Science and Religion: A Very Short Introduction*. Oxford, UK: Oxford University Press, 2008.

Dorrien, Gary. "Dialectics of Difference: Barth, Whitehead, Modern Theology and the Uses of Worldview," *American Journal of Theology & Philosophy*, 30, no. 3 (2009): 244–270.

Evans, John H. *Morals Not Knowledge: Recasting the Contemporary U.S. Conflict Between Science and Religion*. Oakland, CA: University of California Press, 2018.

Farm Community. Retrieved June 24, 2019. http://thefarmcommunity.com

124 The present: 1966 to 2000

Frost, David and Fred Bauer. *Billy Graham: Personal Thoughts of a Public Man*. Colorado Springs, CO: Chariot Victor Publishing, 1997.

Gaustad, Edwin and Leigh Schmidt. *The Religious History of America: The Heart of the American Story from Colonial Times to Today*. San Francisco: HarperCollins, 2004.

Gilbert, James. *Redeeming Culture: American Religion in the Age of Science*. Chicago, IL: University of Chicago, 1997.

Gould, Stephen J. "'Impeaching a Self-Appointed Judge.' Review of Philip Johnson's Darwin on Trial." *Scientific American*, 267 (1992): 118–121.

Gould, Stephen Jay. *Hen's Teeth and Horse's Toes: Further Reflections in Natural History*. New York: W.W. Norton, 1994.

Greenblatt, Stephen. *The Swerve: How the World Became Modern*. New York: W.W. Norton & Company, 2011.

Hammond, Philip E. *Religion and Personal Autonomy: Third Disestablishment in America*. Studies in Comparative Religion. Columbia, SC: University of South Carolina Press, 1992.

John Paul II. "Message to the Pontifical Academy of Sciences," 22 October 1996. Retrieved June 25, 2019. https://www.ewtn.com/library/papaldoc/jp961022.htm

Kitzmiller v. Dover Area School District. Retrieved June 25, 2019. https://law.justia.com/ca ses/federal/district-courts/FSupp2/400/707/2414073

Kruse Kronicle. "Presbyterian Church (USA) On Evolution." Retrieved June 19, 2019. https:// www.krusekronicle.com/kruse_kronicle/2005/09/presbyterian_ch.html#.XQpbpS2ZMWo

Lewis, C.S. *They Asked for a Paper: Paper and Addresses*. London: Geoffrey Bles, 1962.

Lewis, C.S. *Christian Reflections*. Edited by Walter Hooper. Grand Rapids, MI: William B. Eerdmans, 1967.

Lewis, C.S. *On Stories and Other Essays and Literature*. Edited by Walter Hooper. New York: Harvest Book, 1982.

Lovelock, James. *The Gaia: A New Look at Life on Earth*. Oxford Landmark Science. Reprint edition. Oxford, UK: Oxford University Press, 2016.

Malcolm X and Alex Haley. *Autobiography of Malcolm X*. New York: Grove Press, 1965.

Martin, Douglas. "Stephen Gaskin, Hippie Who Founded an Enduring Commune, Dies at 79." Retrieved June 24, 2019. https://www.nytimes.com/2014/07/03/us/stephen-ga skin-hippie-who-founded-an-enduring-commune-dies-at-79.html

McFague, Sallie. *Models of God*. Minneapolis, MN: Fortress, 1987.

McGrath, Alister. *Religion and Science: A New Introduction*. 2nd edition. Oxford, UK: Wiley-Blackwell, 2010.

McKibben, Bill. "The Christian Paradox: How a Faithful Nation Gets Jesus Wrong," *Harper's Magazine*, August 2005.

Miller, Tim. *The 60s Communes: The Hippies and Beyond*, Syracuse Studies on Peace and Conflict Resolution. Syracuse, NY: Syracuse University Press, 1999.

Pike, Sarah. "Nature Religions and the Spiritualization of Science." Chico State Science and Religions conference, April 8, 2017. Retrieved June 19, 2019. https://media.csuchico.edu/m edia/Nature+Religions+and+the+Spiritualization+of+Science/0_6qv681b3/66948482

Reeves, Joshua. *Against Methodology in Science and Religion: Recent Debates on Rationality and Theology*. Routledge Science and Religion Series. Oxford, UK: Routledge, 2018.

Russell, Robert J., Nancey Murphy and Christopher J. Isham, eds. *Quantum Cosmology and the Laws of Nature. Scientific Perspectives on Divine Action*: Volume 1. Berkeley, CA: Vatican Observatory Publications; Center for Theology and the Natural Sciences, 1993.

Russell, Robert J., Nancey Murphy and Arthur R. Peacocke, eds. *Chaos and Complexity. Scientific Perspectives on Divine Action*: Volume 2. Berkeley, CA: Vatican Observatory Publications; Center for Theology and the Natural Sciences, 1995.

Russell, Robert J., Nancey Murphy and William Stoeger, eds. *Scientific Perspectives on Divine Action. Twenty Years of Challenge and Progress*, Berkeley, CA: Vatican Observatory Publications; Center for Theology and the Natural Sciences, 2008.

Russell, Robert J., William R. Stoeger and Francisco J. Ayala, eds. *Evolutionary and Molecular Biology. Scientific Perspectives on Divine Actions*: Volume 3. Berkeley, CA: Vatican Observatory Publications; Center for Theology and the Natural Sciences, 1998.

Russell, Robert J., Philip Clayton, Kirk Wegter-McNelly and John Polkinghorne, eds. *Quantum Mechanics. Scientific Perspectives on Divine Action*: Volume 5. Berkeley, CA: Vatican Observatory Publications; Center for Theology and the Natural Sciences, 2002.

Russell, Robert J., Nancey Murphy, Theo C. Meyering and Michael A. Arbib, eds. *Neuroscience and the Person. Scientific Perspectives on Divine Action*: Volume 4. Berkeley, CA: Vatican Observatory Publications; Center for Theology and the Natural Sciences, 2000.

Russell, Robert J., William R. Stoeger, Francisco J. Ayala and C.V. Coyne, eds. *Physics, Philosophy and Theology: A Common Quest for Understanding*. Berkeley, CA: Vatican Observatory Publications, Center for Theology and the Natural Sciences, 1988.

Schleiermacher, Friedrich. *The Christian Faith*. Edited by H.R. Mackintosh and J.S. Stewart. Edinburgh: T&T Clark, 1989.

Shibley, Mark. "Hammond, Phillip E." Hartford Institute for Religion Research website. Retrieved June 19, 2019. http://hirr.hartsem.edu/ency/Hammond.htm

Sober, Elliott, and David Sloan. *Unto Others: The Evolution and Psychology of Unselfish Behavior*. International Society for Science and Religion, 2007.

Soskice, Janet Martin. *Metaphor and Religious Language*. Oxford, UK: Clarendon, 1987.

Stanford Encyclopedia of Philosophy. "Religion and Science." Retrieved June 24, 2019. https://plato.stanford.edu/entries/religion-science

Stephenson, Douglas. *Out to Change the World: The Evolution of The Farm Community*. Summertown, TN: Book Publishing Co, 2014.

Thompson, William Irwin. *Gaia 2—Emergence: The New Science of Becoming*. Great Barrington, MA: Lindisfarne Books, 1991.

Torrance, Thomas. *Theological Science*. Oxford, UK: Oxford University Press, 1969.

Toumey, Christopher P. *God's Own Scientists: Creationists in a Secular World*. New Brunswick: Rutgers University Press, 1994.

Wallace, Alan B. *Buddhism and Science: Breaking New Ground*. New York: Columbia University Press, 2003.

Wedge Document. Retrieved June 25, 2019. https://ncse.com/creationism/general/wedge-document

Weiss, John. *American Religion*. Boston, MA: Roberts Brothers, 1871.

White, Lynn. "The Historical Roots of our Ecological Crisis." *Science*, 155 (1967): 1203–1207.

Whitehead, Alfred North. *Science and the Modern World*. New York: Free Press, 1925.

Wilcox, Mellisa M. "When Sheila's a Lesbian: Religious Individualism among Lesbian, Gay, Bisexual, and Transgender Christians." *Sociology of Religion*, 63, no. 4 (2002): 497–513.

Wilczek, Frank. *The Lightness of Being: Mass, Ether, and the Unification of Forces*. New York: Basic, 2008.

Wilson, David Sloan. *Darwin's Cathedral: Evolution, Religion, and the Nature of Society*. Chicago, IL: University of Chicago, 2003.

Zukav, Gary. *Dancing Wu Li Masters: An Overview of the New Physics*. New York: HarperOne, 2009.

9

THE PRESENT: THE THIRD MILLENNIUM AND THREE REPRESENTATIVE VOICES

A new century for science and religion

On June 26, 2000, Bill Clinton began his remarks in the East Room of the White House by noting the map that Meriweather Lewis used in his journey across "the American frontier" to the Pacific Ocean:

> Today the world is joining us here in the East Room to behold the map of even greater significance. We are here to celebrate the completion of the first survey of the entire human genome. Without a doubt, this is the most important, most wondrous map ever produced by human kind.[1]

With those words the President presented to many Americans for the first time the Human Genome Project, with its goal of the full mapping and understanding of all the genes of humankind. The project, directed by Francis Collins, completed its work in 2003, "on time and on budget," as I've heard Collins celebrate. Clinton completed these remarks with a nod to a common religious tradition, perhaps what Robert Bellah called "civil religion,"

> What that means is that modern science has confirmed what we first learned from ancient faiths: The most important fact of life on this Earth is our common humanity. My greatest wish on this day for the ages is that this incandescent truth will always guide our actions as we continue to march forth in this, the greatest age of discovery ever known.[2]

And so we simultaneously meet one of the key players in science and religion today, as well as arguably the greatest scientific feat of this century. But there are many more of both, which I will group thematically, continuing on the theme of understanding human beings.

Human origins: In 2002 anthropologists discovered a fossil skull in Chad more than six million years old (perhaps the oldest known human ancestral species), *Sahelanthropus tchadensis*. Two years later, remains of a small humanlike species, nicknamed "hobbits," that lived as late as 18,000 years ago were reported on the Indonesian island of Flores. In 2009 a 4.4-million-year-old partial female skeleton, *Ardipithecus ramidus,* or "Ardi," was found in Africa. In addition, a project sequencing genetic material from Neanderthals turned up evidence in 2010 of prehistoric interbreeding between this hominin species and *Homo sapiens.*

Cosmology and physics: In 2002 astronomers calculated the age range of the universe at 13–14 billion years. And in 2006 researchers reported the evidence of dark matter in space, which makes up about one quarter of the universe. In 2015 scientists discovered traces of liquid on Mars, and in 2016 the LIGO team found gravitational waves from a black hole merger. In 2017 a collaboration project of Virgo and LIGO detected a gravitational wave signal, the first instance of a gravitational wave event, which marked a significant breakthrough for multi-messenger astronomy. In 2012 CERN scientists achieved confirmation (with 99.999% certainty) of the Higgs boson, while in 2014 exotic hadrons are discovered. And in 2019 the first-ever image of a black hole was captured, using eight different telescopes, timed with extremely precise atomic clocks, taking simultaneous pictures.

Computer technology for consumers and social media: When computers, the internet, and social media literally made their way into the hands of consumers, technology became an increasingly important partner in the conversation with religion. And though the smartphone had existed since the mid-1990s, Apple's iPhone, which debuted in 2007, made a hand-held device that could access the internet widely available and desirable for millions of consumers. The social media juggernaut Facebook, begun on the Harvard campus for students in 2003 as Face-Mash, eventually became available to everyone over the age of 13 with a valid email address in 2007.

Evolution and faith: The Clergy Letter Project first appeared in 2004. Michael Zimmerman, the founder and executive director, describes its background. In light of the common misperception of the conflict between science and religion, he wanted the public to know that many clergy and most denominations embrace evolution. "In the fall of 2004, I worked with clergy throughout Wisconsin to prepare a statement in support of teaching evolution.... The response was overwhelming. In a few weeks, nearly 200 clergy signed the statement...."[3] The Clergy Letter Project also sponsors annual Evolution Weekend events and has created a database of scientists working with clergy to answer questions on evolution. Currently there are several versions of the letter from various religions; the Christian Clergy Letter has over 15,000 signatures, the Rabbi Letter almost 800, with Buddhist and humanist versions as well.[4] Similarly, in 2008 the Church of England publicly validated evolutionary theory and offered its apology to Charles

128 Third millennium and three voices

Darwin for initially rejecting his theory, though of course many in the Church of England had long since integrated Darwin into their beliefs.

Focusing on how Christians have received evolutionary theory highlights the complex relationship between religion and science. As I've noted, the rise of fundamentalist opposition to evolution hit a publicly prominent moment in the 1925 Scopes Trial. And yet, there's another story in that scientists, clergy, and popular writers in the United States have continued to work at the reconciliation of science and religion. For example, Biologos, founded in 2007 by Francis Collins, head of the Human Genome Initiative, is an organization that has made evolutionary creation more widely known and one that seeks to reconcile evangelical Christian beliefs and mainstream science by accepting the scientific consensus on issues such as the age of the earth and the process of evolution. In 2014 Geoffrey Mittleman initiated a collaborative venture for Judaism and science, Sinai and Synapses.[5]

In sum, the early twenty-first century brought the interaction of religion and science into an increasing importance of technology, sexuality, and religious pluralism. It also continued the trend toward the assimilation of the teachings of mainstream science by church bodies. And lest it sound like only Christians are creationists, we could consider Adnan Oktar, also known as Harun Yahya and Sami Olcun, the Turkish author and Islamic creationist. Though not American, he made his impact felt in this country when he sent unsolicited letters along with his book, *The Atlas of Creation,* to members of Congress, museums of science, and American scientists as a way to promote Islamic creationism. Similarly, Ken Ham and his organization, Answers in Genesis, have promoted creationism in the more typical mode of conservative Christianity, especially with the opening of his Creation Museum in 2007, as well as his well-publicized debate with Bill Nye, "the science guy," on the topic "Is Creation A Viable Model of Origins?" on February 4, 2014, at its museum in Petersburg, Kentucky (which was to some degree resourced with the funds raised as a result of the debate).

In addition, one of the noteworthy features of the contemporary field of science and religion is that women now lead key organizations. The current director of DoSER (since 2010) is Jennifer Wiseman, who also serves as senior project specialist for the Hubble Space Telescope and senior astrophysicist at the NASA Goddard Space Center. Deborah Haarsma, an MIT-trained astronomer, became director of BioLogos since 2013. Heather Templeton Dill started her presidency of the John Templeton Foundation, the largest funder of research and programs in science and religion, in 2015. And, finally, Leslie Wickman, with a Ph.D. from Stanford in Human Factors and Biomechanics (mechanical engineering), has headed the American Scientific Affiliation (ASA) since 2016.

At this point, in order to establish where we are today with religion and science, I offer three case studies. Since in this book I am steering clear of a simple dichotomy of conflict versus integration in relating science and religion, and even though it would be tempting to set zoologist and arch-atheist Richard Dawkins (born in 1941) against evangelical Christian geneticist Francis Collins (born in 1950), it is critical to bring in at least a third voice, the late Stephen Jay Gould

(1941–2002). The order is simply according to date of birth. (Dawkins was born in March, and Gould in September of the same year.) My apologies that these three primarily represent western religious views, but in the United States that might still be defensible. At least I can hope it is, but I suspect future decades will bring increasing religious variety. Admittedly these three are also white and male, but I hope what I wrote in the last paragraph indicates that a future list will likely be more diverse. With those comments in mind, I intend in these sketches to round out the present state of the conversation of science and religion and the factors when I ponder its future in the next two chapters.

Stephen Jay Gould

Stephen Jay Gould, who died in 2002, was a leading palaeontologist who is worth remembering simply for his scientific contributions both at Harvard University and New York City's Museum of Natural History. Principal among his many scientific accomplishments is the theory he developed with Niles Eldredge in 1972 of *punctuated equilibrium*,

> a revision of Darwinian theory proposing that the creation of new species through evolutionary change occurs not at slow, constant rates over millions of years but rather in rapid bursts over periods as short as thousands of years, which are then followed by long periods of stability during which organisms undergo little further change.[6]

Gould personified the independence model. His 1999 book, *Rock of Ages: Science and Religion in the Fullness of Life*, is a compelling presentation of the independence model for relating science and religion. In it Gould describes NOMA, or Non-Overlapping Magisterial Authority. Science and religion were never at war, but nonetheless are best kept separate. As he described in *Rock of Ages*, each has a domain of teaching authority that does not overlap. "To cite the old clichés, science gets the age of rocks, and religion the rock of ages; science studies how the heavens go, religion how to go to heaven."[7] Why? (And here Gould is reviewing Philip Johnson's *Darwin on Trial*.) "Science can work only with naturalistic explanations, it can neither affirm nor deny other types of actors (like God) in other spheres."[8] He then notes that Darwin was an agnostic and Asa Gray, Darwin's supporter, a "devout Christian," while Charles D. Walcott, who discovered the Burgess Shale Fossils, was "a convinced Darwinian and an equally firm Christian." And then he writes,

> Move on another 50 years to the two greatest evolutionists of our generation G.G. Simpson a humanistic agnostic, Theodosius Dobzhansky, a believing Russian Orthodox. Either half my colleagues are enormously stupid or else Darwinism is fully compatible with religious belief—and equally compatible

130 Third millennium and three voices

with atheism, thus proving that the two great realms of nature's factuality and
the source of human morality do not strongly overlap.[9]

If not the actual paradigm, NOMA as a type represents the dominant view of
official scientific organizations today. (I noted the NAS statement above.) NOMA
declares, "Hey, it's great when science and religion can coexist!" Most of us, if we
don't want the two to play well together, at least don't like to see them at war, and
so it's regrettable that NOMA simply doesn't receive the same amount of press as
conflict narrative ... and thus as the voice of Richard Dawkins.

Richard Dawkins

As I remarked above, Dawkins certainly represents the warfare or conflict view.
Dawkins, an emeritus fellow of New College, Oxford, is an English zoologist and
prominent author. He held Oxford's Professor for the Public Understanding of
Science position from 1995 to 2008 and has sometimes been called "Darwin's
Rottweiler," an allusion to T.H. Huxley, known as "Darwin's Bulldog." He first
came to fame with his 1976 book *The Selfish Gene*, which stated as one of its key
principles that "all life evolves by the differential survival of replicating entities."[10]
Accordingly, he has consistently expressed skepticism about non-adaptive evolutionary processes (such as the "spandrels" that Richard Lewontin and Gould present) and about group selection (here I'm thinking of David Sloan Wilson) as a
way to understand altruism.

In his 1986 *The Blind Watchmaker* Dawkins takes on Paley's Watchmaker analogy. I've cited some of this above, but here I'll offer the longer version.

> An atheist before Darwin could have said, following Hume: "I have no
> explanation for complex biological design. All I know is that God isn't a good
> explanation, so we must wait and hope that somebody comes up with a better
> one." I can't help feeling that such a position, though logically sound, would
> have left one feeling pretty unsatisfied, and that although atheism might have
> been *logically* tenable before Darwin, Darwin made it possible to be an intel-
> lectually fulfilled atheist.[11]

With his winsome, crystal-clear style he popularized a gene-centered view of
evolution and coined the term *meme*. In his 2007 book *The God Delusion*, Dawkins
takes on all kinds of religious faith, but really puts Christianity, and more recently
Islam, in his sights. Since Dawkins is such a brilliant stylist and is fun to quote, I'll
just add another quip he's uttered in various places: "We are all atheists about most
of the gods that societies have ever believed in. Some of us just go one god further."[12] Even though this doesn't entirely make sense, since the God of traditional
western theism is the Source of being and not one god among many, it's brilliant
rhetoric that succeeds in creating a winning assertion. Around the time of this
book, Dawkins joined three other thinkers—Sam Harris, Christopher Hitchens,

and Daniel Dennett—to become the Four Horsemen of New Atheism. Dawkins is the best known of the horsemen and of three voices I'm highlighting here.

Francis Collins

Francis Collins became a leading scientist when he headed the Human Genome Initiative, which decoded the entire genome in 2000 (at least in a "rough draft" form) and then formally presented its findings in 2001. Now director of the National Institutes of Health, Collins lives and breathes the integration of science and religion. He did not grow in a religious home, nor did he subscribe to any religion when he entered medical school at the University of North Carolina. He often recounts an experience as a medical student in which a dying patient had stunningly described her faith in Jesus as the Christ, and then asked, "Doctor, what do you believe?" He realized he had no answer and started reading—at the suggestion of a Methodist minister—C.S. Lewis's famous book (originally talks broadcast on the BBC during World War II) *Mere Christianity*. Collins writes,

> I had always assumed that faith was based on purely emotional and irrational arguments, and was astounded to discover, initially in the writings of the Oxford scholar C.S. Lewis and subsequently from many other sources, that one could build a very strong case for the plausibility of the existence of God on purely rational grounds.[13]

At age 27 he became a Christian. What makes Collins a significant spokesperson is that he is both entirely unassuming and utterly confident in his scientific credentials (holding both a Ph.D in physical chemistry and an M.D). He brings together a world-class understanding of and love for genetics—and thus evolution—with evangelical Christian faith.

Recently I re-read *The Language of God* (2007) and was struck by his rejection of scientific atheism (albeit in a kind, gentler manner appropriate to the man), Intelligent Design, and hardcore creationism. As he wrote in an interview with CNN, "Attaching oneself to such literal interpretations in the face of compelling scientific evidence pointing to the ancient age of earth and the relatedness of living things by evolution seems neither wise nor necessary for the believer."[14] As a result he has found deep reconciliation between religion and mainstream science: "The God of the Bible is also the God of the genome. He can be worshipped in the cathedral or in the laboratory. His creation is majestic, awesome, intricate, and beautiful."[15] Put another way—and I have heard Collins present this view several times publicly—he endorses a two-books view, which I have mentioned a few times above: that God, as the sole author, has written two books, the book of nature and the book of Scripture. Francis Bacon, one of the pioneers of modern science, phrased it this way in the sixteenth century: "God has, in fact, written two books, not just one. Of course, we are all familiar with

132 Third millennium and three voices

the first book he wrote, namely Scripture. But he has written a second book called creation."[16]

Ultimately, Collins came to a reformulation of the traditional phrase *theistic evolution* by coining *Biologos*. "Scholars will recognize *bios* as the Greek word for 'life' (the root word for biology, biochemistry, and so forth) and *logos* as the Greek for 'word.'" Biologos "expresses the belief that God is the source of all life and that life expresses the will of God."[17] (For what it's worth, "Biologos" hasn't really struck a chord. I hear "evolutionary creation" and the older "theistic evolution" much more often from this constituency.) In the same year he wrote the book, Collins founded the BioLogos Foundation (which I mentioned above), and although, as head of the National Institutes of Health, he is no longer directly involved, his imprint remains evident.

These three leading voices validate Ian Barbour's categories, at least in part (even if I've allowed Collins to represent both dialogue and independence). They do indeed speak primarily about monotheistic religion and science, but here I cannot identify a non-western voice of similar influence. Indeed there are limits to Gould, Dawkins, and Collins as representatives. Without trying to be trite or cute, somewhere around the beginning of the second decade of the new millennium we had entered the future. Partly this is revealed in new topics and trends, which I'll outline below. Who will be the next Gould, or Dawkins, or Collins to carry the conversation? How will they be different? What will they talk about? Where then are we headed? These are the questions of the next two chapters.

Notes

1 Bill Clinton, "President Clinton, British Prime Minister Tony Blair Deliver Remarks on Human Genome Milestone," June 26, 2000, retrieved June 19, 2019, http://transcripts. cnn.com/TRANSCRIPTS/0006/26/bn.01.html.
2 Ibid.
3 The Clergy Letter Project, "Background," retrieved June 25, 2019, http://www.the-clergyletterproject.org/Backgd_info.htm.
4 Ibid.
5 Full disclosure: From 2016–2019 I served on the advisory board for BioLogos.
6 Encyclopedia Britannica, "Stephen Jay Gould," retrieved June 25, 2019, https://www. britannica.com/biography/Stephen-Jay-Gould.
7 Stephen Jay Gould, *Rock of Ages: Science and Religion in the Fullness of Life* (New York: Ballantine Books, 1999), 6
8 Stephen J. Gould, "Impeaching a Self-Appointed Judge," review of Philip Johnson's *Darwin on Trial, Scientific American* 267 (1992): 118–21; posted on The Stephen Jay Gould Archive, retrieved June 25, 2019, http://www.stephenjaygould.org/reviews/ gould_darwin-on-trial.html.
9 Ibid.
10 Richard Dawkins, *The Selfish Gene* 2nd edition. (Oxford: Oxford University Press, 1989).
11 Richard Dawkins, *The Blind Watchmaker: Why the Evidence of Evolution Reveals a Universe Without Design* (New York: Norton, 1986), 6.
12 Wikiquote, "Richard Dawkins," retrieved June 25, 2019, https://en.wikiquote.org/ wiki/Richard_Dawkins.
13 Francis Collins, "Why This Scientist Believes in God," *CNN* June 6, 2007, retrieved June 25, 2019, http://www.cnn.com/2007/US/04/03/collins.commentary/index.html.

Third millennium and three voices **133**

14 Ibid.

15 *The Language of God: A Scientist Presents Evidence for Belief* (New York: Free Press, 2006), 211.

16 Francis Bacon; cited in Daniel Buxhoeveden and Gayle Woloschak, eds., *Science and the Eastern Orthodox Church* (Burlington, VT: Ashgate: 2011), 133.

17 Collins, *The Language of God*, 203.

Bibliography

Buxhoeveden, Daniel and Gayle Woloschak, eds. *Science and the Eastern Orthodox Church.* Burlington, VT: Ashgate, 2011.

Clergy Letter Project. Retrieved June 25, 2019. http://www.theclergyletterproject.org

Clinton, Bill. "President Clinton, British Prime Minister Tony Blair Deliver Remarks on Human Genome Milestone," June 26, 2000. Retrieved June 19, 2019. http://transcripts.cnn.com/TRANSCRIPTS/0006/26/bn.01.html

Collins, Francis. *The Language of God.* New York: Free Press, 2006.

Collins, Francis. "Why This Scientist Believes in God." *CNN,* June 6, 2007. Retrieved June 25, 2019. http://www.cnn.com/2007/US/04/03/collins.commentary/index.html

Coyne, Jerry . *Faith Versus Fact: Why Science and Religion Are Incompatible.* New York: Penguin, 2016.

Dawkins, Richard. *The Blind Watchmaker: Why the Evidence of Evolution Reveals a Universe Without Design.* New York: Norton, 1986.

Dawkins, Richard. *The God Delusion.* New York: Mariner, 2008.

Dawkins, Richard. *The Selfish Gene,* 2nd edition. Oxford, UK: Oxford University Press, 1989.

Dennett, Daniel. *Breaking the Spell: Religion as a Natural Phenomenon.* New York: Penguin, 2007.

Dennett, Daniel. *Darwin's Dangerous Idea: Evolution and the Meanings of Life.* New York: Simon & Schuster, 1995.

Dennett, Daniel. "Why the Future of Religion Is Bleak." *Wall Street Journal,* April 26, 2015. Retrieved June 25, 2019. www.wsj.com/articles/why-the-future-of-religion-is-bleak-1430104785

Encyclopedia Britannica. "Stephen Jay Gould." Retrieved June 25, 2019. https://www.britannica.com/biography/Stephen-Jay-Gould

Gould, Stephen J. "'Impeaching a Self-Appointed Judge.' Review of Philip Johnson's Darwin on Trial." *Scientific American,* 267 (1992): 118–121. Posted on The Stephen Jay Gould Archive. Retrieved June 25, 2019. http://www.stephenjaygould.org/reviews/gould_darwin-on-trial.html

Gould, Stephen J. *Hen's Teeth and Horse's Toes: Further Reflections in Natural History.* New York: W.W. Norton, 1994.

Gould, Stephen J. "Nonoverlapping Magisteria." *Natural History* 106 (1997): 16–22.

Gould, Stephen J. *Rock of Ages: Science and Religion in the Fullness of Life.* New York: Ballantine Books, 1999.

Harris, Sam. *The End of Faith: Religion, Terror, and the Future of Reason.* New York: W.W. Norton, 2005.

Hitchens, Christopher. *God Is Not Great: How Religion Poisons Everything.* New York: Twelve, 2009.

Wikiquote. "Richard Dawkins." Retrieved June 25, 2019. https://en.wikiquote.org/wiki/Richard_Dawkins

10

THE FUTURE AND ITS CONTOURS: RELIGIOUS INDIVIDUALISM AND TINKERING

How emerging adults are accelerating a venerable American tradition

"One day I woke up and wondered: maybe today I should be a Christian, or would I rather be a Buddhist, or am I just a *Star Trek* freak?" And so Leigh Eric Schmidt quotes a sociological study and begins his book on American individualized spirituality, *Restless Souls*.[1] He demonstrates that, while plenty of contemporary examples exist, so do precedents in our country's history, charting (as Wade Clark Roof describes it inside the book's cover) the "lineage from Emerson to Oprah." Similarly, in the nineteenth century Philip Schaff described America as "the classic land of sects,"[2] and John Weiss offered this declaration, which summarizes so much: "America is an opportunity to make a Religion out of sacredness of the individual."[3]

The American cultural tradition of religious pluralism, which chooses among various inputs for spirituality, is longstanding and venerable. In this chapter I illustrate how today's emerging adults are accelerating this particularly American tradition of individualism and religious tinkering as a component of our search for the common good. This has a significant impact on the question: what forms of religion will Americans bring to science?

In some sense I have already responded historically, by noting a long history in America of religious pluralism and tinkering. The past directs our present. Americans have always held copious strands of religious threads in our hands, which we weave together in fascinating ways. Emerging adults, influenced by the internet and other digital realities, are accelerating and intensifying this American religious characteristic. In the present, i.e., the past 50 years, science's interaction with religion has been *de facto* with western monotheisms, which led to questions like this posed by the Stanford Encyclopedia of Philosophy: "To what extent can Christian beliefs be brought in line with the results of western science?"[4] I am arguing that even in the period that I've called "the present" this conversation must include an examination of religions outside of Judaism and Christianity, e.g., Hinduism, Buddhism, Islam, as well as many other religious voices. This pluralism undoubtedly represents the future.

I will also respond by looking at the attitudes of emerging adults (age 18–30) through a variety of sociological studies, and some of my own research, with the idea that their attitudes already influence American conceptions of how science and religion relate, and they increasingly define the future. I will look to social science and analyze research on emerging-adults' attitudes about religion and science, including my own surveys and interviews, as signposts. As I've argued elsewhere,[5] a rising, new form of pluralism seems to be the future. Emerging adults are *spiritual bricoleurs*.[6] They tend to create a streaming spirituality mix rather than a monolithic 12-inch vinyl LP religion. (More on that below.) As Zoe, age 20, told me: "I don't ever think of myself as a religious person However, I prefer taking pieces of some different religions." My qualitative interviews clearly support the conclusion that we are turning into a nation with more nones and fewer Christians. This implies new theoretical models, as well as new topics and trends, in the study of science and religion. I'll have much more to say on all this below.

Future changes will not only be driven by attitudes but also by scientific discoveries. I will analyze how scientific discoveries also direct the American cultural conversation of religion and science into the next stage. I'm hoping, as bold and foolish as it might be, to discern the contours of future directions of the relationship of science and religion in America, a world in which the topic evolution will be present but where concerns about sexuality, climate change, technology, AI, and transhumanism will rise in importance. In my boldest and perhaps risky move, I will note trends: there will be a reduction of the influence of the Christian church and a notable rise in the influence of atheism, agnosticism, the nones, as well as other religious and spiritual traditions. The interaction of science and religion could very well witness a decrease in the antipathy that's often been promoted between the two. At least I'll argue why this might be the case.

One might hope that this is an answer to Whitehead's Challenge of negotiating the relationship of science and religion once and for all. Most likely it's another set of responses in an ongoing historical process of Americans arguing over our common good. We may want the path our country has taken to arrive at a final vista. But as we arrive there we realize that the road has a slightly different look, and new travellers have joined us. So let's take a look at who's on the journey, what our companions are like, and where we're headed.

A sketch of emerging adulthood in America

The individualized search for the divine didn't emerge with today's emerging adults *de novo*. But this search has accelerated and morphed through the influence of emerging adults. It also changes the conversation of science and religion. And that brings me to the purpose of looking at emerging-adult attitudes. In forecasting

136 Religious individualism and tinkering

the future I am identifying some key ideas of this demographic because 18–30-year-olds will increasingly be our culture's thought leaders—and of course, to some extent, they already are. In a reasonably straightforward way I am following Robert Wuthnow's study of emerging adults and the next decade of life, which he subtitled "How Twenty- and Thirty-Somethings Are Shaping American Religion."[7]

Before proceeding I need to sketch emerging adulthood and why it's even assigned that particular title. My method synthesizes key sociological research from Wuthnow, Christian Smith, Patricia Snell, Kari Christoffersen, Hillary Davidson, David Kinnaman, Ally Hawkins, Jonathan Hill, and Elaine Howard Ecklund.[8] I will enhance it with my own qualitative interviews with 43 emerging adults and surveys of 18–30-year-olds from an 18-month research grant project for which I served as principal investigator. The Science for Students and Emerging Young Adults (SEYA) project analyzed attitudes of 18–30-year-olds on faith and science, specifically how they are formed and change. In brief, the SEYA team taught on the integration of science and religion with emerging-adult participants and had informal discussions about how they related science and religion. We presented target groups in northern California and New York City with a questionnaire based on surveys from Smith's *Souls in Transition*[9] as well as Kinnaman and Hawkins' *You Lost Me*.[10] During a period of four to six weeks these groups studied and discussed resources such as Alister McGrath's *Science and Religion: A New Introduction*[11] or the DVD *Test of Faith* (developed by the Faraday Institute at Cambridge University[12]). Our team surveyed the participants before and after to discern whether experiencing this curriculum on religion and science made a difference in their attitudes about the possibility of integrating the two. Notably, our analysis of the project mirrored the conclusions of larger sociological studies, and so I will blend the results below.

To move forward, we need to understand who 18–30-year-olds are and what becoming an adult means for them. Synthesizing this research, adulthood is emerging more slowly than it did in the latter half of the twentieth century. In 2000 Jeffery Arnett developed the category of "emerging adulthood"[13] as a stage of life that is no longer adolescence but neither is it fully adulthood. Admittedly, this theory is not beyond criticism,[14] and I am not committed to all its implications. Many in lower socio-economic conditions need to develop job skills and often move into adult responsibilities more quickly.[15] Nevertheless, the paradigm still rightly highlights shifts in American culture that emerging adults are particularly experiencing.

In the past, five milestones defined adulthood: "leaving home, finishing school, becoming financially independent, getting married, and having children."[16] But the age at which these milestones are reached has changed.[17] The Research Network on Transitions to Adulthood and Public Policy completed its work in 2009, having analyzed 40 years of demographic data. It found that, in 1960, two-thirds of men and women had achieved all five of these markers by age 30, but by 2000 less than 50% of females and one-third of males had done so.[18]Wuthnow focused on two markers that are delayed and arrived at a remarkably similar conclusion: Americans are marrying and having children later.[19] If anything, the trajectory has been set: recent research on Gen Z (born in 1996) indicates that, by age 30, only one in four intends to marry and one in six plans to have children.[20] And this is a good moment to emphasize that I am focused more on emerging adulthood as a developmental stage than a particular generation, whether it's millennials or Gen Z. To my mind, the stages are more constant, though they are given contour by the specific historical and cultural events that each generation experiences.

In its traditional formulation, adulthood had its drawbacks but excelled in clear boundaries and commitments. With a longer period to emerge into adulthood, 18–30-year-olds often display five interrelated characteristics: emerging adults seek personal meaning and identity; their lives are marked with instability through regular job relocations, moves, and revisions of life plans; they tend to be self-focused, liberated from parental oversight and significant responsibility for others; they feel "in between"—beyond adolescent life but not yet at full adult status; and, finally, they exist in an "age of possibilities," optimistic about the future and keeping their options open. [21]Arnett's conclusion offers an illuminating perspective for what emerging adults are bringing to the study of science and religion: "Having left the dependency of childhood and adolescence, and having not yet entered the enduring responsibilities that are normative to adulthood, emerging adults often explore a variety of possible life directions in love, work, and worldviews."[22]

In April 2015, as part of the SEYA project, I invited 12 thought leaders in emerging-adult culture—religious theorists and practitioners—to discuss their insights on 18–30-year-olds. These thought leaders portrayed this demographic in various ways and offered a summary of recurring problems in emerging adults, whose lives are "marked by instability in relationships, purpose, and faith." They also noted an openness in emerging adults and that a related anxious stress characterize the life of 18–30-year-olds and set the context for their culture. In addition, it seemed to the assembled group that the multiple forms of information they faced can even make emerging adults "choice phobic" (a jarring phrase, to be sure), which represents the shadow side of possibilities and pluralism.

Emerging adults are free to meditate on their relationship with religious life and practice, or, in a term they use more frequently, spirituality. Along with adulthood itself, approaches to religion are shifting.

Streaming spirituality versus LP religion

If anything characterizes contemporary American religious life, it is pluralism; and emerging adults have been formed by an age of dazzling cultural diversity of all kinds, including innumerable worldviews, as well as sexual and racial–ethnic identities. This reality opens lives to greater possibilities than in the past. Diversity, not unity, is easy for 18–30-year-olds to locate. And, as result, we can better understand that "tolerance"—which I've heard sometimes dismissed as an ineffectual

138 Religious individualism and tinkering

value—embodies a vital strategy for negotiating the challenging interplay of these churning cultural factors.

That characteristically American trait, *individualism*, provides another root for this religious pluralism. In 1985 the Habits of Heart found this in *Sheilaism*. "I believe in God. I'm not a religious fanatic. I can't remember the last time I went to church. My faith has carried me a long way. It's Sheilaism. Just my own little voice...."[23] Wikipedia capably summarizes Sheilaism: "a shorthand term for an individual's system of religious belief which co-opts strands of multiple religions chosen by the individual usually without much theological consideration."[24] Today, Sheila's inner voice seems tame and quite well behaved compared to the cacophony on the web and in social media.

This is a result of the movement in our culture, as Andrew Delbanco expertly described: first the locus of our hope as the basis for the American Dream was in God (the Puritans); then in Nation; and since the 1960s in Self.[25] His meditation on "the real American Dream" concluded with this, "Today, hope has narrowed to the vanishing point of the self alone,"[26] echoing the ontological individualism and its effect on religion that Robert Bellah and his colleagues mourned in the 1980s. Delbanco quite pessimistically decides that the Self alone cannot act as an anchor for hope (although he is also unwilling to promote a repristinated Christianized America).

I could, of course, label this spiritual search through the Self as typical of the "spiritual but not religious" crowd—which, in many ways, it is. For scholars of religion, the terms *spirituality* and *religion*, however, can be reasonably coterminous (as I mentioned in the first chapter). To be religious is to be spiritual. And so the phrase "spiritual, but not religious" can sound vaguely contradictory to those in the guild of religious studies. At any rate, I prefer the way Wuthnow described the lifestyle of many 18–30-year-olds (borrowing from Claude Lévi-Strauss): *bricoleurs*, those who love to "tinker" or assemble a variety of disparate objects to create a composite. "A tinkerer puts together a life from whatever skills, ideas, and resources that are readily at hand."[27] Therefore they often become what Wuthnow describes as "spiritual bricoleurs," by piecing together ideas about spirituality from many sources.[28]

No longer is religious belief a vinyl LP. Sometimes when I come to this point in a lecture I recount the days of old with my college students, specifically when I'd drive to Tower Records on El Camino Real in Palo Alto and thumb through aisles of 12-inch square cardboard record sleeves looking for the perfect vinyl disc. Afterward, the LP tucked under my arm, I would head home, secure some musical refuge in my room, and listen: side A first, then side B. And here's my main point: *it was one recording and almost always one band who set the song sequence.* Thus, to complete the analogy: do we take the Catechism of the Presbyterian Church (USA), play it all the way through and decide to believe the whole thing or not? Not as a rule. Today, the order set by the musical or ecclesiastical authorities neither directs nor constrains church affiliation or decisions about spirituality.

Emerging adults arrange a bricolage of religious inputs, and this creates streaming spirituality (or, perhaps, "Spotify spirituality"). I've heard it proclaimed: "No religion is telling me what to believe or to wear or whom to love." Instead, seekers assemble a variety of spiritual inputs. By using a mix, listeners create a playlist from various artists based on a chosen mood or a feel. "I like listening to Kanye West, but why not throw in some Miles Davis?" We create something new and individualized. Or at least that's what it seems to be. The irony remains that we rarely create this mix; instead we outsource it to a curator or even a curating algorithm assembled by able computer programmers, whether it's music or religious life. In my undergraduate Science and Religion class one student, who had grown up in an evangelical church, commented during a class discussion, "I cherry pick from various religions instead of choosing just one." "Ya," another student added, "I'll stay with being a Catholic, but at times I like Buddhism better. So I'll also go with that."

Tinkering, or bricolage, represents a tactic for realizing one's personal expression—conversely it may also be one strategy for keeping a religious tradition viable. As one student, Taylor, commented, "If someone is Catholic, they may not believe the whole. The way they stay in church is to pick and choose." For example, this can be a strategy for those in religious traditions that don't affirm one's sexual identity, as Melissa Wilcox has argued in her article, "When Sheila's a Lesbian," as a rejoinder to the problems with Sheilaism presented by the Habits of the Heart team.[29] It can also be a way to realize that we don't often live up to the demands of our religion, but we identify with it nonetheless. In some ways this reality overlaps with Catherine Keller and Laurel Schneider's concept of "polydoxy" in its decentering and individualizing of authority, but I am concentrating less on Christian discourse.[30] It also implies that, since emerging adults tend toward digital-streaming spirituality or religious bricolage, there's no one central place of authority, which expands the locus for dialogue and discovery.

Technology, not solely as a metaphor but also as a cultural driver, is indispensable in comprehending this phenomena today. And what I'm arguing is that emerging adults, as digital natives, have grown up in environments saturated with options and possibilities. The explosion of knowledge on the internet, with the number of websites around one billion, only intensifies their array of potential inputs. In various conversations I've heard it argued this is essentially the reality of pluralism and that this is not really a new problem. But this notion strikes me as naïve. Pluralism is not entirely novel, and this has been a thread throughout the book, but it will certainly continue to increase and widen in its scope.

Emerging adults are ratcheting up the machine of cultural change, but my intention is not to overstate this trend as purely a phenomenon of the young. Because, of course, it's not. All ages swim in the pool of religious pluralism. Carol Lee Flinders (born in 1943) has written, "I cannot describe my spiritual practice as Buddhist ... or as Hindu or Catholic or Sufi, though I feel that in a sense it is all of these."[31] As early as 1978 a Gallup poll "found that 80 percent of Americans agreed that 'an individual should arrive at his or her religious beliefs independent of

140 Religious individualism and tinkering

any churches or synagogues.'"[32] And this autonomous spiritual quest creates rampant pluralism. And thus the sweep of our religious history has led to a reality depicted accurately by Edwin Gaustad and Leigh Schmidt: "America's vast religious marketplace—its cornucopia of therapies, advice books, spiritual techniques, retreat centers, angels, Christian diets, and small groups—now shapes religious identities in its own multiplicitous and ever-shifting image."[33]

The change is significant for 18–30-year-olds: they experiment with a variety of religious inputs and therefore often don't affiliate with one single religion. The variety of choices—to phrase this in an alternative way—makes it difficult for emerging adults to decide on *one* religious tradition in light of all the options for spirituality. And increasingly this describes the reality for Americans as a whole. And the hesitation to commit presents difficulties in relating science and *religion*. I've heard or read "I can't commit to any religion until I know more" as a common refrain in surveys and interviews. This probably also expresses the "choice phobia" I described above. Sometimes it also represents consummate humility, but, either way, it has become more complex to know how to bring religion to science. This pluralism moves beyond the hegemony of Christianity in America as we experience growth in other religious traditions, whether "world religions" or indigenous ones. But even more, digital streaming-service spirituality carves up religious practice into a smorgasbord of innumerable slices. The theoretician seeks pure types, and so this bricolage of various beliefs—and even unbelief—can be perplexing and frustrating. Twenty-first century pluralism, as practiced by 18–30-year-olds, can feel complicated and dizzying to grasp, but that is the reality of emerging-adult religion. We must choose not what is theoretically expedient but what is inherently empirical.

With Smith and Snell—who are certainly influential in describing emerging adults—I agree that this creates confusion:

> Very many emerging adults simply don't know how to think about things, what is right, or what is deserving for them to devote their lives to. On such matters, they are very often paralyzed, wishing they could be more definite, wanting to move forward, but simply not knowing how they might possibly know anything worthy of conviction and dedication. Instead, very many emerging adults exist in a state of basic indecision confusion, and fuzziness.[34]

This is part of their famous phrase about emerging-adults' belief in a vague deity that creates "Moralistic Therapeutic Deism" (MTD).[35] But they missed that the variety of choices creates this condition. It's not vagueness, but individualized specificity, that leads to choice phobia. In fact the reality is not about a broad underlying strand of unity—MTD—but about a pluralism that exists in all levels of emerging-adult consciousness. The book seems frustrated by the lack of good thinking—and I agree—and looks for clearer thinking and a unity beyond bad cognition. And that's a weakness, because the spiritual tinkering is a response to entirely too much information. In this respect, Wuthnow's religious bricolage is much closer to the reality, in which venues for religious inquiry and discussion are also changing. As Wuthnow writes,

> We have seen that spiritual choices are not limited to the kinds of denominational switching that some scholars are content to emphasize. Spiritual tinkering involves a minority of young adults in church shopping and church hopping. It also takes the form of searching for answers to the perennial existential questions in venues that go beyond religious traditions and in expressing spiritual interests through music and art as well as through prayer and devotional reading.[36]

This searching is not simply about knowledge, but mainly about ethics (here John Evans returns, with Jonathan Haidt accompanying him[37]), and even more about "intuitive cognitions" or "feelings of certainty" that we find in community. The rejection of any particular scientific conclusions often overrides rational concerns because those in "my tribe" don't subscribe.[38] Venues are shifting, and emerging adults arrive at their conclusions in new ways. When seeking truths about science outside of religious communities, 18–30-year-olds—and increasingly Americans in general—are often distrustful of the church, synagogue, or mosque as a place to seek out answers about science and religion. This phenomenon expands the variety of curators of the conversation between science and religion. In the past we could assume that people discuss science and religion in congregations, and in academic institutions such as seminaries, Christian colleges, and sometimes public universities. This is shifting.

But what does this mean for how emerging adults see science and religion? And, thus, where this conversation is headed? Is there any specific research that can help us?

Signs pointing in opposite directions?

In analyzing the research on emerging-adult views on science and religion I came to a dilemma about six years ago. As I mentioned in the first chapter, Christian Smith and Kyle Longest found more than half (57%) of 2,381 18–23-year-olds they surveyed disagreed with the statement, "My views on religion have been strengthened by discoveries of science,"[39] and that 70% "agree" or "strongly agree" with the statement that the teachings of religion and science "ultimately conflict." On the other hand, Christopher Scheitle's analysis of the Spirituality in Higher Education Survey (SHEP) of 10,810 undergraduates arrived at a seemingly opposite conclusion: "The analysis finds that, despite the seeming predominance of a conflict-oriented narrative, the majority of undergraduates do not view the relationship between these two institutions [religion and science] as one of conflict."[40] Of those surveyed, 69% agreed that independence or collaboration was the best way to relate religion and science. A subsequent study of over 10,241 participants conducted by Scheitle and Ecklund found this number among US adults at 73%,

142 Religious individualism and tinkering

with 35% choosing Independence ("They refer to different aspects of reality") and 38% Collaboration ("Each can be used to help support the other").[41] And the SHEP undergraduates mirror their science professors. Ecklund and Jerry Park found, when they surveyed 1,646 scientists at 21 elite US research universities, "In contrast to public opinion and scholarly discourse, most scientists do *not* perceive a conflict between science and religion."[42]

At first it wasn't immediately clear to me how to reconcile these competing claims. With closer analysis I realized it was a function of the question: is it about the culture at large (Smith and Longest's study) or about views that are personally held? (Scheitle's analysis). Critically important are the surveys' questions. Scheitle analyzed the response to this statement from SHEP, which reads as follows: "*For me*, the relationship of science and religion is one of...." Longest and Smith presented this question: "*The teachings of science and religion* often ultimately conflict with each other. (Do you strongly agree, agree, disagree, or strongly disagree?)" The SHEP statement embeds a personal tone with the phrase "to me." It examines personally held attitudes. The second question, from Longest and Smith, is stated more generally. It describes the "teachings of science and religion," which is about seeing a conflict of systematic knowledge.

What did I conclude? Simply put, emerging adults sense that there is conflict in the culture "out there," but they themselves seek an alternative way, one that moves from conflict and toward independence or reconciliation.

In this case, emerging-adults' views seem to match in the country as a whole. In 2015 Pew Research Center found that:

> People's sense that there generally is a conflict between religion and science seems to have less to do with their own religious beliefs than it does with their perceptions of *other* people's beliefs. Less than one-third of Americans polled in the new survey (30%) say their personal religious beliefs conflict with science, while fully two-thirds (68%) say there is no conflict between their own beliefs and science.[43]

It's probably not a surprise that the synopsis for the piece reads: "Highly religious Americans are less likely than others to see conflict between faith and science."

Is this another nail in the coffin of the conflict thesis? Perhaps. Notably these findings present problems for Barbour's conflict category and for the warfare thesis. The latter emphasize *systematic knowledge* in the clash between science and religion—here we learn that the conflict, where it exists, is specifically *perception*. But, of course, perception is a psychological reality that is then shared. Perception means that there is conflict, if nothing else, in the way that people discuss science and religion. We have a situation where the current consensus among emerging adults on science and religion is that they sense that religion is against—is at war with—science (and vice versa, to some degree), but they don't feel that it's the best path. They hear it in the news and especially on the internet, but may not actually feel it themselves.

Technology, especially social media, plays a critical role in hammering home the conflict between science and religion. Despite proclamations from prestigious organizations such as the National Academy of Sciences that "Attempts to pit science and religion against each other create controversy where none needs to exist,"[44] the internet fills the smartphones of twenty-somethings—and thus their assessment is that the world, defined as it is by science and technology, oozes antagonism toward religion. Atheists and the religious conservatives present these views for their own agendas.[45] Memes like "God—for people who are not strong enough to cope with reality" and "If Jesus is the answer, it must be a stupid question" appear on their Reddit feeds. Why? If you want followers on Twitter, Instagram, or Facebook (should an emerging adult be found at the latter), create controversy. They've overheard another conversation than that of NAS and AAAS—maybe it's Bill Nye and Ken Ham on TV, or they have seen some YouTube clips of Kent Hovind or Lawrence Krauss. These comments create great "click bait" in the social media because—as I've heard numerous times from book publishers and journalists—"conflict sells news." (Interestingly, this fact seems itself to have a scientific basis: through the stimulation of the amygdala in the limbic system of human beings, among other bodily systems, *Homo sapiens* is evolved to be highly attuned to threats. We are, it seems, prone to see conflict when we sense that it might threaten our survival.) The *Kulturkampf* of science and religion is *virtually* perceived and has a quite *real* effect.

The conservative Christian church has also done its part in its unwillingness to engage mainstream science, as David Kinnaman's study of formerly churched and now disaffected emerging adults demonstrated.[46] Kinnaman's more recent findings present an even starker picture: 49% of *churchgoing* teens agree with the statement, "The church seems to reject much of what science tells about the world."[47] In post-Trump America, public perception of religious resistance to science has been even more marked, since the terms *white evangelicals* and *Christian* seem to be coterminous for many in the wider public. That's the best way for me to comprehend the growing voice of anti-evolutionists and climate change deniers who combine their resistance to mainstream science with conservative politics. Notably, it stands in contrasts with those in the mainline religions, who are more likely to accept evolutionary theory than the American public at large—at 78% versus 60%.[48]

If I had to solely lean on popular culture or Smith and Longest's study, I'd conclude with the 70%, that there exists an enduring and irresolvable war between science and religion. But I don't, and neither do 18–30-year-olds. Rumors of the war between science and religion are certainly in the air, but, when asked, seven out of ten early emerging adults are not personally convinced. Scheitle's work and my own interviews with students revealed to me another view: 18–30-year-olds don't personally hold to a fundamental incompatibility between these two cultural forces. And I've also heard this in my interviews. After learning about the nuances of historical and philosophical approaches to science and religion, Travis concluded, "I'm really interested to hear from someone who's thought about these issues."

144 Religious individualism and tinkering

Many emerging adults want to hear thoughtful voices that head beyond warfare and shrill dogmatic debate. They've been exhausted by the culture wars.

In sum, a broad and multiform pluralism radically marks emerging adults, and the implications of this reality head in three directions. First of all, this has created a digital-streaming spirituality. Second, 18–30-year-olds, like the wider American public, perceive conflict between science and religion out there, but vastly prefer independence or collaboration between the two. Third, these changes resonate through American culture and define the future of the relationship of science and religion, even the topics that these two will bring to argument over the common good for America.

Top eleven topics today and for the future

With these comments about emerging adults and their cultural influence in mind, I arrive at two questions: first of all, where is the relation between science and religion headed, and, second, what specifically will be the topics? I'll answer the second in this section and the first in the next chapter. The attitudes of emerging adults are the key since they mark the future, but they do not exhaust the reasons why I'm highlighting certain issues and directions—some are presented by the scientific discoveries themselves.

As we've seen throughout these pages, several key topics have wound their way through the history of our country and how we argue about and struggle for the common good. Today some new ones emerge, and some diehard ones remain. Every once in a while—like the heliocentric view of the universe—we can declare that a topic becomes settled. And even then there will always be holdouts. For example, one evening at a monthly meeting on science, theology, and philosophy, which I've convened at my house for the past decade and half, a reasonably inconsistent participant promoted the idea of a flat earth as a "disputed" topic that we should study. That, admittedly perplexing and reasonably depressing example, however, represents an exception.

With those comments in mind, here are my notes on the eleven key topics of the future.[49] Why eleven? Given space limitations, I've given myself a constraint for how much to write because, to state the obvious, each of these are worthy of its own book. Have I missed some? Certainly. I'm fairly confident in the general set of topics, though I'm less so about the specific future issues and questions. Undoubtedly there will be scientific discoveries that today we know nothing of and are genuine surprises. For that reason, in light of the inevitable specific changes and discoveries I can't predict, I will simply list the eleven with a general, simple description here (with the caveat that, because of space limitations, I'll sometimes note their relationship to one or two religious traditions and not all possible connections). In Appendix B I've set out more specifics about what these eleven look like in 2020.

My list opens with the stalwarts and then moves to newer, trending topics as it proceeds.

1. Religion and rationality

A common slogan I hear from my college students and read in various kinds of media is, "Science is about evidence. Faith is about having none, but believing anyway"; or the gauntlet that Richard Dawkins threw down, "Faith means blind trust, in the absence of evidence, even in the teeth of evidence."[50] Naturally, many religions look to an unseen reality, God or gods, while science seeks to understand the workings of the natural world,[51] and so there needs to be a healthy analytical independence. Nonetheless, *faith* in monotheistic religions such as Judaism, Christianity, and Islam is essentially reliance or trust. Or as C.S. Lewis defined it, "the art of holding on to things your reason has once accepted, in spite of your changing moods."[52] And, certainly, not all religious traditions emphasize faith, and so an anti-religious cavil against "faith" can represent a category error. Buddhism, for example, focuses on *enlightenment*, since indeed the word *Buddha* has as its root "enlighten" or "awaken." In addition, Buddhism offers an openness to change its teachings based on new information (cf. my citations from the 250 BCE Kalama Sutta and the Dalai Lama in Appendix B). Fruitful conversations need to continue unfolding in at least two directions: how to integrate various sciences and technologies with religious traditions that do not privilege faith; and how to engage with mature definitions of monotheistic faith and avoid simplistic, unhelpful slogans.

2. Divine action

David Sloan Wilson once commented in a discussion about evolution and religious faith, "I can see how some sort of deity is possible with evolution, but not a personal God who intervenes in the world" (my paraphrase). As I wrote above, not all religions believe in a deity, but for those who do, how do they conceive of God's action? As outlined in Chapter Eight, quantum physics in supplanting Newtonian mechanics described a new concept of the world, and some thinkers find in quantum indeterminancy fresh opportunities to frame God's work. Others, through a process of Whiteheadian metaphysics, portray a deity who is persuasive and non-coercive. And still others take recourse in the more traditional Thomistic dual causation. To be sure, I'm listing just three of several possible religious options. Others head in an opposite direction and talk about science as "atheistic," meaning God doesn't play a factor (e.g., Lawrence Krauss), which also contrasts markedly with some scientists (e.g., Francis Collins) who see nature as a place to witness God's creative action. The bottom line is this question: does God act in the world? Most religious Americans answer by saying that scientific descriptions should include God's action and that scientists should be open to miracles.[53]

3. Evolution

To many it's either the Bible or Darwin. The problem is that the clear consensus of mainstream science is with evolution as a theory that has guided scientific research

146 Religious individualism and tinkering

in a variety of fields for over a century and a half. The topic of evolution naturally encompasses more than simply origins—i.e., how can we put Genesis 1–3 together with evolution and the Big Bang? It also raises the question of human uniqueness, since evolutionary thought connects all life. Hindus commonly affirm that, "All living things have Ātman (self or soul), and all Ātman are parts of one Brahman, the one universal mind or consciousness that is the source of all things," and the Jains hold that "*all* living things have a soul of *jiva*."[54] Which religious views then connect most effectively with evolution?

4. Genetics, medicine, and the specter of eugenics

This is the first topic that I see trending; that is, entering into the conversation of science and religion with a new prominence. Here I will note a specific discovery in genetic editing, CRISPR (Clustered Regularly Interspaced Short Palindromic Repeat). Francis Collins remarked in 2019 that CRISPR "came out of nowhere five years ago," a technique that works via an "enzyme like what you have in a word processor that does search and replace,"[55] which makes it relatively easy. And he added, "High school students can do this. And that should worry you." CRISPR makes *germline* interventions, which affect future generations, unlike *somatic cell* interventions, which do not. This leads to the question of how to use this powerful and simple technology and whether to cure diseases or create "designer babies." It also raises issues of what to do about undesirable traits. And who decides what or who needs to be edited out? The specter of eugenics is on the horizon. Finally, who will be given the power to decide? Will religious ideas play any part in these conversations?

5. Psychology, neuroscience, and the cognitive science of religion

Functional Magnetic Imaging Resonances (FMRIs) seem to show what's happening inside our brains. Is God all in our head? And do the insights of neuroscience finally rid us of believing there's a soul? Here Buddhist approaches to the non-self, or *anatta,* and some forms of cognitive science and neuroscience seem to have striking similarities. In addition there's a growing interest in appropriating the Buddhist practice of mindfulness and its relationship to secular psychology, and especially positive psychology. Finally, the Cognitive Science of Religion, which powerfully brings together the cognitive sciences in the service of understanding religious belief and practice, has also provided fruitful insights for further discussion and research.

6. Cosmology and astrobiology

Key to many religious traditions is an emphasis on the nature of the world, or the universe, and our place in it. Recent astronomical discoveries have highlighted the vast number of exoplanets (planets beyond our own solar system).[56] In the seventeenth century the scientifically and theologically minded Blaise Pascal considered his "brief span of life" and "the small space I occupy and which I see swallowed up in the infinite immensity of spaces of which I know nothing and which know nothing of me, I take fright and am amazed...."[57] And there are medieval hints and certainly eighteenth-century antecedents.[58] Still, some assert that exoplanets and the possible (or probable) existence of extraterrestrial life mean the sudden death of the Christian scheme of salvation since, according to the biblical texts, Jesus came to save this world (such as in John 3:16). The biblical cosmos was vanishingly small compared to our current understanding. Where is our place in the universe? Conversely, if this seems like a loss for Christianity, could it be a gain for other religions?

7. Big Data

I don't see much religious writing or speaking in the popular press or in academic circles on this stealth topic. Big Data is (via a reasonably garden variety definition) "data sets, typically consisting of billions or trillions of records, that are so vast and complex that they require new and powerful computational resources to process."[59] This new reality bequeathed to us by the power of computing has profound religious significance. First of all, some promote Big Data as the scientific cutting edge with almost religious zeal. Pat Gelsinger, CEO of VMware, commented, "Data is the new science. Big Data holds the answers." That sounds like a fairly grandiose, even religious, claim. Since this is such a new topic (at least to me), I'll simply lay out three sets of questions: 1) How do we as human beings conceive of the sheer volume of information? What tools do we possess? 2) What should we do with this information? Who owns each person's data—the individual or powerful, multinational corporations? This is an especially tricky ethical question with healthcare. 3) How does the Eye of Big Data relate to the omnipresence of our God? Is it benevolent? Does this give us comfort, concern, or some mixture of both?

8. Technology, AI, and transhumanism

Technology is increasingly central to the science and religion dialogue. Cell phones, laptops, video conferencing, social media, etc. must be increasingly at the forefront as we consider science, especially for emerging adults. Simply put, 18–30-year-olds have only known a technologically-saturated world; and technology must be brought to the top three or four topics, where formerly scientific and theological method, interactions with evolutionary biology, and cosmology have often appeared. And this certainly connects with *transhumanism*, a term Julian Huxley coined in 1967 to describe the belief that the creation, development, and use of technology will improve human physical, intellectual, and psychological capacities.[60] Add Ray Kurzweil's vision, which promotes a singularity where *artificial intelligence* (AI) and human thinking will merge by 2045,[61] and this would take humankind toward something like omniscience. Science Daily defines AI as "the study and design of intelligent agents where an intelligent agent is a system that perceives its environment and takes action which maximizes its chances of success."[62] Kurzweil quite clearly seeks a form of immortality by uniting brains with the Cloud and living forever. This drive toward immortality fascinates me, as it brings to mind whether religions are indelibly invested in death and afterlife. Will religions survive if human beings can survive indefinitely? Put another way, the issue is one of *technological salvation*. Can technology be a means of enlightenment and salvation? Can AI pass the Turing Test and thus become indistinguishable from human intelligence? If so, does this mean we have become creator gods? What does AI imply for the existence of the soul? These are hot topics, and high-tech firms are investing loads of capital to answer many of them. As these rapidly advancing fields expand, they will surely create questions with significant religious implications.

9. Race and (again) a possible eugenics redux

Above, I've noted where the construction of race, and especially racial superiority, has been tied to science and thus scientific racism.[63] Today I'm hearing a growing questioning of the status of race as a scientific category,[64] part of which is the reason that those who study science and religion are predominantly, and disproportionately, Caucasian (and male). In this respect we—and by "we" I mean those of religious and scientific insight— have to grapple with the social construction of race. And with race arrive many other ills. Already, in the 1990s, Marouf A. Hasian, Jr. noted a "revival of eugenics."[65] One of the surprises of cultural life in post-Trump America is the return of white supremacists and nationalists. And today's anti-immigration rhetoric highlights certain countries (in this case, Latin American ones) and religions (Islam). Some will connect this rhetoric with genes, which has significant flaws. "Genomics—reading DNA—is showing that all human populations carry most of the same genetic variations, contrary to what we would expect if 'races' existed," (Dave Unander).[66] My hope is that skilled and informed contributors to this conversation, including those who understand religious sensibilities and beliefs, will emerge. At any rate it will continue to rise in importance for science and religion.

10. Sex and sexuality

Although we used to think science wasn't that sexy, that's changed. One of the unexpected results that arose in my qualitative interviews is that emerging adults believe that LGBTQ issues are clearly part of science and religion. Whenever I talk about science with emerging adults I hear questions like, "Doesn't science tell us that we don't choose to be gay?" Are religious communities that reject gay and lesbian members or participants bigoted and scientifically ignorant? As a result, topics previously considered secondary will become primary. And yet the themes of sexuality and gender, and particularly their relationship to science and religion, have not made it into textbook-length treatments of core issues in standard textbooks, because these sources move more gradually.[67]

11. Climate change

Many in the field of science and religion see *this*—global climate change—as *the issue* for science and religion. As Philip Clayton has written, "There is universal agreement among scientists that humans are causing the climate of our planet to change; and there are clear teachings within every major religious tradition, from indigenous lifeways to New Age spiritualities, that the earth is to be protected and valued."[68] Indeed human-caused, or *anthropogenic*, climate change represents a topic that increasingly comes to mind in science and religion discussions, and the consensus among scientists is overwhelmingly that climate change really exists and that we human beings have caused it. As a result, the AAAS has moved beyond its usual roles into more public advocacy and communication. In 2018 it launched "How We Respond," a communication initiative to highlight how communities are actively and effectively responding to climate change at local, state and regional levels, and to demonstrate the critical role of science and scientists in informing these activities."[69] The three monotheistic religions of Judaism, Christianity, and Islam prioritize their call to stewardship.[70] Eastern religions also have their own contributions. Buddhism, for example, emphasizes compassion and the interconnection of all life. Hindus and Jains describe a soul in all things, and the latter's accent on *ahimsa* can contribute a deep reverence for all life.

Those are my Top Eleven, briefly noted, and I'm confident that many readers of this book will have others. Who then will be determining the responses to these questions? What kind of trends will emerge in the process? Those are the themes of the next chapter.

Notes

1 Leigh Eric Schmidt, *Restless Souls: The Making of American Spirituality* (Berkeley: University of California Press, 2012), 1.
2 Cited in Andrew Delbanco, *The Real American Dream: A Meditation on Hope* (Cambridge, MA: Harvard, 2000), 49.
3 John Weiss, *American Religion,* (Boston: Roberts Brothers, 1871), 47.
4 Stanford Encyclopedia of Philosophy, "Religion and Science," retrieved June 24, 2019, https://plato.stanford.edu/entries/religion-science.
5 Greg Cootsona, "Some Ways Emerging Adults are Shaping the Future of Science and Religion," *Zygon: Journal of Religion and Science* 51, no. 3 (2016): 557–72.
6 I've adapted this term from Robert Wuthnow, *After the Baby Boomers: How Twenty- and Thirty-Somethings Are Shaping the Future of American Religion* (Princeton and Oxford: Princeton University Press, 2007), 14; cf. Melissa M. Wilcox, "When Sheila's a Lesbian: Religious Individualism among Lesbian, Gay, Bisexual, and Transgender Christians," *Sociology of Religion* 63, no. 4 (2002), 498.
7 Wuthnow, *After the Baby Boomers.*

8 Wuthnow, *After the Baby Boomers*; Christian Smith with Patricia Snell. *Souls in Transition: The Religious and Spiritual Lives of Emerging Adults* (Oxford: Oxford University, 2009); Christian Smith, Kari Christoffersen, and Hillary Davidson, *Lost in Transition: The Dark Side of Emerging Adulthood* (Oxford: Oxford University, 2011); Jonathan Hill, *Emerging Adulthood and Faith* (Grand Rapids: Calvin College Press, 2015).
9 Smith with Snell, *Souls in Transition, 2009.*
10 David Kinnaman with Aly Hawkins, *You Lost Me: Why Young Christians Are Leaving Church … and Rethinking Faith* (Grand Rapids: Baker Books, 2011).
11 Alister McGrath, *Religion and Science: A New Introduction*, 2nd edition. (Oxford: Wiley-Blackwell, 2010).
12 For more info, see Test of Faith, retrieved June 25, 2019, http://www.testoffaith.com.
13 Jeffrey Arnett, "Emerging Adulthood: A Theory of Development From the Late Teens Through the Twenties," *American Psychologist* 55. no. 5 (2000): 469–80.
14 Jeffrey Arnett, Marion Klepp, Leo B. Hendry, and Jennifer L. Tanner, *Debating Emerging Adulthood: Stage or Process?* (New York: Oxford University Press, 2011).
15 David P. Setran, and Chris A. Kiesling, *Spiritual Formation in Emerging Adulthood: A Practical Theology for College and Young Adult Ministry* (Grand Rapids: Baker Books, 2013), 242, n. 12.
16 Ibid., 2.
17 A 2019 article from *The Guardian* is even more clear, "Five Markers of Adulthood Millennials Have Had to Give Up On," retrieved June 13, 2019, https://www.the-guardian.com/lifeandstyle/2016/mar/10/five-markers-of-adulthood-millenials-have-had-to-give-up-on.
18 Setran and Kiesling, *Spiritual Formation*, 2.
19 Wuthnow, *After the Baby Boomers*, 11.
20 Barna Group, *Gen Z: The Culture, Beliefs and Motivations Shaping the Next Generation* (Barna Group, 2018), 32.
21 Arnett "Emerging Adulthood"; summarized by Setran and Kiesling, *Spiritual Formation*, 3–4.
22 Arnett, "Emerging Adulthood," 469.
23 Robert Bellah, Richard Madsen, William Sullivan, Ann Swidler, and Steven Tipton, *Habits of the Heart* (Berkeley: University of California Press, 1985), 221.
24 Wikipedia, "Sheilaism," retrieved June 13, 2019, https://en.wikipedia.org/wiki/Sheilaism.
25 See Delbanco, *The Real American Dream.*
26 Ibid., 103.
27 Wuthnow, *After the Baby Boomers*, 13. Incidentally, it is probably worth noting that, since Wuthnow wrote his study in 2007, many of his subjects are now older than 30, but his research on emerging adults is nonetheless relevant. I am analyzing 18–30-year-olds primarily from the angle of psychological development more than from a particular demographic.
28 Ibid., 135.
29 Wilcox, "When Sheila's a Lesbian."
30 Catherine Keller and Laurel Schneider, *Polydoxy: Theology of Multiplicity and Relation* (New York: Routledge, 2010).
31 Cited in Edwin Gaustad and Leigh Schmidt, *The Religious History of America: The Heart of the American Story from Colonial Times to Today* (San Francisco: HarperCollins, 2004), 424.
32 Bellah et al., *Habits of the Heart*, 228.
33 Gaustad and Schmidt, 426.
34 Smith with Snell, *Souls in Transition*, 293.
35 Ibid., 154ff.
36 Wuthnow, *After the Baby Boomers*, 135.
37 Jonathan Haidt, *The Righteous Mind: Why Good People Are Divided by Politics and Religion* (New York: Vintage, 2013), esp. ch. 3.

38 Minsu Ha, David L. Haury, and Ross H. Nehm, "Feeling of Certainty: Uncovering a Missing Link between Knowledge and Acceptance of Evolution," *Journal of Research in Science Teaching* 49 (2011): 95–121. This study was about evolutionary science, but it could be extended to science in general that threatens our social group.

39 Kyle Longest and Christian Smith, "Conflicting or Compatible: Beliefs About Religion and Science Among Emerging Adults in the United States," *Sociological Forum*, vol. 26, no. 4, (2011): 846–69, especially 854.

40 Christopher P. Scheitle, "U.S. College Students' Perception of Religion and Science: Conflict, Collaboration, or Independence? A Research Note," *Journal for the Scientific Study of Religion* 50 (2011): 175. Even those that leaned toward conflict register a notable division between those who side with religion (17%) and those with science (14%); Ibid., 178–9.

41 Elaine Howard Ecklund and Christopher P. Scheitle, *Religion vs. Science: What Religious People Really Think* (Oxford: Oxford University Press, 2018), 28.

42 Elaine Howard Ecklund and Jerry Z. Park, "Conflict Between Religion and Science Among Academic Scientists?" *Journal of the Scientific Study of Religion* 48 (2009): 276.

43 Pew Research Center, October 22, 2015, "Religion and Science," https://www. pewresearch.org/science/2015/10/22/science-and-religion.

44 Under Evolution Resources, "Compatibility of Science and Religion," http://www.nas. edu/evolution/Compatibility.html.

45 For brief description, see Becky Ham, "Religious and Scientific Communities May Be Less Combative Than Commonly Portrayed," February 17, 2014, retrieved June 25, 2019, http://www.aaas.org/news/religious-and-scientific-communities-may-be-less-combative-commonly-portrayed.

46 Kinnaman and Hawkins, *You Lost Me*, chapter 7, which is simply entitled, "Antiscience."

47 Barna, *Gen Z*, 71.

48 Pew Research Center, "Public's Views on Human Evolution," December 30, 2013, retrieved June 24, 2019, https://www.pewforum.org/2013/12/30/publics-views-on-human-evolution.

49 These have been compiled in conversation with Drew Rick-Miller, Se Kim, and Robert John Russell, among others.

50 Richard Dawkins, *The Selfish Gene*, 2nd edition. (Oxford: Oxford University Press, 1989), 198.

51 See my definitions in chapter one for more detail.

52 C.S. Lewis, *Mere Christianity*. (New York: MacMillan, 1952), 141.

53 Ecklund and Scheitle, *Religion vs. Science*, 28.

54 Philip Clayton, *Science and Religion: The Basics*. 2nd edition. (New York: Routledge, 2019), 103.

55 Francis Collins, "What do YOU Believe, Doctor?" April 19, 2019, BioLogos 10th Anniversary Conference, retrieved June 25, 2019, https://biologos.org/resources/what-do-you-believe-doctor.

56 See NASA website, "Exoplanet Exploration," retrieved June 25, 2019, https://exoplanets.nasa.gov.

57 Blaise Pascal, *Pensées*, trans. A.J. Krailsheimer, Penguin Classics (New York: Penguin, 1995), 19.

58 See Olli-Pekka Vainio, *Cosmology in Theological Perspective* (Grand Rapids: Baker, 2018), chs. 3 and 4.

59 Dictonary.com, "Big Data," retrieved June 25, 2019, https://www.dictionary.com/browse/big-data.

60 "The human species can, if it wishes, transcend itself…. We need a name for this new belief. Perhaps transhumanism will serve." Julian Huxley, *Religion Without Revelation* (London: C.A. Watts, 1967), 195, cited in Ted Peters, "Theologians Testing Transhumanism," Theology and Science 13, no. 2 (2015): 132.

61 Ray Kurzweil, *The Singularity is Near* (New York: Penguin, 2005), 136.

152 Religious individualism and tinkering

62 See *Science Daily*, "Artificial Intelligence," retrieved June 25, 2019, https://www.sciencedaily.com/terms/artificial_intelligence.htm.

63 The American Society of Human Genetics (ASHG), "ASHG Denounces Attempts to Link Genetics and Racial Supremacy," *The American Journal of Human* Genetics 103, Issue 5 (2018): 636, retrieved June 25, 2019, https://www.ncbi.nlm.nih.gov/pmc/articles/PMC6218810; Amy Harmon, "Why White Supremacists Are Chugging Milk (and Why Geneticists Are Alarmed)," *New York Times*, October 17, 2018, retrieved June 25, 2019, https://www.nytimes.com/2018/10/17/us/white-supremacists-science-dna.html?module=inline, and "Geneticists Criticize Use of Science by White Nationalists to Justify 'Racial Purity.'" *New York Times*, October 19, 2018, retrieved June 25, 2019, https://www.nytimes.com/2018/10/19/us/white-supremacists-science-genetics.html.

64 E.g., the ground-breaking work of Alan Templeton, *Human Population Genetics and Genomics* (Cambridge, MA: Academic Press, 2018), and "Biological Races in Humans," *Studies in the History and Philosophy of Biology and Biomedical Sciences* 44 (2013): 262–71.

65 Marouf A. Hasian, *The Rhetoric of Eugenics in Anglo-American Thought* (Athens and London: University of Georgia Press, 1996), 23.

66 Dave Unander, "Race: A Brief History of its Origin, Failure and Alternative," February 21, 2018, retrieved June 25, 2019, https://biologos.org/articles/race-a-brief-history-of-its-origin-failure-and-alternative.

67 E.g., Barbour, *Issues in Science and Religion* (New York: HarperCollins, 1971 [1966]); Philip Clayton, *Religion and Science*; Christopher Southgate et al. *God, Humanity, and the Cosmos: A Textbook in Science and Religion* (Harrisburg, PA: Trinity, 1999); Alister McGrath, *Religion and Science*; Holmes Rolston, *Science and Religion: A Critical Survey* (West Conshohoken, PA: Templeton Press, 2006); Mark Richardson and Wesley J. Wildman, eds. *Religion and Science: History, Method, Dialogue* (New York: Routledge, 1996).

68 Clayton, *Science and Religion*, xi. I added a "to" before "relate" in the quotation, which was missing in the original.

69 American Association for the Advancement of Science (AAAS), "Climate Change Communication," retrieved June 25, 2019, https://www.aaas.org/pes/climate-change-communication.

70 See Greg Cootsona, "Christian Faith and Sustainability: Friends or Foes? Christian Theology and Stewardship of Creation," unpublished paper presented at Chico State University Sustainability Conference, November 10, 2008.

Bibliography

American Association for the Advancement of Science (AAAS). "Climate Change Communication." Retrieved June 25, 2019. https://www.aaas.org/pes/climate-change-communication

American Society of Human Genetics (ASHG). "ASHG Denounces Attempts to Link Genetics and Racial Supremacy." *The American Journal of Human Genetics*, 103, Issue 5 (2018): 636. Retrieved June 25, 2019. https://www.ncbi.nlm.nih.gov/pmc/articles/PMC6218810.

Arnett, Jeffrey. "Emerging Adulthood: A Theory of Development From the Late Teens Through the Twenties." *American Psychologist*, 55, no. 5 (2000): 469–480.

Arnett, Jeffrey, Marion Klepp, Leo B. Hendry, and Jennifer L. Tanner. *Debating Emerging Adulthood: Stage or Process?* New York: Oxford University Press, 2011.

Bagir, Zainal Abidin. "The 'Relation' between Science and Religion in the Pluralistic Landscape of Today's World." *Zygon*, 50 (2015): 403–417.

Barbour, Ian. *Issues in Science and Religion.* New York: HarperCollins, 1971 [1966].

Barna Group. *Gen Z: The Culture, Beliefs and Motivations Shaping the Next Generation.* Barna Group, 2018.

Bellah, Robert, Richard Madsen, William Sullivan, Ann Swidler and Steven Tipton. *Habits of the Heart*. Berkeley, CA: University of California Press, 1985.

Bolger, Daniel, Robert A. Thomson Jr. and Elaine Howard Ecklund. "Selection versus Socialization? Interrogating the Sources of Secularity in Global Science." *Sage*, 2019. https://journals.sagepub.com/doi/pdf/10.1177/0731121419835507

Cantor, Geoffrey and Chris Kenny. "Barbour's Fourfold Way: Problems with His Taxonomy of Science-Religion Relationships." *Zygon*, 36 (2001): 765–781.

Collins, Francis. "What do YOU Believe, Doctor?" April 19, 2019. BioLogos 10th Anniversary Conference. Retrieved June 25, 2019. https://biologos.org/resources/what-do-you-believe-doctor

Cootsona, Greg. "Christian Faith and Sustainability: Friends or Foes? Christian Theology and Stewardship of Creation." Unpublished paper presented at Chico State University Sustainability Conference, November 10, 2008.

Cootsona, Gregory S. "How Nature, and Beauty Can Bring Scientists and Theologians Together." *Theology and Science*, 9, no. 4 (2011): 379–393.

Cootsona, Greg. "Some Ways Emerging Adults Are Shaping the Future of Religion and Science." *Zygon: Journal of Religion and Science*, 51, no. 3 (September 2016): 557–572.

Dawkins, Richard. *The Selfish Gene*, 2nd edition. Oxford, UK: Oxford University Press, 1989.

Delbanco, Andrew. *The Real American Dream: A Meditation on Hope*. Cambridge, MA: Harvard, 2000.

Dictonary.com. "Big Data." Retrieved June 25, 2019. https://www.dictionary.com/browse/big-data

Ecklund, Elaine Howard and Christopher P. Scheitle. *Religion vs. Science: What Religious People Really Think*. Oxford, UK: Oxford University Press, 2018.

Finke, Roger. "Religious Deregulation: Origins and Consequences." *Journal of Church and State*, 32 (Summer 1990): 609–626.

Gaustad, Edwin and Leigh Schmidt. *The Religious History of America: The Heart of the American Story from Colonial Times to Today*. San Francisco: HarperCollins, 2004.

Geertz, Clifford. *The Interpretation of Cultures*. New York: Basic Books, 1973.

Gilbert, James. *Redeeming Culture: American Religion in the Age of Science*. Chicago, IL: University of Chicago, 1997.

Guardian, The. "Five Markers of Adulthood Millennials Have Had to Give Up On." Retrieved June 13, 2019. https://www.theguardian.com/lifeandstyle/2016/mar/10/five-markers-of-adulthood-millenials-have-had-to-give-up-on

Ha, Minsu, David L. Haury and Ross H. Nehm. "Feeling of Certainty: Uncovering a Missing Link between Knowledge and Acceptance of Evolution." *Journal of Research in Science Teaching*, 49 (2011): 95–121.

Haidt, Jonathan. *The Righteous Mind: Why Good People Are Divided by Politics and Religion*. New York: Vintage, 2013.

Ham, Becky. "Religious and Scientific Communities May Be Less Combative Than Commonly Portrayed." February 17, 2014. Retrieved June 25, 2019. http://www.aaas.org/news/religious-and-scientific-communities-may-be-less-combative-commonly-portrayed

Harmon, Amy. "Why White Supremacists Are Chugging Milk (and Why Geneticists Are Alarmed)." *New York Times*, October 17, 2018. Retrieved June 25, 2019. https://www.nytimes.com/2018/10/17/us/white-supremacists-science-dna.html?module=inline

Harmon, Amy. "Geneticists Criticize Use of Science by White Nationalists to Justify 'Racial Purity'." *New York Times*, October 19, 2018. Retrieved June 25, 2019. https://www.nytimes.com/2018/10/19/us/white-supremacists-science-genetics.html

154 Religious individualism and tinkering

Hasian, Marouf A. *The Rhetoric of Eugenics in Anglo-American Thought*. Athens and London: University of Georgia Press, 1996.

Kinnaman, David with Aly Hawkins. *You Lost Me: Why Young Christians Are Leaving Church ... and Rethinking Faith*. Grand Rapids, MI: Baker Books, 2011.

Keller, Catharine and Laurel C. Schneider, eds. *Polydoxy: Theology of Multiplicity and Relation*. New York: Routledge, 2010.

Kinsley, David. *Ecology and Religion: Ecological Spirituality in Cross-Cultural Perspective*. Englewood Cliffs, NJ: Prentice, 1995.

Kurzweil, Ray. *The Singularity is Near*. New York: Penguin, 2005.

Lewis, C.S. *Mere Christianity*. New York: MacMillan, 1952.

Longest, Kyle and Christian Smith. "Conflicting or Compatible: Beliefs About Religion and Science Among Emerging Adults in the United States." *Sociological Forum*, 26, no. 4 (2011): 846–869.

McGrath, Alister. *Religion and Science: A New Introduction*. 2nd edition. Oxford, UK: Wiley-Blackwell, 2010.

Mead, Sidney. *The Old Religion in the Brave New World*. Berkeley and Los Angeles, CA: University of California Press, 1977.

NASA. "Exoplanet Exploration." Retrieved June 25, 2019. https://exoplanets.nasa.gov

Pascal, Blaise. *Pensées*. Translated by A.J. Krailsheimer, Penguin Classics. New York: Penguin, 1995.

Peters, Ted. "Theologians Testing Transhumanism." *Theology and Science*, 13, no. 2 (2015): 130–149.

Pew Research Center. "Defining generations: Where Millennials end and Generation Z begins." http://www.pewresearch.org/fact-tank/2019/01/17/where-millennials-end-and-generation-z-begins

Pew Research Center. "Millennials." http://www.pewresearch.org/topics/millennials

Pew Research Center. "Millennials increasingly are driving growth of 'nones'." http://www.pewresearch.org/fact-tank/2015/05/12/millennials-increasingly-are-driving-growth-of-nones

Pew Research Center. "Public's Views on Human Evolution." December 30, 2013. Retrieved June 24, 2019. https://www.pewforum.org/2013/12/30/publics-views-on-human-evolution

Prothero, Stephen. *God is Not One: The Eight Rival Religions That Run the World*. San Francisco: HarperOne, 2010.

Richardson, Mark and Wesley J. Wildman, eds. *Religion and Science: History, Method, Dialogue*. New York and London: Routledge, 1996.

Rolston, Holmes. *Science and Religion: A Critical Survey*. West Conshohoken, PA: Templeton Press, 2006.

Scheitle, Christopher P. "U.S. College Students' Perception of Religion and Science: Conflict, Collaboration, or Independence? A Research Note." *Journal for the Scientific Study of Religion*, 50, no. 1 (2011): 175–186

Schmidt, Leigh Eric. *Restless Souls: The Making of American Spirituality*. Berkeley, CA: University of California Press, 2012.

Science Daily. "Artificial Intelligence." Retrieved June 25, 2019. https://www.sciencedaily.com/terms/artificial_intelligence.htm

Setran, David P. and Chris A. Kiesling. *Spiritual Formation in Emerging Adulthood: A Practical Theology for College and Young Adult Ministry*. Grand Rapids, MI: Baker Books, 2013.

Smith, Christian with Patricia Snell. *Souls in Transition: The Religious and Spiritual Lives of Emerging Adults*. Oxford, UK: Oxford University, 2009.

Smith, Christian, Kari Christoffersen and Hillary Davidson. *Lost in Transition: The Dark Side of Emerging Adulthood*. Oxford, UK: Oxford University, 2011.

Smith, Huston. *The World's Religions*. San Francisco: HarperOne, 1991.

Southgate, Christopher et al. *God, Humanity, and the Cosmos: A Textbook in Science and Religion*. Harrisburg, PA: Trinity, 1999.

Stanford Encyclopedia of Philosophy. "Religion and Science." Retrieved June 24, 2019. https://plato.stanford.edu/entries/religion-science

Templeton, Alan. "Biological Races in Humans." *Studies in the History and Philosophy of Biology and Biomedical Sciences*, 44 (2013): 262–271.

Templeton, Alan. *Human Population Genetics and Genomics*. Cambridge, MA: Academic Press, 2018.

Test of Faith. Retrieved June 25, 2019. http://www.testoffaith.com

Unander, Dave. "Race: A Brief History of its Origin, Failure and Alternative." February 21, 2018. Retrieved June 25, 2019. https://biologos.org/articles/race-a-brief-history-of-its-origin-failure-and-alternative

Vainio, Olli-Pekka. *Cosmology in Theological Perspective*. Grand Rapids, MI: Baker, 2018.

Weiss, John. *American Religion*. Boston, MA: Roberts Brothers, 1871.

Wikipedia. "Sheilaism." Retrieved June 13, 2019. https://en.wikipedia.org/wiki/Sheilaism

Wilcox, Melissa M. "When Sheila's a Lesbian: Religious Individualism among Lesbian, Gay, Bisexual, and Transgender Christians." *Sociology of Religion*, 63, no. 4 (2002): 497–513.

Wuthnow, Robert. *After the Baby Boomers: How Twenty- and Thirty-Somethings Are Shaping the Future of American Religion*. Princeton and Oxford: Princeton University Press, 2007.

11

THE FUTURE AND ITS CONTOURS: MAJOR TRENDS

The perils of prediction

Trends are notoriously tricky to identify. At times it seems we squint our eyes and make our best guess at what's on the horizon. Andrew Delbanco, in a lecture at Harvard on *The Real American Dream*, invited his audience to ponder Disney's Tomorrowland, which had to be rebuilt because of its limited success at predicting the future.[1] My own memory of Tomorrowland at the original Anaheim Disneyland in the 1970s was that it would hardly match today's world. Instead it would look vaguely like the TV show I loved as a kid, or as Delbanco phrased it, "a hokey replica of a stage set for the Jetsons."[2]

In this final chapter, I'm looking for sources and signs to discern the contours of the future, but proceed with caution. "It's tough to make predictions," as Yogi Berra once cautioned, "especially about the future."

Still I will try. I'm fascinated by what's to come and I believe that, though history is highly contingent, we can find clues today for the outlines of tomorrow. How do I know how the contingencies of thought and history will play out? I admit this final chapter is fraught with the dangers of trying to navigate between the Scylla of presumption and the Charybdis of ignorance. Seeking to make my way between these perils I journey ahead toward the future home of science and religion, letting the oars of future trends and topics, as well as the surveys and analysis of emerging-adults' attitudes, guide the ship.

The first two sections begin with comments particular to the religious makeup of our country and then move to science and religion.

A decreasing influence of Christianity and a splintering of American religious life

That the Christian church will have a decreasing influence in the United States and that America's religious will become more splintered and individualized—those two conclusions seem irresistible. Almost every major poll of the past five to ten years, along with leading scholarship I've discussed in this book, demonstrates that as a nation we are less religiously affiliated and therefore less Christian. I'll return to the nones in a moment, but it's important to take in the state of Christian influence in America because that has been the dominant (though, of course, not the only) theme in our history.

First of all let it be said that most Americans consider themselves at least nominally within the Christian fold, whether it's three-quarters (2017 Gallup poll[3]) or just over seven in ten (2014 Pew's 70.6%).[4] Either way, even if the iceberg is melting it's still a big iceberg.

Nevertheless, as I've argued above, the vector of how to relate science and religion leads away from Christian-centric and toward an increasingly pluralistic model. Put another way, of the specific religious traditions that will play an increasingly significant role, many of those will be non-Christian. If trends continue, Muslims and Hindus will about double from 2010 to 2050 (from 0.9% to 2.1% and 0.6% to 1.2%, respectively) and, most interestingly, "other religions" (which includes, for Pew, Bahai, Jainism, Wicca, Zoroastrianism, Shintoism, Sikhism, etc.) will grow by 150%.[5] Another way to see this is that the young are definitely in the ranks outside of Christianity, as the Public Religion Research Institute (PRRI) found in its 2017 survey. "Muslims, Hindus, and Buddhists are all far younger than white Christian groups. At least one-third of Muslims (42%), Hindus (36%), and Buddhists (35%) are under the age of 30." And as we've seen, about a third of nones are under 30, while white Christians are greying.

> Slightly more than one in ten white Catholics (11%), white evangelical Protestants (11%), and white mainline Protestants (14%) are under 30. Approximately six in ten white evangelical Protestants (62%), white Catholics (62%), and white mainline Protestants (59%) are at least 50 years old.[6]

Americans appear to be gradually aging out of Christianity.

Here's how I read the data on the shape shifting of religion in America. Christian influence in this country, though powerful, will decline. Even as I see the rise of a variety of religious traditions and their contributions, I cannot help but note—as a Christian theologian—that Christianity is also shifting. Naturally, the presence of religious fundamentalism will continue, as demonstrated by the surprise election of Donald Trump in 2016 and the influence of the American religious right, especially white evangelicals, who simply show up for elections and punch way beyond their weight. But gradually they cannot escape the wider trends and soon there will be fewer in the ring.

158 Major trends

The bigger story is the broader demographic tides that will gradually take America away from white evangelical shores. The trends signal a hard crash on the rocks for white evangelicals in both ethnicity (i.e., white) and religious identification (evangelical). As PRRI found in 2017, "Fewer than one in five (17%) Americans are white evangelical Protestant, but they accounted for nearly one-quarter (23%) in 2006."

In addition, despite the strong association of President Trump with white evangelicals, other groups are markedly less supportive,[7] and an under-emphasized trend in my view are countervailing voices even among evangelicals—such as Beth Moore—and prominent progressive Christian leaders (and some former evangelicals) such as Jen Hatmaker, the late Rachel Held Evans, and Rob Bell, many of whom skew toward a younger demographic.

Whether from Buddhist, Christian, neopagan, or other sources—and remembering the definition of *religion* in Chapter Two, especially that it's reasonably synonymous with popular usage of *spirituality*—our religious life is transforming, but not dying. Consequently, an observer of American religion has to admit that the secularization thesis (often associated with Max Weber, although I would certainly include Auguste Comte) has been much less clearly realized than most scholars could foresee. As societies progress, the argument goes, they become modernized and "rationalized," and thus the authority of religion diminishes in all aspects of social life and governance, as the spheres previously assigned to religion are spun off to other structures. The full extent of this secularization thesis has failed to materialize as predicated after more than 100 years. To be sure, it's true that the formal structural power of religions has diminished, particularly as demonstrated in the rise of the unaffiliated—and I will comment on the phenomenon of the nones below in light of secularization—but that does not mean that religion *per se*, as defined by scholars in the field, is wasting away.

This is worth a pause, given how well the secularization thesis continues to endure in the hallways of US sociology and religious studies departments, which is one reason that the conflict thesis endures.[8] It was just a few decades ago that Jürgen Habermas could announce, following Weber, "not only the secularisation of Western *culture*, but also and especially the development of modern *societies* from the viewpoint of rationalisation."[9] And he continued by describing that the "new structures of society were marked by the differentiation of the two functionally intermeshing systems that had taken shape around the organisational cores of the capitalist enterprise and the bureaucratic state apparatus."[10] More recently, however, Habermas has realized that he's wiser to speak of a "post-secular" society[11] and that we have not become entirely secularized, fully disentangled from religious life. And so, as he phrased it, "Both religious and secular mentalities must be open to a complementary learning process if we are to balance shared citizenship and cultural difference."[12] Religion is here to stay, but those remaining have changed their shapes, and this reality is wound into the fabric of American society alongside a growing religious disaffiliation. Secularization is morphing as well.

Delbanco wondered what will replace the Christian story that has defined America and particularly American hope. How will we fight off "melancholy" (to use Delbanco's word) that lurks around the edges of American consciousness, and especially our fixation on consumption and technological distractions? To respond, he looked to the perennially insightful commentator on America, Alexis de Tocqueville, who observed that religion represents "only one particular form of hope, and it is as natural as the human heart as hope itself."[13] Tocqueville represented both a keen eye for religion in our country as well as a marked incredulity and distance, characteristic of an early nineteenth-century French intellectual, when he continued,

> It is by a sort of intellectual abstraction, and in a way, by doing moral violence to their own nature, that men detach themselves from religious beliefs, and invincible inclination draws them back. Incredulity is an accident; faith is the only permanent state of mankind.[14]

"According to this axiom," Delbanco added, "the question is never whether some kind of faith will remerge. The question is, what will it be?"[15] I do certainly see new commitments that might resemble traditional religions but do not include a Transcendent Reality or God. I'm often in conversations with people, especially twenty- and thirty-somethings with Christian leanings, who can't find a new religious thinker that resonates. Here I'm specifically struck with the lack of any one compelling voice on the American religious scene for engaging the sciences—to date this has been primarily *Christianity*. Moreover, in my reading at least, even thinkers as prominent as Fritjof Capra or the Dalai Lama have failed to inspire a movement, even if Buddhist voices seem likely poised to provide future leadership. Given an enduring Christian majority in America and to focus on voices within Christianity, it's worth considering the continuing prominence of various liberation theologies. Since, by nature, they focus on God's priority toward the poor and oppressed, they do not present themselves as major players in the dialogue with science generally, though they could have targeted influence on the topics of the science of race. I've read and heard attempts to return to Aristotelian-Thomistic thought as a source,[16] to evangelicalism,[17] to more popular voices like Bell and Richard Rohr, as well as to process thought and its cousin, "open theism."[18] None has quite replaced the Great Trio I learned to revere: Ian Barbour, Arthur Peacocke, and John Polkinghorne. Besides Francis Collins, whom I highlighted in Chapter Nine, it is beyond my abilities to discern that new voice or those voices.

And although I'm not sure which Christian voice is on the horizon, I'm reasonably certain a digital streaming spiritualty is on the rise. But so are some other factors as well. I turn to the anti-religious, or at least the atheists and agnostics.

160 Major trends

A rise in atheism and agnosticism

It's undeniable—as I'll note below—that the nones will continue to increase markedly. Atheism and agnosticism will rise as well, but it is important not to make *nones* and *agnostics/atheists* coterminous. Michael Lipka has written for the Pew Research Center, "one thing is for sure: Along with the rise of religiously unaffiliated Americans (many of whom believe in God), there has been a corresponding increase in the number of atheists."[19] But note the phrase in parenthesis, *many of whom believe in God*. Pew did find an uptick from 2007 to 2014 in those who call themselves atheist or agnostic, but their growth is not tracking with that of the nones. "The share of Americans who identify as atheists has roughly doubled in the past several years. Pew Research Center's 2014 Religious Landscape Study found that 3.1% of American adults say they are atheists when asked about their religious identity, up from 1.6% in a similarly large survey in 2007. An additional 4.0% of Americans call themselves agnostics, up from 2.4% in 2007."[20] The "corresponding increase" that Lipka notes in the first citation has a coefficient of about .3. In other words, for every 100 new nones, 30 will be atheist or agnostic.

Notably, Elaine Howard Ecklund and Christopher Scheitle also have pointed out that agnostics and atheists in science are not entirely against spirituality. "We found that more than 22% of atheist scientists and more than 27% of agnostic scientists are still interested in spirituality."[21] One of their interviewees clarified, "If anything, my own spirituality might be closer to almost an Eastern kind of tradition than a Western tradition, even though I was raised a Catholic."[22] And according to the Pew Research Center, in 2016 "8% of those who call themselves atheists also say they believe in God or a universal spirit. Indeed, 2% say they are 'absolutely certain' about the existence of God or a universal spirit."[23]

Such declarations make the category of *atheism* a bit slippery. Nonetheless, atheism can claim a birthright here, even if the US is unusually religious for a developed country. Atheists represent the hardcore warfare adherents, and so this voice will be with us in our country. And the denial of God constitutes a part of our country's life. In fact, denying the Deity (or any deity) is indeed protected by the Constitution and its First Amendment. The voice represented in various centuries by Robert Ingersoll, Madalyn Murray O'Hare, and Jerry Coyne will always be with us, but here's the change I see: this hard-edged atheism will gradually give way to a kinder, gentler naturalism. And the shift in language is important—*atheism*, with its alpha privative leading the way, fundamentally denies Something, while *naturalism* or *materialism* affirms that the material world, nature, is all there is and all there ever needs to be. And, yes, I am alluding to Carl Sagan's famous phrase "The Cosmos is all that is or was or ever will be," as well as thinking of the brilliant work of the humanist scholar Stephen Greenblatt in *The Swerve* as offering a somewhat subtle plea to recover Lucretius's materialism as the way for us to move forward.[24] Allison, age 19, quite calmly told me that she was an atheist—there was no edge as there might have been in Robert Ingersoll's time 150 years ago, or even in my experience as a student at UC Berkeley in the 1980s. She stated matter-of-factly and without irony, "If they want to believe, more power to them." The hard-edged atheism of Richard Dawkins and Jerry Coyne will fade because religion represents less to fight over.

The spiritual yearning that has characterized our country (and I'll stick with America, as I have throughout this book), as well as our entrepreneurial spirit for satisfying that yearning, shows no signs of abating, only of transforming. And so, even with the rising percentage of nones, practitioners and theorists in science and religion face an exciting, dizzying, and challenging future. This brings me to another observation.

With the nones' increase, antipathy both increases and decreases

The rising percentage of nones will likely result in the bifurcated trend I described in the last chapter: they will drive an increased antipathy toward the collaboration of science and religion in the culture at large, or "out there," and a decreased antipathy between science and an individual's personal religion or spirituality, or "in here."

To envision the religious future of America I simply have to bring to mind the San Francisco Bay Area of my past. As I've mentioned in other places[25] (and for whatever it's worth), I grew up in a happy, secular Silicon Valley, which regularly emerges as the region of our country with the lowest religious affiliation. Although I was a twenty-something before the nones became a trend, I grew up with no religious affiliation. So, in short, I am born and bred to be comfortable with the nones and the future they bring. With the increase in scientific and technological thinking, unaffiliation or disaffiliation (sometimes called "nones and dones") already runs at one-third (and perhaps more) for 18–30-year-olds.

In researching and reflecting on this chapter I wondered if there is any way to forestall this trend. I couldn't find any reason to doubt it, and a 2014 Pew Research study offered me a clear outline; 36% of younger millennials (1990–1996) and 34% of older millennials (1981–89) were unaffiliated, while only 11% of the silent generation (1928–1945) could be placed in that category. In between these two fell Generation X (1965–1980) at 23% and baby boomers (1946–1964) at 17%.[26] Through the 60 years between the first and the last of these generations, the percentage of nones in America has more than tripled. The report continued by noting that this is partly a generational reality.

> While some Millennials are leaving their childhood religion to become unaffiliated, most Millennials who were raised without a religious affiliation are remaining religious "nones" in adulthood. Two-thirds of Millennials who were raised unaffiliated are still unaffiliated (67%), a higher retention rate than most other major religious groups—and much higher than for older generations of "nones."[27]

162 Major trends

I have heard it presented that "Oh, they'll come back to church or synagogue when they get older, get married, and have kids" (which, as I noted, has been correlated with religious affiliation in the past). Pew doesn't give religious communities much comfort for the future:

> It is possible that more Millennials who were raised unaffiliated will begin to identify with a religion as they get older, get married and have children, but previous Pew Research Center studies suggest that generational cohorts typically do not become more religiously affiliated as they get older. And the new survey finds that most generational cohorts actually are becoming less religiously affiliated as they age. [28]

Consequently, the future seems largely unaffiliated with formal religious structures, but that doesn't mean uninterested in God, Ultimate Reality, or spirituality.

In fact, most nones believe in God and some still worship in traditional congregations. And even those who don't believe in God find a bigger Something at the core of existence. Pew Research found in 2018 that 72% of nones still believe in God or a Higher Power, which can be compared to about 90% of Americans:

> The overwhelming majority of Americans, including a majority of the religiously unaffiliated – those who describe themselves, religiously, as atheists, agnostics or "nothing in particular" – say they believe in God or a higher power, according to a new Pew Research Center survey conducted in December of 2017. [29]

As Devan, one of the older persons I interviewed at age 33, put it, "I don't believe in God, but there is a spiritual component to life." And as Maria, age 18, said, "When it comes to religion and spirituality, I think I would describe myself as more religious than spiritual. I attend mass occasionally and spend time praying when I am troubled or thankful." One must make this claim because too often the nones are thrown in with the atheists and agnostics. This is a category error if we mean that they are all against belief in God or even participation in worship services. They do belong in the same category only if the topic is the answer to "Do you affiliate with a particular religion?"

And so I move to my most contentious assertion: the interaction of science and religion will most likely find a decrease in the antipathy "in here," that is, personally, but not "out there," in the culture.

I'll first start with the problem and a brief glance in my rearview mirror. More atheists (or really anti-theists) than religious fundamentalists see a conflict between science and religion.[30] Ecklund and Scheitle found that the most likely to hold a conflict view of religion and science are the religiously unaffiliated, at 52%, which is significantly higher than evangelicals, at 31%.[31] But will this deeper connection work? In other words, will those who look find that they can connect with science (and technology) and religion? It's important to recall John Evans's observation that

Major trends   163

the line of hardest resistance to mainstream science is with conservative Protestants and their ilk.[32] And zooming out to a wider religious landscape, a majority of Catholics (58%) and mainline Protestants (51%) subscribe to evolution as the best explanation for human origins, and Buddhists (81%), Hindus (80%), and Jews (77%) are even higher, according to a poll taken 150 years after publication of Charles Darwin's 1859 *Origin of Species.* [33]

As we've seen, all groups think that the conflict is *their problem and not my problem.* And the "their" is either the conservative "Bible thumpers" or "godless scientists." We don't tend to be tolerant of the intolerant, and this predisposition could rise.

Let's return to the nones. It's possible to assert that as we grow decreasingly religious in our country we will see increasing conflict. Dawkins and Coyne revel in such notions. My conclusion, however, heads partly in the opposite direction: as nones remain more open to religion without the hard edges—and even the spirituality of science—a closer collaboration is on the horizon. In reviewing the research noted above I've discovered that the majority of emerging adults find a conflict between science and religion unnecessary and ineffectual. To be sure, they've heard others argue, and they're certainly aware that warfare is in the air. But many emerging adults are not convinced about this approach. They have become fatigued with the culture wars. And even those emerging adults that identify with the church don't want it to teach defective science. This is how I make sense of Pew findings from 2015: "Respondents who have no religious affiliation are the most likely to think that science and religion, in general, are often in conflict, with 76% expressing this view."[34]

In this book I have focused on research of millennials, those who became adults in the twenty-first century (born 1981–1996) because that's the state of the art.[35] (As I've mentioned above—but it is worth repeating—I'm less invested in the specifics of each generation than in how they will help us see the contours of the future.) There is also some emerging research to indicate that the next wave of churchgoing teens, born between 1999 and 2015 and dubbed "Gen Z" by some, including the Barna Group, are deeply concerned that "The church seems to reject much of what science tells us about the world." Forty-nine percent of churchgoing teens, according to Barna, perceive this to be true of the church.[36]

Overall, emerging adults seem discontent with either religious or anti-religious intolerance. If we can conclude anything, as nones increase there will be an uptick in antipathy toward antipathetic views of science and religion. That last sentence was, of course, a double negative stated positively. I foresee a modest, but discernible, increase in those who see a positive relationship between science and religion for themselves. As Americans become less conventionally religious they also become less personally conflicted with science. The numbers here are hard to find, but one 2015 Pew poll discovered, without distinguishing age demographics, "Among those with a religious affiliation, 34% say their religious beliefs conflict with science, down from 41% in 2009."[37] Even among the affiliated, antipathy toward science is decreasing, and this could be the increasing influence of aging

164 Major trends

millennials (and, frankly, death among older generations). Moreover, the data on those outside congregations supported a similar conclusion—of a decreasing conviction, and even appetite, for enmity: "Among the religiously unaffiliated, 16% say their own religious beliefs sometimes conflict with science while fully 81% say they do not."[38]

Philip Clayton's comments make particular sense of the growth of the nones along with a greater spiritual openness. He recognizes that only a minority of nones are actually atheistic. More characteristic of the nones is their spiritual openness, and since we are in such agreement—and he's also willing to make observations that support my forecasts—I'll cite him at length (and notice the sentences that sounds like bricolage or streaming spirituality, which I'll italicize):

> Interest in the spiritual approach to science has grown rapidly in recent years. It's no coincidence that these same years have seen a rapid decrease in participation in organized religion. The no-longer-affiliated or "Nones" have described themselves as "spiritual but not religious" or "spiritual independents." *They may practice yoga or meditation without much attention to traditional Hindu or Buddhist teachings. They may find spirituality in different places: in nature or music, in being with friends or making love. They may tie together bits of sacred texts and practices without feeling that they have to be at home in just one.* [39]

The nones will bring, as far as I can tell, an openness that will defuse conflict so often brought by fundamentalisms, both religious and atheistic.

Will this be at the level of intense systematic truth claims between these fields of knowledge? Note here that it is not critical for the emerging adults I've interviewed to achieve consistency in systems of knowledge or in epistemic claims.[40] Although this is certainly possible, ethical and emotional concerns present more possibilities. They want collaboration or independence on an emotional level.

Put another way, will Whitehead's Challenge be answered? Will this be the resolution to the conflict between science and religion? Not exactly, but it holds some intriguing possible results, and theorists and practitioners need new methods for this new reality.

Toward new modes, new models

These emerging-adult attitudes clearly leave room for those who work in the interaction of religion and science—both as practitioners (priests, pastors, rabbis, imams, and less formally recognized authorities) and theorists (religious studies professors, journalists, public intellectuals)—to embrace all its complexity. This implies, from my argument throughout this book, that as scholars we can move beyond merely reporting and analyzing within the warfare thesis toward something more generative and integrative.

One caveat for scholars: America is experiencing a growing and continuing antipathy toward experts, which came to the foreground in the election of Donald

Trump, a President with no political or military experience who boasted that his intuition takes precedence over experts and whose Republican Party represents an outlier as the only political party of a developed nation to reject the science of climate change. I have noted American individualism throughout this book, which doesn't work with scientific consensus. "You're entitled to your own opinion, but you're not entitled to your own facts" (to cite a saying I've seen attributed to Daniel Patrick Moynihan). Edward Larson commented on the Scopes Trial and brilliantly extended this insight: "Indeed, the issues raised by the Scopes trial and legend endure precisely because they embody a characteristically American struggle between individual liberty and majoritarian, and cast it in the timeless debate over science and religion."[41] The sovereignty of individual authority resists mainstream scientific consensus and will not produce the common good in America. Added to that characteristic our conviction that democracy means "don't listen to anyone simply because they're in charge" and we see the antipathy toward experts that's bound up with resistance to climate change, vaccines, and evolution.

It also means that many old models are defective, as Joshua Reeves has recently argued quite persuasively.[42] Today, he concluded, "philosophers of science spend much of their time working on specific issues arising from scientific theories," and so, "It is time for the field of science and religion to make a similar shift away from essentialism."[43] He presents three anti-essentialist models. "The first possibility is that the field should become more descriptive in orientation, producing research to explore the shifting boundaries of science and religion over time and describing how the categories function in current controversies."[44] The main issue here is that Christian scholars often presented putatively "scientific" approaches but smuggled in Christianized "religion-in-general." "A second way forward for religion and science scholars would be to embed themselves as much as possible in active scientific research programs."[45]

The third way (and, as these typologies work, the final most often represents the author's proposal) notes that an essentialist approach to categories has to be rejected, but "the lesson of essentialism is that we should reform our use of categories, rather than abandon them all together."[46] This approach takes seriously that religion is not a natural kind, but a social construction, which doesn't need to create a vicious circle—we define what we then continuously reject. Indeed (and this is my language) it can lead toward a humble approach in connecting science and religion. Along these lines, Reeves prefers to speak of *maps*:

> Maps filter out most features of the terrain in order to represent objects of cartographical significance to the person and communities that produced it. In the same way, our categories can be judged on how well they help travelers through the tangled brush of Western intellectual history and can be revised as we discover uncharted territories or improve our techniques.[47]

Certainly, the problem of *essentialism* that Reeves proposes, following Harrison's proposal for *territories,* is reasonably clear to many scholars of science and religion. It

166 Major trends

presents another crumbling of Barbour's well-worn typology. We are no longer in the present of science and religion (as I've defined it), but the future. Following Harrison, Reeves presents a kind of open and in-process interface between science and religion, which is alluring but, given my analysis, falls short. This methodology cannot fully comprehend today's streaming spirituality and the changes in science and technology since the mid-1960s.

Thus I will add to Reeves's and Harrison's insights. In light of growing pluralism, we need new theoretical models to curate this conversation with religious bricoleurs and their streaming-service mix of spiritual inputs. Previously we could take refuge in the "science and religion" model. Two entities, or things, have one relationship, which is easy conceptually to grasp. And even if we add a *tertium quid* of philosophy, that still essentially represents one relationship, albeit mediated by a third party. A splintered American religious life, however, as well as a greater sensitivity to the nuance of what constitutes "science" and "technology" and the inability to find a monolithic "scientific method," all make the task dizzyingly and excitingly pluriform. Zainal Abidin Bagir rightly noted that this simple "and" between "science *and* religion" conceals a plethora of complications, principal among them that both are primarily about ideas.[48] (We return again to Evans's insights.) But there are other concerns: as Americans we are not only facing the situation of *religion* (in the singular) and the way it interacts with science, we are coming to grips with the variety of *religions*—not only the five classic world religions of Hinduism, Judaism, Buddhism, Christianity, and Islam, but also religious traditions with large numbers of adherents such as Sikhism, Wicca, and neopaganism generally, and indigenous religions as well. What does it mean to bring religious pluralism to scientific insights? Bagir rightly highlights we need to take in "the pluralistic landscape" and concludes that this approach "requires not simply inviting more participants from different religious traditions but also demands the expansion of the conceptions of 'science' and 'religion.'"[49] If it sounds like I'm returning to a theme I raised in the Introduction, my point has not been lost. American individualism affects all that we think and do culturally. It leads to rampant pluralism—and all its complexity, wonder, and, to some degree, dread—and that significantly affects how we view this simple *ménage à deux*, "science and religion."

Would it be possible to construct a religion and science model, which emerging-adult spiritual bricoleurs bring, that is decentered and takes in the various slices of religion while countenancing the pluriform, non-essentialist nature of the topic?

Toward a truly pluralist model

Drawing on Michael Welker's analysis of Whitehead's philosophy, here are some directions toward a truly pluralist model for integrating science and religion.[50]Welker appropriated Whitehead's metaphysical model through two key characteristics: it is *polycontextual* and *multiperspectival*, with no single perspective being privileged.

What do these terms mean? *Polycontextual* means that each context sets its own "relative actual world" (to employ Whitehead's language). It refers to the concrete coordinates in time and space of the individual entities that experience the world. I remember experiencing the devastating 2018 Camp Fire centered in Paradise, California, adjacent to Chico, where I live. What was *the* context? Was it the houses consumed by the flames? Was it the eerie quiet at Chico State as I walked to class and a black cloud gradually filled the skies? Was it—as I've talked with several students later who told me "the Camp Fire didn't affect me"—that life was reasonably normal? There appears to be no one "world" on November 8, 2018, and there is no one universal perspective to find the unity of the world; as Welker summarizes, "The objective unity of the world is mediated by nothing except concrete individual occasions."[51]

Thus, Welker continues, as these individual "occasions" (to use Whitehead's language) or events perish, they integrate with other occasions and unify into a "relative actual world."[52] Noteworthy is that this theme of "perishing" for Whitehead is the process for this mediated unity: only in light of continual perishing, the inescapable reality of the process of becoming, do actual occasions attain unity. Whitehead reflected on his philosophy of organism and highlighted the concept of "perishing": "Almost all of *Process and Reality* can be read as an attempt to analyze perishing on the same level as Aristotle's analysis of becoming."[53]

Where then is the unity of this world of science and religion? Only in the interactive network of individual occasions. Again I cite Welker, "the world remains polycontextual and thinkable only in this 'network' which is to be multi-perspectivally adjusted. Yet Whitehead's cosmology lets us comprehend the "dynamic effort of the World into everlasting unity.'"[54]

This, I assume, needs some translation or at least explication. The *multiperspectival* adjustment takes in that no single perspective is privileged and represents the exchange from all standpoints that produces a network of interconnections. Only in this network of relations does the world attain unity. Does this sound complicated? Yes. Would it be easier to assemble the world of science and religion in a monolithic framework? Absolutely. But I hope everything I've written to this point stands as an angel at the east of Eden preventing a return to the garden of unity.

Instead, the task before us is to create a framework for a world of streaming spirituality that needs the particular contexts while countenancing a many-to-many metaphysics. In principle (because I haven't achieved this yet), I advocate a Lakatosian-type *research programme* [55] that develops a similar polycontextual and multi-perspectival model specifically addressing sciences and religions. The polycontextuality would frankly extend a dialogue to establish how to understand a particular environment or context (which has some resonance with Reeves's second category). For example, what is the relative actual world in which a streaming mix of Christian teaching with Buddhist practice engages the insights of Artificial Intelligence? In fact, this task is so complex that it would take another book, and so I'll leave it with those notes here.

And, yet, I'm quite sure this task needs to be accomplished.

168 Major trends

Final thoughts on what I've learned

The experiment of our country is exhibited in its rugged founding through the Puritans (and many others), as well as the exclusion of those not considered participants, such as Native Americans, African slaves, women. This is the dialectic of expansive exploration and freedom along with oppressive restriction to these very goods. These countervailing forces mark the dream of America and its limitations. It's this context in which we have negotiated the relationship of science and religion—where we have blended various forms of belief with unbelief, rationality and emotion, in a sometimes uneasy mix that produces shrill voices like Robert Ingersoll and Charles Finney in the nineteenth century and Ken Ham and Jerry Coyne in the twentieth.

We seem to love both religion and science, and their ongoing presence in our culture is secure, even if our recalcitrant individualism gives us license to pick and choose its findings and implications. Moreover, because of our unrelenting insistence on freedom and the power of the market, we will also innovate in how we promote religion. Given our propensity for religious life in the United States, albeit modified by the streaming-service approach, our future will certainly hold a new blending of various inputs.

In some ways this turbulent mix represents a fundamental component to American life, in which we negotiate science and religion's relationship; and here I return to James Gilbert's insight, "The dialogue between science and religion in America expresses essential ideas and deep-seated structures of culture."[56] I've learned, in the process of writing this book, that it's better for us when neither religion nor science dominates, but when they exist in healthy tension.

And what we do in this country resonates throughout the world. We are, to be sure, a remarkably religious people with indicators of religiosity much higher than should be the case for an industrialized nation. Though some will strive to separate religious or spiritual life from humanity, this seems to be a task with limited effect. We are *Homo religioso*—a fact undergirded by contemporary scientific studies.[57] Or as Lewis Mumford (1895–1990) once quipped, "Man does not live by machine alone."[58] What we know and discover must be set within a larger context of narrative (or myth), community, and ethos. I've learned that trying to negotiate the relationship between these two poles, represented conveniently, and sometimes quite loosely, by *religion* and *science*—the rational, taxonomizing, and analytic, alongside the emotional, integrating, and synthetic—constitutes a key part of what it means to be human, and not simply what it means to be American. If these are struggling, it's due to a struggle we face as human beings.

In order to find the right dialectic between religion and science in America, some will blend a variety of spiritual inputs while others will find they can hold to a traditional religion and make necessary adjustments, which doesn't imply eschewing our Christianity entirely. Even as it wanes, the characteristically Christian, and even Protestant, character of America will endure. As for those, like myself, who hold to a religious tradition, I want my faith to engage with mainstream science. And most Americans, religious or otherwise, do not see a conflict. As Ecklund and Scheitle commented, "After five years of research, here is what we know: Religious Americans of all types are interested in and appreciate science."[59] In fact, science and religion have a long, worthy history together.

Of course, others find themselves heading in a more pluralistic direction, which blends in streaming spirituality. This indeed summarizes a great deal of what I have sought to do in these pages. For the sake of our souls individually and as a nation—and I mean *soul* in the broadest definition possible, as that elevating aspect in human life—we will do best when we learn to bring together science and religion into the integrated whole, or at least into a détente. It does not seem warranted to insist, along the lines of Dawkins and Johnson, and White and Draper before them, that these two must fight it out to the death. That might signal the death of our culture's vitality.

We might have hoped for a conclusive answer to Whitehead's Challenge, but it's most likely another set of responses in an ongoing historical process. Nevertheless, this unique American vitality—found in negotiating "the force of our religious intuitions, and the force of our impulse to accurate observation and logical deduction," (per Whitehead)—is what I believe we're after. It might even define a key component of what it means to be an American. We need both in our culture in a vital interplay. And, thankfully, I think that's where we're headed.

In Chapter Three I dedicated a few pages to analyzing Jonathan Edwards, especially his emphasis on beauty, because that's where a fruitful dialogue occurs: around beauty as a nexus.[60] If a rapprochement, a reconciliation, or even an integration can be found between these two cultural forces, beauty is an essential component. There we find the common good for America, "life, liberty, and the pursuit of happiness." And the response is inherently beautiful as well.

Notes

1 Andrew Delbanco, "Andrew Delbanco: The Real American Dream: A Meditation on Hope," a lecture at the Gilder Lehrman Institute, Harvard University, December 10, 2010, retrieved June 20, 2019, https://vimeo.com/17684400. It also appears in his book.

2 Andrew Delbanco, *The Real American Dream: A Meditation on Hope* (Cambridge, MA: Harvard, 2000), 97–8.

3 Frank Newport, "2017 Update on Americans and Religion," retrieved June 24, 2019, https://news.gallup.com/poll/224642/2017-update-americans-religion.aspx.

4 Pew Research Center, "Religious Landscape Study," retrieved June 26, 2019, https://www.pewforum.org/religious-landscape-study.

5 Pew Research Center, "The Future of World Religions: Population Growth Projections, 2010–2050," APRIL 2, 2015, retrieved July 29, 2019, https://www.pewforum.org/2015/04/02/religious-projections-2010-2050.

6 Daniel Cox and Robert Jones, "America's Changing Religious Identity," Public Religion Research Institute (PRRI), retrieved June 26, 2019, https://www.prri.org/research/american-religious-landscape-christian-religiously-unaffiliated.

7 Philip Schwadel and Gregory A. Smith, March 18, 2019, "Evangelical approval of Trump remains high, but other religious groups are less supportive," http://www.

170 Major trends

pewresearch.org/fact-tank/2019/03/18/evangelical-approval-of-trump-remains-high-but-other-religious-groups-are-less-supportive.

8 I came across this idea in an article by Thomas H. Aechtner entitled very succinctly "Social Scientists" in Jeff Hardin, Ronald L. Numbers, and Ronald A. Binzley, eds., *The Warfare Between Science and Religion: The Idea That Wouldn't Die* (Baltimore: Johns Hopkins University Press, 2018), 302ff. Aechtner notes that sociologists and anthropologists, especially in introductory college texts on their fields, produce wildly hyperbolic statements about the warfare between science and religion.

9 Habermas, *The Philosophical Discourse of Modernity*, trans. Frederick G. Lawrence. (Cambridge: Polity Press, 1990), 2.

10 Ibid.

11 Jürgen Habermas, *An Awareness of What is Missing: Faith and Reason in a Post-secular Age* (Cambridge: Polity Press, 2010).

12 Habermas, "Notes on a post-secular society." *New Perspectives Quarterly* 25 (2008): 17–29. Cf. Charles Taylor's massive study, *The Secular Age* (Harvard: Harvard University Press, 2007).

13 Delbanco, *Real American Dream*, 116, citing *Democracy in America*.

14 Ibid.

15 Ibid.

16 E.g., Ric Machuga, *Three Theological Mistakes* (Eugene, OR: Wipf and Stock, 2015); Stephen Mumford, "Causal Dispositionalism," in *Properties, Powers, and Structures: Issues in the Metaphysics of Realism*, ed. Alexander Bird, B.D. Ellis, and Howard Sankey (New York: Routledge, 2012); W. R. Stoeger, "Contemporary Physics and the Ontological Status of the Laws of Nature," Robert Russell, Nancey Murphy, Christopher Isham, eds., *Quantum Cosmology and the Laws of Nature*, Scientific Perspectives on Divine Action: vol. 1 (Berkeley, CA: Vatican Observatory Publications; Center for Theology and the Natural Sciences, 1993), 209–34.

17 E.g., Olli-Pekka Vainio, *Cosmology in a Theological Perspective* (Grand Rapids: Baker, 2018); Joshua Swamidass, *The Genealogical Adam and Eve: The Surprising Science of Universal Ancestry* (Downers Grove, IL: IVP Academic, 2019); Gary Fugle, *Laying Down Arms to Heal the Creation-Evolution Divide* (Eugene, OR: Wipf & Stock, 2015).

18 Thomas Oord, *The Uncontrolling Love of God: An Open and Relational Account of Providence* (Downers Grove, IL: IVP Academic, 2015).

19 Michael Lipka, "10 facts about atheists," Pew Research Center June 1, 2016, retrieved June 26, 2019, https://www.pewresearch.org/fact-tank/2016/06/01/10-facts-about-atheists.

20 Ibid.

21 Elaine Howard Ecklund and Christopher P. Scheitle, *Religion vs. Science: What Religious People Really Think* (Oxford: Oxford University Press, 2018), 57.

22 Ecklund and Scheitle, *Religion vs. Science*, 57.

23 Liptka, "10 facts about atheists."

24 Stephen Greenblatt, *The Swerve: How the World Became Modern* (New York: W.W. Norton & Company, 2011).

25 Greg Cootsona, *Mere Science: Bridging the Divide with Emerging Adults* (Downers Grove, IL: InterVarsity, 2018), chapter one.

26 Michael Lipka, "Millennials Increasingly are Driving Growth of 'Nones,'" Pew Research Center, May 12, 2015, retrieved June 26, 2019, http://www.pewresearch.org/fact-tank/2015/05/12/millennials-increasingly-are-driving-growth-of-nones.

27 Ibid.

28 Ibid.

29 Dalia Fahmy, "Key Findings about Americans' Belief in God," Pew Research Center, April 25, 2018, retrieved May 23, 2019, https://www.pewresearch.org/fact-tank/2018/04/25/key-findings-about-americans-belief-in-god.

30 See, for example, John H. Evans, *Morals Not Knowledge: Recasting the Contemporary U.S. Conflict Between Science and Religion* (Oakland: University of California Press, 2018), 86–96.
31 Ecklund and Scheitle, *Religion vs. Science*, 16.
32 E.g., Evans, *Morals Not Knowledge*, 86–96, 108–09, 119–36, 147–48.
33 Pew Research Center, "Religious Differences on the Question of Evolution," February 4, 2009, https://www.pewforum.org/2009/02/04/religious-differences-on-the-question-of-evolution, retrieved July 29, 2019.
34 Pew Research Center, "Religion and Science," October 22, 2015, retrieved June 26, 2019, https://www.pewresearch.org/science/2015/10/22/science-and-religion.
35 Michael Dimock, "Defining generations: Where Millennials end and Generation Z begins," Pew Research Center, January 17, 2019, retrieved May 23, 2019, http://www.pewresearch.org/fact-tank/2019/01/17/where-millennials-end-and-generation-z-begins.
36 Barna Group, *Gen Z: The Culture, Beliefs and Motivations Shaping the Next Generation* (Barna Group, 2018), 71.
37 Pew Research Center, "Perception of Conflict Between Science and Religion," October 22, 2015, retrieved June 26, 2019, https://www.pewresearch.org/science/2015/10/22/perception-of-conflict-between-science-and-religion.
38 Ibid.
39 Philip Clayton, *Science and Religion: The Basics*, 2nd edition. (New York: Routledge, 2019), 59–60.
40 This parallels what John Evans writes in "The View from the Street," Hardin et al., eds., *The Warfare Between Science and Religion: The Idea That Wouldn't Die* (Baltimore: Johns Hopkins University Press, 2018), 330ff.
41 Edward Larson, *Summer for the Gods: The Scopes Trial and America's Continuing Debate Over Science and Religion* (New York: Basic, 1997), 265.
42 Joshua Reeves, *Against Methodology in Science and Religion: Recent Debates on Rationality and Theology*, Routledge Science and Religion Series (Oxfordshire: Routledge, 2018).
43 Ibid., 126.
44 Ibid., 129.
45 Ibid., 131.
46 Ibid., 133.
47 Ibid., 135.
48 Zainal Abidin Bagir, "The 'Relation' between Science and Religion in the Pluralistic Landscape of Today's World" *Zygon*, 50 (2015):405–7, especially 406; cf. Geoffrey Cantor and Chris Kenny, "Barbour's Fourfold Way: Problems with His Taxonomy of Science-Religion Relationships," *Zygon*, 36 (2001): 778.
49 Bagir, "The 'Relation,'" 216.
50 Gregory Cootsona, *God and the World: A Study in the Thought of Alfred North Whitehead and Karl Barth* (Frankfurt: Peter Lang, 2001), which builds on Michael Welker, "Alfred North Whitehead's Basic Philosophical Problem: The Development of a Relativistic Cosmology." *Process Studies* 16 (1987): 1–25.
51 Welker, "Whitehead's Basic Philosophical Problem," 24.
52 Ibid.
53 A.N. Whitehead, *Essays in Science and Philosophy* (New York: Philosophical Library, 1948), 87.
54 Welker, "Whitehead's Basic Philosophical Problem," 24, citing A.N. Whitehead, *Process and Reality:* Corrected Edition, David Ray Griffin and Donald W. Sherburne, eds. (New York: Free Press, 1978 [1929]), 349/530.
55 I am alluding to the philosophy of science that Imre Lakatos presented, centered around "research programmes." See Imre Lakatos, "Falsification and the Methodology of Scientific Research Programmes," in *Criticism and the Growth of Knowledge*, ed. Imre Lakatos and Alan Musgrave (Cambridge: Cambridge University Press, 1970), 91–106.

172 Major trends

56 James Gilbert, *Redeeming Culture: American Religion in an Age of Science* (Chicago: University of Chicago, 1997), 332,
57 Justin Barrett, *Born Believers: The Science of Children's Religious Belief* (New York: Free Press, 2012).
58 Gilbert, *Redeeming Culture*, 61.
59 Ecklund and Scheitle, *Religion vs. Science*, 139
60 See my article, "How Nature and Beauty Can Bring Scientists and Theologians Together." *Theology and Science* 9. Vol. 4 (2011): 379–93.

Bibliography

Bagir, Zainal Abidin. "The 'Relation' between Science and Religion in the Pluralistic Landscape of Today's World." *Zygon*, 50 (2015): 403–417.

Barna Group. *Gen Z: The Culture, Beliefs and Motivations Shaping the Next Generation*. Barna Group, 2018.

Barrett, Justin. *Born Believers: The Science of Children's Religious Belief*. New York: Free Press, 2012.

Bell, Rob. *What We Talk About When We Talk About God*. San Francisco, CA: HarperOne, 2014.

Cantor, Geoffrey and Chris Kenny. "Barbour's Fourfold Way: Problems with His Taxonomy of Science-Religion Relationships." *Zygon*, 36 (2001): 765–781.

Clayton, Philip. *Science and Religion: The Basics*. 2nd edition. New York: Routledge, 2019.

Cootsona, Gregory S. *God and the World: A Study in the Thought of Alfred North Whitehead and Karl Barth*. Frankfurt: Peter Lang, 2001.

Cootsona, Gregory S. "How Nature and Beauty Can Bring Scientists and Theologians Together." *Theology and Science*, 9, vol. 4 (2011): 379–393.

Cootsona, Gregory S. *Mere Science: Bridging the Divide with Emerging Adults*. Downers Grove, IL: InterVarsity, 2018.

Cox, Daniel and Robert Jones. "America's Changing Religious Identity." Public Religion Research Institute (PRRI). Retrieved June 26, 2019. https://www.prri.org/research/american-religious-landscape-christian-religiously-unaffiliated

Delbanco, Andrew. *The Real American Dream: A Meditation on Hope*. Cambridge, MA: Harvard, 2000.

Delbanco, Andrew. "Andrew Delbanco: The Real American Dream: A Meditation on Hope." A lecture at the Gilder Lehrman Institute, Harvard University. December 10, 2010. Retrieved June 20, 2019. https://vimeo.com/17684400

Dimock, Michael. "Defining generations: Where Millennials End and Generation Z Begins." Pew Research Center. January 17, 2019. Retrieved May 23, 2019. http://www.pewresearch.org/fact-tank/2019/01/17/where-millennials-end-and-generation-z-begins

Ecklund, Elaine Howard and Christopher P. Scheitle. *Religion vs. Science: What Religious People Really Think*. Oxford, UK: Oxford University Press, 2018

Fahmy, Dalia. "Key Findings about Americans' Belief in God." Pew Research Center. April 25, 2018. Retrieved May 23, 2019. https://www.pewresearch.org/fact-tank/2018/04/25/key-findings-about-americans-belief-in-god

Fugle, Gary. *Laying Down Arms to Heal the Creation-Evolution Divide*. Eugene, OR: Wipf & Stock, 2015.

Gilbert, James. *Redeeming Culture: American Religion in an Age of Science*. Chicago, IL: University of Chicago, 1997.

Greenblatt, Stephen. *The Swerve: How the World Became Modern*. New York: W.W. Norton & Company, 2011.

Habermas, Jürgen. *The Philosophical Discourse of Modernity*. Translated by Frederick G. Lawrence. Cambridge, UK: Polity Press, 1990.

Habermas, Jürgen. "Notes on a post-secular society." *New Perspectives Quarterly*, 25 (2008): 17–29.

Habermas, Jürgen. *An Awareness of What is Missing: Faith and Reason in a Post-secular Age*. Cambridge, UK: Polity, 2010.

Hardin, Jeff, Ronald L. Numbers and Ronald A. Binzley, eds. *The Warfare Between Science and Religion: The Idea That Wouldn't Die*. Baltimore, MD: Johns Hopkins University Press, 2018.

Lakatos, Imre. "Falsification and the Methodology of Scientific Research Programmes." *Criticism and the Growth of Knowledge*. Edited by Imre Lakatos and Alan Musgrave. Cambridge, UK: Cambridge University Press, 1970, 91–106.

Larson, Edward. *Summer for the Gods: The Scopes Trial and America's Continuing Debate Over Science and Religion*. New York: Basic Books, 2006.

Lipka, Michael. "Millennials Increasingly are Driving Growth of 'Nones'." Pew Research Center. May 12, 2015. Retrieved June 26, 2019. http://www.pewresearch.org/fact-tank/2015/05/12/millennials-increasingly-are-driving-growth-of-nones

Lipka, Michael. "10 facts about atheists." Pew Research Center. June 1, 2016. Retrieved June 26, 2019. https://www.pewresearch.org/fact-tank/2016/06/01/10-facts-about-atheists

Machuga, Ric. *Three Theological Mistakes*. Eugene, OR: Wipf and Stock, 2015.

Mumford, Charles. "Causal Dispositionalism." *Properties, Powers, and Structures: Issues in the Metaphysics of Realism*. Edited by Alexander Bird, B.D. Ellis and Howard Sankey. New York: Routledge, 2012.

Newport, Frank. "2017 Update on Americans and Religion." Retrieved June 24, 2019. https://news.gallup.com/poll/224642/2017-update-americans-religion.aspx

Oord, Thomas. *The Uncontrolling Love of God: An Open and Relational Account of Providence*. Downers Grove, IL: IVP Academic, 2015.

Pew Research Center. "Religious Differences on the Question of Evolution." February 4, 2009. Retrieved July 29, 2019. https://www.pewforum.org/2009/02/04/religious-differences-on-the-question-of-evolution

Pew Research Center. "The Future of World Religions: Population Growth Projections, 2010–2050." April 2, 2015. Retrieved July 29, 2019. https://www.pewforum.org/2015/04/02/religious-projections-2010-2050

Pew Research Center. "Religion and Science." October 22, 2015. Retrieved June 26, 2019. https://www.pewresearch.org/science/2015/10/22/science-and-religion

Pew Research Center. "Perception of Conflict Between Science and Religion." October 22, 2015. Retrieved June 26, 2019. https://www.pewresearch.org/science/2015/10/22/perception-of-conflict-between-science-and-religion

Pew Research Center. "Religious Landscape Study." N.d. Retrieved June 26, 2019.https://www.pewforum.org/religious-landscape-study

Reeves, Joshua. *Against Methodology in Science and Religion: Recent Debates on Rationality and Theology*. Routledge Science and Religion Series. Oxford, UK: Routledge, 2018.

Rohr, Richard. *Immortal Diamond: The Search for Our True Self*. San Francisco, CA: Jossey-Bass, 2013.

Russell, Robert J., Nancey Murphy, Christopher J. Isham, eds. *Quantum Cosmology and the Laws of Nature. Scientific Perspectives on Divine Action*: Volume 1. Berkeley, CA: Vatican Observatory Publications; Center for Theology and the Natural Sciences, 1993.

174 Major trends

Swamidass, Joshua. *The Genealogical Adam and Eve: The Surprising Science of Universal Ancestry.* Downers Grove, IL: IVP Academic, 2019.

Taylor, Charles. *The Secular Age.* Cambridge, MA: Harvard University Press, 2007.

Vainio, Olli-Pekka. *Cosmology in a Theological Perspective: Understanding Our Place in the Universe.* Grand Rapids, MI: Baker, 2018.

Welker, Michael. "Hegel and Whitehead: Why Develop a Universal Theory?" In George R. Lucas Jr., ed. *Hegel and Whitehead: Contemporary Perspectives on Systematic Philosophy.* Albany, NY: State University of New York, 1986.

Welker, Michael. "Cosmic Piety in Whitehead's Works." *American Journal of Theology and Philosophy,* 7 (1986): 121–131.

Welker, Michael. "Alfred North Whitehead's Basic Philosophical Problem: The Development of a Relativistic Cosmology." *Process Studies,* 16 (1987): 1–25.

Welker, Michael. *Universalität Gottes und Relativität der Welt: Theologische Kosmologie im Dialog mit dem amerikanischen Prozessdenken nach Whitehead.* 2nd edition. Neukirchen-Vluyn: Neukirkener, 1988

Whitehead, Alfred North. *The Concept of Nature.* Cambridge, UK: Cambridge University Press, 1920.

Whitehead, Alfred North. *Science and the Modern World.* New York: Free Press, 1925.

Whitehead, Alfred North. *Religion in the Making.* Cambridge, UK: Cambridge University Press, 1927.

Whitehead, Alfred North. *Essays in Science and Philosophy.* New York: Philosophical Library, 1948.

Whitehead, Alfred North. *Process and Reality: Corrected Edition.* Edited by David Ray Griffin and Donald W. Sherburne. New York: Free Press, 1978 [1929].

APPENDIX A: SUMMARY OF *NEGOTIATING SCIENCE AND RELIGION IN AMERICA*

In 1925 the Harvard philosopher-scientist Alfred North Whitehead stated that the future of our civilization depended, to some degree, on how effectively we were able to relate science and religion, which he described as "the force of our religious intuitions, and the force of our impulse to accurate observation and logical deduction."

And thus the burden of this book: if indeed religion and science are central to America, where is their future relationship? (This would be a worthwhile question without its centrality, but that fact intensifies the need for an answer.) What do we do with the fact that about 70% of Americans see ultimate conflict between the teachings of science and religion, but that same percentage of believers don't see science conflicting with *their* faith? The past provides us with a guide to the present.

My Introduction highlights Whitehead's 1925 Challenge. I then outline the subsequent chapters. In Chapter Two I define key words. For example, the definitions of *science* and *religion* don't map exactly onto our usage. (The word *scientist*, for example, was not coined until the 1830s.) I then adapt Ian Barbour's iconic typology of how to relate the two: *conflict, independence,* and *integration.* Finally, despite challenges, I use the relation between science and religion as a way to understand American cultural life and the common good that we promote to define our country.

I sketch the answer out to how we've related science and religion in three phases: past, present, and future.

The **past** I define as approximately 1687 to 1966, with a division of 1859 in between, which comprise Chapters Three and Four. I freely admit that every historical division is clunky, somewhat arbitrary, and therefore distorting; nonetheless, I am employing three publication dates, Isaac Newton's *Principia* (1687), Charles Darwin's *Origin of Species* (1859), and Ian Barbour's *Issues in Science and Religion*

176 Appendix A

(1966). Between Newton and Darwin, the United States was officially founded and in that time it maintained a tensive relationship between rationality and *religious affections*, to use Jonathan Edwards's term. It was a period marked by an Enlightenment rationality, featured prominently in our nation's core documents, while at the same embodying a warmth of emotional life no less characteristic of America. In fact, I look at Edwards as an exemplary thinker who employed his impressive intellectual skills to hold together these two American cultural forces, even as the early eighteenth-century Great Awakening was booming. I contrast Edwards with Thomas Paine, who saw no way to combine rationalism with revealed religion, which marked our Revolutionary period. Grasping these two is an effective way to understand America culturally. In the early eighteenth century, though largely a time of cultural contentment combining science and religion, especially through Baconian induction and Scottish Common Sense Realism, one can discerns signs of a brewing discontent.

In Chapters Five through Seven I note that the Civil War interrupted the early reception of Darwin in America, and then chart what happened post-Darwin through to the modern study of science and religion with characters such as Andrew Dickson White, John William Draper, Charles Hodge, and Asa Gray, as well as events such as the rise of eugenics, modernism, the fundamentalist-modernist split, and the 1925 Scopes Trial. Here the United States was coming of age intellectually and culturally, and continued to find an uneasy relationship with a variety of impulses. Put another way, both religious expansion and scientific advances such as relativity and quantum theories sometimes worked in alliance, sometimes in antagonism, and sometimes in contented independence—and this blend marked a period of about 100 years from 1859 to 1966.

For the **present**, I begin in Chapter Eight with Barbour's 1966 *Issues* because—at least for the academic study of religion and science—this book defined the field. It emerged in the massive splintering that characterizes the Sixties, when the Christian church became increasingly disestablished and a variety of religious traditions more mainstreamed. Barbour helped us understand a more nuanced and effective approach to religion and science (than, for example, White's), even if scholars now see its significant limitations. During these years we saw the emergence of ideas that broaden the dialogue, such as Capra's *The Tao of Physics* and the Gaia Hypothesis. Chapter Nine takes us to the new millennium (a term I like because it sounds so grand) and analyzes the early twenty-first century interaction of religion and science through three key voices: Stephen Jay Gould, Richard Dawkins, and Francis Collins.

The final part peers into the **future** (which started somewhere around the second decade of the twenty-first century) by first—in Chapter Ten—analyzing research from key scholars on emerging adult attitudes about religion and science (seasoned with my own interviews and surveys) as signposts for the future. Chapter Eleven analyzes these views as a way to discern the contours of these future directions of science and religion in the United States: first of all, a world of new topics in science and religion—in which evolution and creation will be present—

but with concerns about topics such as sexuality, climate change, AI, and transhumanism increasing in importance. I then note some trends: the decreasing influence of Christianity and the further splintering of American religious life, a modest rise in atheism and agnosticism with a marked increase of the religious nones, and, finally, a decreased antipathy in the interaction of science and religion. And I close with final thoughts.

APPENDIX B: 2020 NOTES ON TOPICS TODAY AND FOR THE FUTURE

I've asked throughout this book: where is the relation between science and religion headed? What will be the topics? The attitudes of emerging adults are the key, since they mark the future, but they do not exhaust the reasons why I'm highlighting certain issues and directions—some are presented by the scientific discoveries themselves and by changes in religious sensibilities. What are the topics—or, perhaps better, set of topics?

I listed those topics, and here are my 2020 notes on the eleven key topics of the future.[1] In other words, I sensed that my specific answers would soon become dated, but they were worth setting in an appendix. But why eleven? I decided that it was a suitable constraint for how much to write because, to state the obvious, each of these are worthy of its own book. (In addition, even here I'm limiting myself to approximately 500–1,000 words each, and even sometimes I fail in this limitation.) Nonetheless, my goal is to provide a sufficient set of notes for your consideration, thus I've limited myself by not seeking to achieve the impossible goal of describing every possible question and subtopic. I try to sound them out with only one or two religious traditions, although, of course, this means I'm just beginning. This also means that in relaxing my intention to be thorough I'll become somewhat less academic and therefore perhaps less restrained and more user-friendly. To keep things brief, I'll focus on *why* a topic is important, with a few comments on *who* is currently setting the agenda and *what* they are talking about.

Have I missed some? Without a doubt. Still, I begin with the stalwarts, and move to newer, trending topics starting with the fourth (genetics et al.).

Religion and rationality

"Science is about evidence. Faith is about having none, but believing anyway." I hear that slogan from my college students, and frankly it continues to dominate

Appendix B   179

many of my classroom discussions. If they didn't think of it themselves, they may have Richard Dawkins to thank, who produces the perfect quotation: a gauntlet thrown down? "Faith means blind trust, in the absence of evidence even in the teeth of evidence."[2] Or to paraphrase Mark Twain, faith is "believing what you know ain't true."

And, of course, some measure of these challenges includes truth: theistic religious faith looks to an unseen reality, God, while science seeks to understand the workings of the natural world.[3] We must keep a healthy ingredient of independence of science and religion even as sometimes we see how they relate.

First of all I need to define *faith*, a virtue emphasized by the monotheism, e.g, Judaism, Christianity, and Islam. Faith is often misunderstood and misrepresented. It essentially represents reliance, fidelity, or trust (exemplified in the key New Testament word *pistis*). In this respect, the noted twentieth-century Christian author C.S. Lewis defined faith as "the art of holding on to things your reason has once accepted, in spite of your changing moods."[4] Faith in this case is fiduciary, holding on to sacred values, and thus a relationship with one's Creator.

Of course, not all religious traditions emphasize faith (and thus not all religions are "faiths"), which means an anti-religious cavil against "faith" can represent a category error. Buddhism, for example, focuses on *enlightenment*, since indeed the word *Buddha* has as its root "enlighten" or "awaken." For this and other reasons Buddhism and science will continue to draw interest, e.g., the Dalai Lama's *The Universe in a Single Atom: The Convergence of Science and Spirituality*,[5] *Buddhism and Science: Breaking New Ground*, edited by B. Alan Wallace,[6] and, more recently, Robert Wright's *Why Buddhism is True: The Science and Philosophy of Meditation and Enlightenment.*[7]

And this too is the place to engage with the question of faith in *sacred texts and science*. Another putative anti-rational element in religions is that their texts always look back, but science continually looks forward. In this respect Buddhism offers an openness to change its teachings based on new information. From the Kalama Sutta (ca. 250 BCE),

> Do not go upon what has been acquired by repeated hearing; nor upon tradition; nor upon rumor; nor upon what is in a scripture; nor upon surmise; nor upon an axiom; nor upon specious reasoning; nor upon a bias towards a notion that has been pondered over; nor upon another's seeming ability; Rather, when you yourselves know that these things are good; these things are not blamable; undertaken and observed, these things lead to benefit and happiness, then and only then enter into and abide in them.[8]

And, more recently, the Dalai Lama,

> Suppose that something is definitely proven through scientific investigation, that a certain hypothesis is verified or a certain fact emerges as a result of scientific investigation. And suppose, furthermore, that that fact is incompatible

180 Appendix B

with Buddhist theory. There is no doubt that we must accept the result of the scientific research.[9]

This has led Diana Eck to conclude that "there is a common agenda and method in the fact that both mind science of the Buddhist tradition and the exploration of the medical researchers are based on the traditions of experimentation. [Buddhism is] an experimental practice."[10]

A conversation needs to unfold further on integrating the varieties of sciences and technologies with various religious traditions that do not privilege faith. In addition, there needs to be a realization that even those religious traditions that privilege faith don't obviate scrutiny and rational reflection; in fact, following Anselm of Canterbury's famous dictum, faith seeks understanding (*fides quaerens intellectum*).

Divine action

I remember a comment, really an assertion, by David Sloan Wilson at a colloquium in which I participated several years ago. He was addressing participants in our discussion group, many of whom were conventionally Christian, and stated, "I can see how some sort of deity is possible with evolution, but not a personal God who intervenes in the world." This, of course, mirrors the God of Albert Einstein (and many other scientists) who commented: "I do not believe in a personal God and I have never denied this but have expressed it clearly. If something is in me which can be called religious then it is the unbounded admiration for the structure of the world so far as our science can reveal it."[11] Or as the late Stephen Hawking once declared, "One can't prove that God doesn't exist. But science makes God unnecessary ... The laws of physics can explain the universe without the need for a creator."[12]

As I've already written above, not all religions believe in a deity. But for those that do, there's a topic related to the rationality of religious belief in a scientific and technological age: God's action. Since the advent of Newton's mechanistic universe—and despite any contributions or adjustments from quantum physics—if science finds that we live in a closed box of cause and effect, then God cannot work, and theistic religion makes no sense.[13]

Robert John Russell has done some significant work on this topic. Taking into account a variety of scientific fields in the multi-volume series he co-edited, he presented NIODA, or Non-Interventionist Divine Action, in which God's action takes place in quantum indeterminancy. Other current models are Whitehead's persuasive non-omnipotent Deity, who lures each actual occasion toward Beauty and the Good but cannot act unilaterally.[14] In addition there is Thomistic dual causation, where God acts as primary cause and we and the rest of nature present secondary causation.[15] This is sometimes classified as *divine concurrentism*, in which natural events are caused by God and creatures, both directly and fully involved (or concurring) in bringing an effect, with proper awareness of the ontological difference between God and creatures.[16]

Islamic science emphasizes the powerful and unilateral actions of God in all events, and has sometimes edged toward—if not entered all the way into—occasionalism, as in the philosophy of Al Ghazali's rejection of causation.[17] Minimally, as Muzaffir Iqbal comments in *The Study Quran,*

> Built into the Quranic description of the cosmos is a teleology that anchors the physical cosmos in a metaphysical realm, thereby establishing an incontrovertible nexus between God and the cosmos, on the other hand, and whatever exists in the cosmos and its raison d'être, on the other ... anchoring of the physical cosmos and all that exists in it in a realm beyond the physical is utterly lost in modern science.[18]

Once again, careless talk problematizes a religious and scientific search for the common good. It also excludes a thoughtful discussion of divine action. The biologist J.B.S. Haldane wrote in 1934,

> My practice as a scientist is atheistic. That is to say, when I set up an experiment I assume that no god, angel, or devil is going to interfere with its course and this assumption has been justified by such success as I have achieved in my professional career.[19]

Lawrence Krauss, who quoted Haldane in an op-ed piece in the 2015 *New Yorker,* continues with this conclusion, "It's ironic, really, that so many people are fixated on the relationship between science and religion: basically, there isn't one. In my more than thirty years as a practicing physicist, I have never heard the word 'God' mentioned in a scientific meeting."[20] Even if Francis Collins can declare, "I am a scientist and a believer, and I find no conflict between those world views," and that "God can be found in the cathedral or in the laboratory. By investigating God's majestic and awesome creation, science can actually be a means of worship"[21]—those statements don't always seem like enough for Krauss and those of similar mind.

Many Americans, however, want God in science. Elaine Ecklund and Christopher Scheitle's research provides insight into what this means. They found that when they asked respondents to agree or disagree with this statement, "scientists should be open to considering miracles in their theories and explanations," 38% of Americans agreed, 21% disagreed, and 41% responded with no opinion. "Among evangelicals, *60% agreed that scientists should be open to considering miracles.*"[22] This, of course, makes Richard Dawkins go apoplectic: "Any belief in miracles is flat contradictory not just to the facts of science but to the spirit of science."[23] In addition, two-thirds of Americans and almost half of evangelicals (48%) also believe science and religion have a collaborative relationship, and this may imply a corollary, *when scientists allow God's action,* which also explains a related point of tension. Ecklund and Scheitle discovered that what they termed a

182   Appendix B

creator theology narrative focuses on God's role as master creator and maintains firmly established boundaries and a clear hierarchy between God's role and human role. Thus, technologies that appear to intervene at the beginning of human life and influence the direction of that life are seen as morally and theologically wrong because they place humans in a God-like creator role (i.e., "playing God").[24]

Some want God in science. Others are convinced that it's a mistake.

On a related note, science and religion cannot answer all questions. As for science, it's not clear to me that science can answer moral questions, which is patently evident from the history of eugenics in America, if nothing else. As I've written elsewhere, *science can inform, but not dictate ethics.* [25] In addition, science is always embedded in some metaphysics and is therefore incapable—without the help of philosophical reflection—to make general statements about meaning and reality.

In fact, science properly studies the natural world and its relations and its power of science resides in its limitations. As John Polkinghorne commented,

> Science's success has been purchased by the modesty of its explanatory ambition. It does not attempt to ask and answer every question that one might legitimately raise. Instead, it confines itself to investigating natural processes, attending to the question of how things happen. Other questions, such as those relating to meaning and purpose, are deliberately bracketed out. This scientific stance is taken simply as a methodological strategy with no implication that those other questions, of what one might call a "why" kind, are not fully meaningful and necessary to ask if complete understanding is to be attained.[26]

Evolution

To many, it's either the Bible or Darwin. And thus, to paraphrase Jesus's words about the poor (Mark 14:7), "Debates about evolution you will always have with you." This is *the* issue when I talk with people about science and religion on planes, in coffee shops, in the classroom, etc. Some, in fact, may assert that evolution represents an eternal hot button issue. Among those, a selected few, like David Jeremiah, can claim that by accepting evolutionary theory we may be placing ourselves in an eternally hot place: "modern evolutionism is simply the continuation of Satan's long war against God."[27]

But I will head in another, more mundane, direction. The consensus of mainstream science is clearly with evolution, as a theory that has guided scientific research in a variety of fields for over a century and a half. With that as a given, certain questions arise in relation to evolution: what does it mean to assert that God creates through evolutionary processes? What do we do with those who see this as contradictory to God's creation? How does this make us, as *Homo sapiens,* nothing entirely special in the animal kingdom?

Appendix B   183

On the face of it, Genesis 1–3 and the long evolution of the universe offer strikingly contrasting pictures of our biological origins, and one theological strategy has been to conceded the physical territory to the scientific picture and take solace in one's "absolute dependence" on God (Friederich Schleiermacher[28]) or "in an authentic stance toward [our] earthly predicament" (Rudolph Bultmann[29]). But I sense that's a bit too simple and convenient.

The topic of evolution also encompasses more than origins—e.g., the question of *human uniqueness:* Is *Homo sapiens* unique among the animals, descendants of Adam and Eve, and thus made in "God's image"?[30] Speaking of human uniqueness—which places us as separate from the rest of creation—other religious traditions, such as Hinduism and Jainism, connect all living creatures together. According to the former, "All living things have Ātman (self or soul), and all Ātman are parts of one Brahman, the one universal mind or consciousness that is the source of all things." Going one step further, "The Jains hold some of the most radical standards in this regard, based (again) on the belief that *all* living things have a soul of *jiva.*"[31] Does that provide a better foundation for connecting with scientific studies?

We now enter the region of topics that are trending. Because these are emerging, I can only briefly note their potential silhouettes and others will have to paint the cleaner and finer lines in years to come. These constitute topics under-represented in past studies of "science and religion."

Genetics, medicine, and the specter of eugenics

When I first began to write this book a colleague offered the topic of CRISPR (Clustered Regularly Interspaced Short Palindromic Repeat) as "one discovery away," and yet, in the meantime, it has already become a topic of great interest. CRISPR gene editing represents a powerful means of changing ourselves through gene therapies in ways that will affect future generations. In a March 30, 2019, lecture, Francis Collins described it as "coming out of nowhere five years ago," and offering a technique via an "enzyme like what you have in word processors that does search and replace." The technique is relatively easy and, as Collins also phrased, "High school students can do this. And that should worry you." [32] This plays on the important distinction between germline interventions, which affect future generations and which CRISPR can make, versus somatic cell interventions, which do not affect future generations.

This does seem like we've entered a brave new world. Fears abound, as do questions. Why not use this technology for the good? Why are religious people standing in the way like they've always done? Should we do something about this? Who decides what is an improvement? How do we strike the balance—to paraphrase Collins—between proper use for cures and reprehensible ones to create designer babies for the rich?

As of the writing and to answer the first question, CRISPR has been employed to great effect for sickle cell anemia, as *Nature* reported as early as 2016.[33] (To put

184 Appendix B

this in perspective, in the United States there are 100,000 people suffering from sickle cell anemia.) In March 2019, at the tenth anniversary conference for Bio-Logos (the religion and science organization that he helped start), Collins highlighted this significant contribution in CRISPR's use for cancer immunotherapy as well as spinal muscular atrophy, where a child is born with something akin to ALS and dies within a year or two.

And yet, on November 26, 2018, in Hong Kong there was the case of the Chinese scientist, He Jiankui, employing CRISPR to clone a baby.[34] And because He is Chinese, United States laws have no effect. Collins subsequently initiated a public discussion, as well as collaboration with leading scientists from other countries, on the possibility of a moratorium on germline experiments, particularly in light of CRISPR.[35] This controversy represents exactly the critical questions faced by gene editing.

In principle, eugenics in America is dead. For example, in May 2002, as Governor of Virginia, Mark Warner declared, "The eugenics movement was a shameful effort in which state government never should have been involved," and offered an apology to the 8,000 or so Virginia citizens sterilized from 1924 to 1979. And yet I am concerned that a new genetic zombie is rising. The power of these genetic interventions is that they arrive with a significant cost-benefit because there is always some standard of humanity inherent in their use. As our ability to modify human genetics increases, we could also weed out putatively undesirable traits like Down syndrome, a condition virtually eliminated in Iceland, where almost all mothers of the 80%–85% of those who take the test and receive a positive test abort fetuses with the condition. Termination rates after fetal diagnoses of Down syndrome in Denmark may be as high as 98%, and the rate is about two-thirds in the United States.[36] Could these technologies again be applied in veiled or overtly racist modes? Edwin Black poses this chilling question in light of the history of eugenics in America: "Will the twenty-first-century successor to the eugenics movement, now known as 'human engineering,' employ enough safeguards to ensure that the biological crimes of the twentieth century will never happen again?"[37]

It's worth adding another question. Will religious leaders and scientists be allowed to participate in the discussion of these scientific technologies? The Human Genome Initiative included a percentage of its funds to explore ethical ramifications, including theological assessments. When I was a Ph.D student at Berkeley's Graduate Theological Union it was exciting to hear Robert Russell and Ted Peters communicate some of these ethical deliberations.[38] I'm reminded of Christian Rosen's assessment, largely accurate in my view, about future conversations of genetic engineering.

> Although religious leaders were among some of the most vigorous participants in early debates about the new genetics, today they are largely marginalized, supplanted by a new class of professional bioethicists who work in the halls of academe, not the sanctuaries of churches or synagogues.[39]

This leads to the broader questions of medicine, which, to my mind, are often forgotten or underemphasized in the field of science and religion, and, along with those, end of life decisions and reproductive technologies. John Evans, in sensitizing me to the importance of morality in science and religion, demonstrated how this comes to a head with medical technologies, or "Technology Applied to the Body," where scientists are accused of "playing God"[40] by conservative Christians and most religious respondents when asked about whether the ability to change our genes should not be left to God alone. "There were three major reasons: that God works through humans; that we should transform the human if limited to God, God-given purposes; and that we have God-given free will to do both good and bad."[41]

Psychology, neuroscience, and the cognitive science of religion

Functional Magnetic Imaging Resonances (FMRIs) seem to show some fairly clear things about what happens inside our noggins. As the Harvard scientist Stephen Pinker asserts, "I want to convince you that our minds are not animated by some godly vapor or single wonder-principle."[42] Is Pinker right? Is God all in our heads? Or, even more, are my thinking and feeling—the components that make me— simply physical processes like digestion? And does science rid us finally of believing there's a soul?

The convergence between Buddhist approaches to the non-self or *anatta* and some forms of modern cognitive and neuroscience is striking, as is the openness in Buddhism to test religious truth or discard it. Moreover, the interest in the Buddhist practice of mindfulness has gained ground, and Matthieu Ricard's excellent article, "On the Relevance of Contemplative Science," offers a stunning connection between Buddhist meditation and science, concluding with their ultimate complementarity:

> Scientific and contemplative knowledge are not antagonistic to one another. However, there is a hierarchy not to be overlooked. Science gives priority to understanding outer phenomena and acting on the world, while contemplative traditions emphasize inner peace, the elimination of mental suffering, and making the mind lucid, serene, and altruistic. One experiences with things, the other with consciousness.[43]

The Cognitive Science of Religion (CSR), a term coined by Justin Barrett in 2000[44] and developed by many others (e.g., E. Thomas Lawson and Robert McCauley, Pascal Boyer, Harvey Whitehouse, and S.E. Guthrie[45]), brings together the cognitive sciences in the service of understanding religious belief and practice. Some believe that CSR leads to a naturalistic, positivistic explanation of religion. I've written elsewhere that CSR reinforces our notion that *Homo sapiens* is naturally religious,[46] and, particularly, we even have something like the "awareness of divinity" that John Calvin described.[47]

186 Appendix B

Cosmology and astrobiology

A key emphasis of religious traditions lies in their focus on the nature of the world, or the universe, and our place in it; to cite Immanuel Kant's oft-quoted phrase, "Two things fill me with wonder: the starry sky above and the moral law within." That starry sky above will remain a fascination. Certainly, any further insights via scientific cosmology will spark discussion. Recent astronomical discoveries have also highlighted the vast number of exoplanets (that is, planets beyond our own solar system)—currently running at almost 4,000.[48] Some assert that this means the sudden death of the Christian scheme of salvation since, according to the biblical texts, Jesus came to save this world (*kosmos* in Greek, e.g., John 3:16), but the cosmos was vanishingly small compared to our current understanding. Where is our place in the universe? Conversely, if this seems like a loss for Christianity could it be a gain for other religions?

In some ways the logic is disastrously circular—the known world of biblical times was small, and so why should we assume that the texts would address a twenty-first century universe? In addition, this concern is not entirely new. In the seventeenth century the scientifically and theologically minded Blaise Pascal considered his "brief span of life" and "the small space I occupy and which I see swallowed up in the infinite immensity of spaces of which I know nothing and which know nothing of me, I take fright and am amazed...."[49]

As one example, which I choose because it's decades old and predates (among other things) the discovery of exoplanets, C.S. Lewis took on these claims in his 1958 essay, "Religion and Rocketry." (Lewis himself was an avid amateur astronomer, who mounted a telescope on the balcony of his bedroom at The Kilns, his home near Oxford.) Lewis addressed Fred Hoyle's claims (like those of several other thinkers) who asserted that life must have originated in many times and places, given the vast size of the universe. Referring to a series of broadcast talks that Hoyle had given in 1950 (later published as *The Nature of the Universe*), Hoyle argued against a Christian view of origins and the uniqueness of the Christian faith, based on the size of the universe. Lewis also noted that, as a child, he learned an antiphonal view of the cosmos.

> When we were boys all astronomers, so far as I know, impressed upon us the antecedent improbabilities of life in any part of the universe whatever. It was not thought unlikely that this earth was the solitary exception to a universal reign of the inorganic. Now Professor Hoyle, and many with him, say that in so vast a universe life must have occurred in times and places without number. The interesting thing is that we have heard both these estimates used against Christianity.[50]

Lewis then addresses what the Christian Gospel might mean to these "hypothetical rational species."[51] They might be good and not need redemption (as the fallen human race does). They might be "strictly diabolical," but it seems most likely that this species might contain both good and bad. Like any missionary work, he concludes that the Christian duty is to preach the Gospel. And then he ends with this question,

> Would this spreading of the Gospel from earth, through man, imply a pre-eminence for earth and man? Not in any real sense. If a thing is to begin at all, it must begin in some particular time and place; and any time and place raises the question: "Why then and just then?" One can conceive an extraterrestrial development of Christianity so brilliant that earth's place in the story might sink to that of a prologue.[52]

How do we evaluate this proposal?[53] If nothing else, it demonstrates that concerns about life outside our solar system aren't new—speculating about life in other worlds goes back to the Middle Ages, as Olli-Pekka Vainio (and others) have recently demonstrated.[54] In any event, this is an exploding field and new astronomical discoveries will bring new questions and insights.

Big Data

As yet I don't see much writing or speaking on this in the popular press or in academic circles: religion and Big Data is a stealth topic. Big Data is explained (via a reasonably garden variety definition) as "data sets, typically consisting of billions or trillions of records, that are so vast and complex that they require new and powerful computational resources to process."[55] This new reality bequeathed to us by the power of computing has profound religious significance.

Admittedly, the presence of Big Data (as well as the field of Data Science) doesn't have the directness of creation and evolution (How do we read Genesis 1–3 as authoritative revelation and take in human evolution?) or astrobiology (If there is life on other planets, what does that mean about God's coming in a human being to save the world?). And yet, with a moment's reflection, if you're one of the 250 million or so smartphone users in the US then we must realize that our little, seven-ounce device tracks us at virtually every moment, records what it finds, and presents a data picture of who we are, what we like, and what we do.[56]

Some certainly promote Big Data as the scientific cutting edge. Consider two quotations. The first is from Pat Gelsinger, the Chief Executive Officer of VMware, who says, "Data is the new science. Big Data holds the answers," The second (to quote a phrase used for other purposes) is like unto it: "I keep saying that the sexy job in the next 10 years will be statisticians, and I'm not kidding," claims Hal Varian, Chief Economist at Google. When I, appropriately enough, googled "big data" I also found this: "Even Napoleon is reported to have quipped, 'War is 90% information.'"[57]

This topic is huge and emerging, and so I will simply lay out three sets of questions: 1) How do we as human beings conceive of the sheer volume of information? What tools do we need to help us manage these teraflops of data?; 2)

188 Appendix B

What should we do with this information? Who's is it—the individual's or an enormous, powerful, multinational high-tech corporation's? This is an especially tricky ethical question with healthcare. If my genetic information, for example, might lead a healthcare insurer to drop me from my coverage, do they have a right to know? 3) How do we cope with the "roving eyes" on us at all times? How does the Eye of Big Data relate to the omnipresence of our God? Is this deity benevolent? Does this give us comfort, concern, or some mix of both? Should information ever be discarded, especially that which reveals our sin, and then separated from us (to quote Psalm 103:12) "as far as the east is from the west"?

Technology, AI, and transhumanism

"Steam and electricity have tremendously increased the pace of life. Everybody is in a hurry. People have, indeed, been busy since the world began, but never have they rushed ahead in a haste so frantic as in this present," reported George Hodges, Dean of the Episcopal School of Cambridge, Massachusetts, in his 1896 Lowell Lectures.[58] And so the growth of technology and its effects are hardly new, but we need to add them as another category to science and religion. Earlier I noted the remark by Willem Drees, that the practice of science is embedded in technology, and for this reason at least it is increasingly central to the science and religion dialogue. Cell phones, laptops, video conferencing, and social media must be increasingly at the forefront as we consider science, especially for emerging adults. Simply put, 18–30-year-olds have only known a technologically saturated world, and technology must be brought to the top three or four topics, where formerly scientific and theological method, interactions with evolutionary biology, and cosmology have often appeared. This certainly connects with transhumanism and Artificial Intelligence (AI), which I will focus on here.

With technology, we gain mastery over the world, but the question is whether technology will soon master us. Films such as *Her* (about a man who falls in love with his operating system) and *Ex Machina* (about the creation of a beautiful, and ultimately dangerous, AI robot, Ava) are part of the landscape that affects emerging-adults' conceptions of science and religion. Add to this Ray Kurzweil's vision, which promotes a singularity where AI and human thinking will merge by 2045.[59]

What do I mean by *transhumanism*? Julian Huxley coined the term in 1967 to describe the belief that the creation, development, and use of technology will improve human physical, intellectual, and psychological capacities.[60] More contemporarily, Nick Bostrom writes that transhumanism

> promotes an interdisciplinary approach to understanding and evaluating the opportunities for enhancing the human condition and the human organism opened up by the advancement of technology. Attention is given to both present technologies, like genetic engineering and information technology, and anticipated future ones, such as molecular nanotechnology and artificial intelligence.[61]

But what do transhumanists promote? In addition to Bostrom's list, they also raise the topic of radical life extension, with Kurzweil quite clearly seeking a form of immortality where he is able to merge his brain with the Cloud and live forever. We shouldn't, however, equate transhumanism with radical life extension. According to one survey by Hank Pellissier, managing director of the Institute for Ethics and Emerging Technologies, about a quarter of transhumanists (23.8%) did not seek immortality; other reasons were our planet's overpopulation, boredom, and the yearning for an afterlife.[62] On the other hand, this drive toward immortality fascinates me, as it brings to mind whether religions are indelibly invested in death and afterlife. Will religions survive if human beings can survive indefinitely? Put another way, the question is one of *technological salvation*. Can technology be a means of enlightenment and salvation, and will we receive it?

Finally, AI brings the promise of technology to create minds like we have (or at least something that works the voice interface on my car). There are several definitions out there, and so I'll simply use *Science Daily*'s: "The modern definition of artificial intelligence (or AI) is 'the study and design of intelligent agents' where an intelligent agent is a system that perceives its environment and takes actions which maximizes its chances of success." And for what it's worth, John McCarthy coined the term in 1956 and defined it as "the science and engineering of making intelligent machines."[63] Moreover, the goal of strong AI is: "To develop artificial intelligence to the point where the machine's intellectual capability is functionally equal to a human's. Weak or narrow AI is that focused on one specific or narrow task (e.g., Siri on the iPhone)."[64]

AI also brings out the question: if we do create intelligence robots, will they be persons? And thus, will they have to pay taxes? More seriously, AI has garnered the attention of several high-tech firms, raising questions around the Turing Test, whether this means we have become gods as creators, and the existence of the soul.

The Turing Test,[65] which has continued to be a critical element in discussions of AI, particularly its philosophical and religious implications, deserves some measure of attention. The mathematician and computer scientist Alan Turing (1912–54) made a proposal to determine a machine's ability to exhibit intelligent, human-like behavior, indistinguishable from that of a human. He presented this test in his 1950 paper "Computing Machinery and Intelligence." It opened with the words: "I propose to consider the question, 'Can machines think?'" Because "thinking" is especially difficult to define, Turing chose to "replace the question by another, which is closely related to it and is expressed in relatively unambiguous words." Turing's new question was: "Are there imaginable digital computers which would do well in the *imitation game*?" This question, Turing believed, was one that could actually be answered. In the remainder of the paper he argued against all the major objections to the proposition that "machines can think." He proposed that a human evaluator would evaluate natural language conversation between a human and a machine designed to generate human-like responses. The evaluator would be aware that one of the two partners in conversation was a machine, and all participants would be separated from one another. The conversation would be limited to a text-only channel, such as a computer

190 Appendix B

keyboard and screen, so the result would not depend on the machine's ability to render words as speech. If the evaluator could not confidently tell the machine from the human, the machine would be said to have passed the test. The test results would not depend on the machine's ability to give correct answers to questions, only how closely its answers resembled those a human would give.

So where are we with the Turning Test? Has it been, or will it be, passed? In a 2017 *Futurism* article, Kurzweil was quoted as follows: "2029 is the consistent date I have predicted for when an AI will pass a valid Turing test and therefore achieve human levels of intelligence. I have set the date 2045 for the 'Singularity' which is when we will multiply our effective intelligence a billion fold by merging with the intelligence we have created."

Will we arrive? There is consistent speculation, but, even more, this will create questions with significant religious implications.

Race and a potential eugenics redux

Above, I've noted a few places where the construction of race, and especially racial superiority, has been tied to science; for that reason it's also promoted (as noted above) as "scientific racism."[66] Today I'm hearing a growing questioning of the status of race as a scientific category—for example, in the influential work of Alan Templeton. [67] The reason is partly that those who study science and religion are predominantly, and disproportionately, Caucasian (and male). In this respect we have to grapple—and by "we" I mean those of religious and scientific insight—with the social construction of race.

And with race arrives many other ills. One of the surprises of cultural life in contemporary America is the return of white supremacists and nationalists and the anti-immigration rhetoric that highlights certain countries (in this case, Latin American ones) and religions (Islam). I am concerned about the rhetoric against the immigrant that led to Donald Trump's election as President and how it mirrors the social concerns of the early twentieth century. "The essence of bigotry, including racism, is the belief that easily identified categories reliably predict behavior, intelligence, and character," wrote Dave Unander. [68] And Marouf A. Hasian, Jr., in his 1996 *The Rhetoric of Eugenics*, had already noted a "revival of eugenics" (and this, of course, before the mapping of the human genome and CRISPR). I see no reason to miss the same parallel in post-Trump America:

> Just as Americans in the 1990s are confronted with the specter of armies of homeless, dependent AIDS patients, and violent inner-city gangs, in the 1910s and 1920s the nation was concerned with what it termed problems of the feeble-minded, the congenital defectives, and other degenerates.[69]

In his study of race and eugenics in the southern states, Edward Larson examines how southern eugenicists were more vexed about "the deterioration of the Caucasian race than about any threat from the African race" and then presents this 1919 quotation from a white Louisiana physician: "What language can express the humiliation we should feel at seeing [our] race, physically, mentally and morally, slowly going to decay?"[70] As a grade-school child in the 1960s and early 1970s I remember growing up and learning about three primary human races: "Caucasoid, Negroid, and Mongoloid." How confusing those easy distinctions have become in light of the reality of mixed racial compositions and the fact that the relevant sciences don't support commonly held discriminating features distinctions based on race. Unander continues: "Genomics—reading DNA—is showing that all human populations carry most of the same genetic variations, contrary to what we would expect if 'races' existed."[71] In a related vein, Templeton concluded in his study of any biological basis for race, "Humans are an amazingly diverse species, but this diversity is not due to a finite number of subtypes or races. Rather, the vast majority of human genetic diversity reflects local adaptations and, most of all, our individual uniqueness."[72]

My hope is that skilled and informed contributors to this conversation will emerge. At any rate, it will continue to rise in importance for science and religion.

Sex and sexuality

We used to think science wasn't that sexy, now that's changed. Science has taught me to be sensitive to unexpected results in my hypotheses, and one of the results that arose in my qualitative interviews with emerging adults is they believe LGBTQ issues are plainly within the domain of science and religion. "Doesn't science tell us that we don't choose to be gay?" "Any church that doesn't embrace gay and lesbian Christians is bigoted and ignorant." What then does science tell us about transgender persons and transbinarity?

In addition, particularly in the interaction of traditional Christian sexual ethics, the science of psychology finds its way into discussions around same-sex orientation and ex-gay therapy, as Antony Alumkal outlined in his new book, *Paranoid Science*,[73] which came across my desk in writing this book. Alumkal describes how quickly, in terms of scientific paradigms, views about homosexuality changed among professional psychologists in the 20th century.

Any title that includes the word "paranoid" is probably a clue that the topic is still contested, and I've also learned that, because sex is a consistently hot topic with an immensity of possible directions, brevity can be helpful. And so I'll simply note for now that sex and sexuality, once considered secondary, need to become primary. Naturally, there has already been brilliant work done in journals, more so than in books since the former can more quickly integrate developing topics. The themes of sexuality and gender, and particularly their relationship to science and religion, have not made it into textbook-length treatments of core issues in standard textbooks because these sources move more gradually.[74]

Climate change

There are many in the field of science and religion that see *this*—global climate change—as *the* issue for science and religion. I can affirm that, at recent years'

192 Appendix B

meetings of the American Academy of Religion, near catholic consensus exists around this view. In his introduction to *Religion and Science: The Basics*, Philip Clayton writes,

> People used to tell me that discussions of how to relate science and religion are too abstract. No longer. Around the globe we are witnessing the strangest phenomena: there is universal agreement among scientists that humans are causing the climate of our planet to change; and there are clear teachings within every major religious tradition, from indigenous lifeways to New Age spiritualities, that the earth is to be protected and valued.[75]

Indeed, human-caused, or "anthropogenic," climate change represents a topic that increasingly comes to mind in science and religion discussions. The consensus among scientist is overwhelming, or well-nigh overpowering, that climate change really exists and that we human beings have caused it. As Clayton notes, many current models of climate change indicate effects that could last 1,000 years.[76] In that light, scientists can describe the consensus; as indeed the AAAS has done recently with increased vigor, even moving beyond its usual roles into more public advocacy and communication in 2018 when it launched How We Respond, "a new communication initiative to highlight how communities are actively and effectively responding to climate change at the local, state and regional levels, and demonstrate the critical role of science and scientists in informing these activities."[77]

On the religious side of the ledger, the three monotheistic religions of Judaism, Christianity, and Islam prioritize their call to stewardship, which is how I—along with many others—interpret the "dominion mandate" in Genesis 1.[78] Eastern religions have their own contributions. Buddhism, with its emphasis on compassion and the interconnection of all life, represents relevant teachings. Hindus and Jains describe a soul in all things, and the latter's accent on *ahimsa* can contribute a respect for all life.

The subject of climate change leads to the question of whether we have entered a new geological age, the Anthropocene, in which the dominant influence on climate, environment, and biological life is human activity. And herein lies a deep and tragic irony: *Homo sapiens* (i.e., us) is the most powerfully intelligent species on the planet, and we will probably not exist as long as other hominin ancestors. Fossil evidence for *Homo erectus* stretches over more than 1.5 million years, dwarfing the 400,000 years of our own species. As the Natural History Museum in London has remarked on *Homo erectus,* "we begin to appreciate their ability to survive over a long period marked by many changes to the environment and climate."[79] Indeed we seem to be causing our own short span of *species*.

And so my last scientific topic ends on an apocalyptic note, which may be itself a connection with religious themes.

In sum, those are my Top Eleven, somewhat briefly noted. I'm sure many readers of this book will have more ideas and topics, which I hope will become future contributions to the vital conversation of science and religion.

Notes

1 These have been compiled in conversation with Drew Rick-Miller, Se Kim, and Robert John Russell, among others.
2 Richard Dawkins, *The Selfish Gene*, 2nd edition. (Oxford: Oxford University Press, 1989), 198.
3 Cf. my definitions in chapter one for more detail.
4 C.S. Lewis, *Mere Christianity*. (New York: MacMillan, 1952), 141.
5 Dalai Lama, *The Universe in a Single Atom: The Convergence of Science and Spirituality* (New York: Morgan Road Books, 2005).
6 Alan B. Wallace, ed., *Buddhism and Science: Breaking New Ground* (New York: Columbia University Press, 2003).
7 Robert Wright, *Why Buddhism is True* (New York: Simon & Schuster, 2018).
8 Kalama Sutta, cited in Jake H. Davis and Owen Flanaga, *A Mirror is for Reflection: Understanding Buddhist Ethics* (Oxford: Oxford University Press, 2017), 106–7.
9 Wallace, *Buddhism and Science*, 77.
10 Diana Eck in Dalai Lama, Herbert Benson, Robert Thurman, Howard Gardner, Daniel Goleman, *MindScience: An East-West Dialogue* (Boston: Wisdom, 1999), 106.
11 Helen Dukas, *Albert Einstein the Human Side* (Princeton: Princeton University Press, 1981), 43.
12 Nick Watt, "Stephen Hawking: 'Science Makes God Unnecessary,'" September 7, 2010, retrieved June 26, 2019, https://abcnews.go.com/GMA/stephen-hawking-science-makes-god-unnecessary/story?id=11571150.
13 See "Causation" in Gary B. Ferngren, *Science and Religion: A Historical Introduction* (Baltimore: Johns Hopkins, 2002), 377–94.
14 A.N. Whitehead, *Process and Reality: Corrected Edition*, David Ray Griffin and Donald W. Sherburne, eds. (New York: Free Press, 1978 [1929]).
15 Ric Machuga, *Three Theological Mistakes* (Eugene, OR: Wipf and Stock, 2015); cf. Stephen Mumford, "Causal Dispositionalism," in *Properties, Powers, and Structures: Issues in the Metaphysics of Realism*, ed. Alexander Bird, B.D. Ellis, and Howard Sankey (New York: Routledge, 2012); W.R. Stoeger, "Contemporary Physics and the Ontological Status of the Laws of Nature," Robert Russell, Nancey Murphy, Christopher Isham, eds., *Quantum Cosmology and the Laws of Nature*, Scientific Perspectives on Divine Action: vol. 1 (Berkeley, CA: Vatican Observatory Publications; Center for Theology and the Natural Sciences, 1993), 209–34.
16 John Henry and Mariusz Tabaczek, "Causation" in Ferngren, *Science and Religion* 382.
17 Ibid., 380; cf. Stanford Encyclopedia of Philosophy, "Occasionalism," retrieved June 26, 2019, https://plato.stanford.edu/entries/occasionalism.
18 Muzaffir Iqbal, "Scientific Commentary on the Quran," in Seyyd Hossein Nasr, ed., *The Study Quran: A New Translation and Commentary* (San Francisco: HarperOne, 2015), 1693.
19 Quoted by Lawrence Krauss in "All Scientists Should Be Militant Atheists," *The New Yorker,* September 8, 2015, retrieved May 23, 2019, https://www.newyorker.com/news/news-desk/all-scientists-should-be-militant-atheists.
20 Ibid.
21 Francis Collins, "Why This Scientist Believes in God," *CNN* June 6, 2007, retrieved June 25, 2019, http://www.cnn.com/2007/US/04/03/collins.commentary/index.html.
22 Elaine Howard Ecklund and Christopher Scheitle, *Religion vs. Science: What Religious People Really Think* (Oxford: Oxford University Press, 2018), 28.
23 Ibid., 28.
24 Ibid., 125.
25 Greg Cootsona, *Mere Science: Bridging the Divide with Emerging Adults* (Downers Grove, IL: InterVarsity, 2018), 133–47
26 John Polkinghorne, "The Universe as Creation," in Michael L. Peterson, William Hasker, and Bruce Reichenbach, *Philosophy of Religion: Selected Readings* (Oxford: Oxford University Press, 2014), 551.

194 Appendix B

27 In his foreword to Henry Morris's *The Long War Against God*; cited by Alister McGrath, *Religion and Science: A New Introduction*, 2nd edition. (Oxford: Wiley-Blackwell, 2010), 46.

28 Friedrich Schleiermacher, *The Christian Faith*, H.R. Mackintosh and J.S. Stewart, eds. (Edinburgh: T&T Clark, 1989).

29 Bultmann in John Hedley Brooke, *Science and Religion: Some Historical Perspectives,* The Cambridge History of Science Series. (Cambridge: Cambridge University Press, 1991), 4.

30 I've written more on this in *Mere Science and Christian Faith, esp. chapter 5.*

31 Philip Clayton, *Science and Religion: The Basics.* 2nd edition. (New York: Routledge, 2019), 103.

32 Francis Collins, "What do YOU Believe, Doctor?" April 19, 2019, BioLogos 10th Anniversary Conference, retrieved June 25, 2019, https://biologos.org/resources/what-do-you-believe-doctor.

33 Heidi Ledford, "CRISPR Deployed to Combat Sickle-Cell Anaemia," *Nature News,* October 12, 2016, retrieved June 26, 2019, https://www.nature.com/news/crispr-deployed-to-combat-sickle-cell-anaemia-1.20782.

34 Antonio Regalado, "EXCLUSIVE: Chinese Scientists are Creating CRISPR Babies," *MIT Technology Review*, November 25, 2018, retrieved June 29, 2019, https://www.technologyreview.com/s/612458/exclusive-chinese-scientists-are-creating-crispr-babies.

35 Cf. Ariana Eunjung Cha, "CRISPR Babies Spur NIH Director to Call for Public Debate, New Oversight," *Washington Post,* December 28, 2019, retrieved June 29, 2019, https://www.washingtonpost.com/health/2018/12/20/crispr-babies-spur-nih-director-call-public-debate-new-oversight/?utm_term=.ec721662601e.

36 Julian Quinones Arijeta Lajka, CBS News, August 14, 2017, "'What Kind of Society Do You Want to Live in?' Inside the Country Where Down Syndrome is Disappearing," Aug 15, 2017, retrieved June 29, 2019, https://www.cbsnews.com/news/down-syndrome-iceland; cf. Snopes Fact Check, retrieved June 29, 2019, https://www.snopes.com/fact-check/iceland-eliminated-syndrome-abortion.

37 Edwin Black, *War Against the Weak: Eugenics and America's Campaign to Create a Master Race* (New York: Thunder's Mouth Press, 2003), 8.

38 One outcome, though not directly a part of the Human Genome Initiative, was Ted Peters's book, *Playing God? Genetic Determinism and Human Freedom,* 2nd edition. (London: Taylor & Francis, 2014).

39 Christine Rosen, *Preaching Eugenics: Religious Leaders and the American Eugenics Movement* (Oxford: Oxford University Press, 2004), 187

40 See John H. Evans, *Morals Not Knowledge: Recasting the Contemporary U.S. Conflict Between Science and Religion* (Oakland: University of California Press, 2018), 146, 145.

41 Ibid., 156.

42 Stephen Pinker, *How the Mind Works* (New York: W.W. Norton, 1997), 4.

43 Ricard in Wallace, *Buddhism and Science*, 278.

44 Justin Barrett, "Exploring the Natural Foundations of Religion," *Trends in Cognitive Sciences* 4, vol. 1 (2000): 29–34.

45 E.T. Lawson and R.N. McCauley, *Rethinking Religion: Connecting Cognition and Culture* (Cambridge: Cambridge University Press, 1990); Pascal Boyer, *The Naturalness of Religious Ideas* (Berkeley: University of California Press, 1994) and *Religion Explained: The Evolutionary Origins of Religious Thought* (New York: Basic Books, 2002); Harvey Whitehouse, *Modes of Religiosity: A Cognitive Theory of Religious Transmission*, Cognitive Science of Religion (Walnut Creek, CA: AltaMira Press, 2004); S.E. Guthrie, *Faces in the Clouds: A new theory of religion* (New York: Oxford University Press, 1993).

46 See Justin Barrett, *Born Believers: The Science of Children's Religious Belief* (New York: Free Press, 2012).

47 See Greg Cootsona, "Science and the *Sensus Divinitas*: The Promise and Problem of the Natural Knowledge of God," Connecting Faith and Science: Philosophical and Theological Inquiries (Claremont: Claremont School of Theology Press, 2018).

48 See NASA's website on "Exoplanet Exploration," retrieved June 25, 2019, https://exoplanets.nasa.gov.

49 Blaise Pascal, *Pensées*, trans. A.J. Krailsheimer, Penguin Classics (New York: Penguin, 1995), 19.

50 C.S. Lewis, "The Seeing Eye," *Christian Reflections*, Walter Hooper, ed. (Grand Rapids: William B. Eerdmans, 1967), 174.

51 Ibid.

52 Ibid.

53 See Joshua Moritz, *Science and Religion: Beyond Warfare and Toward Understanding* (Winona, MN: Anselm Academic, 2016).

54 Olli-Pekka Vainio, *Cosmology in Theological Perspective* (Grand Rapids: Baker, 2018), ch. 4, 59ff.

55 Dictonary.com, "Big Data," retrieved June 25, 2019, https://www.dictionary.com/browse/big-data.

56 Statista, "Number of Smartphone Users in the United States from 2010 to 2023 (in Millions)," retrieved June 26, 2019, https://www.statista.com/statistics/201182/forecast-of-smartphone-users-in-the-us.

57 Manu Jeevan, "50 Amazing Big Data and Data Science Quotes to Inspire You," retrieved June 26, 2019, https://www.edvancer.in/50-amazing-big-data-and-data-science-quotes-to-inspire-you.

58 George Hodges, *Faith and Social Service* (New York: Thomas Whitaker, 1896), 6.

59 Ray Kurzweil, *The Singularity is Near* (New York: Penguin, 2005), 136.

60 Julian Huxley, "The human species can, if it wishes, transcend itself.... We need a name for this new belief. Perhaps transhumanism will serve," *Religion Without Revelation* (London: C.A. Watts, 1967), 195, cited in Ted Peters, "Theologians Testing Transhumanism," *Theology and Science* 13, no. 2 (2015): 132.

61 Nick Bostrom, "Transhumanist Values," *Review of Contemporary Philosophy* 4, nos. 1–2 (2005): 87–101; available at www.nickbostrom.com/ethics/values.pdf.

62 Pellissier's survey had 818 respondents. See Hank Pellissier, "Do all Transhumanists Want Immortality? No? Why Not?" Institute for Ethics and Emerging Technologies. August 12, 2012, retrieved June 26, 2019, https://ieet.org/index.php/IEET2/more/pellissier20120801.

63 See *Science Daily*, "Artificial Intelligence," retrieved June 25, 2019, https://www.sciencedaily.com/terms/artificial_intelligence.htm.

64 Aric Huang, "A Holistic Approach to AI," retrieved June 26, 2019, https://www.ocf.berkeley.edu/~arihuang/academic/research/strongai3.html.

65 Cf. A. M. Turing, "Computing Machinery and Intelligence," *Mind* 49 (1950): 433–60, retrieved June 27, 2019, https://www.csee.umbc.edu/courses/471/papers/turing.pdf.

66 The American Society of Human Genetics (ASHG), "ASHG Denounces Attempts to Link Genetics and Racial Supremacy," *The American Journal of Human* Genetics 103, Issue 5 (2018): 636, retrieved June 25, 2019, https://www.ncbi.nlm.nih.gov/pmc/articles/PMC6218810; Amy Harmon, "Why White Supremacists Are Chugging Milk (and Why Geneticists Are Alarmed)," *New York Times*, October 17, 2018, retrieved June 25, 2019, https://www.nytimes.com/2018/10/17/us/white-supremacists-science-dna.html?module=inline; and "Geneticists Criticize Use of Science by White Nationalists to Justify 'Racial Purity.'" *New York Times*, October 19, 2018, retrieved June 25, 2019, https://www.nytimes.com/2018/10/19/us/white-supremacists-science-genetics.html.

67 E.g., Templeton, *Human Population Genetics and Genomics* (Cambridge, MA: Academic Press, 2018).

68 Dave Unander, "Race: A Brief History of its Origin, Failure and Alternative," February 21, 2018, retrieved June 25, 2019, https://biologos.org/articles/race-a-brief-history-of-its-origin-failure-and-alternative.

69 Marouf A. Hasian, *The Rhetoric of Eugenics in Anglo-American Thought* (Athens and London: University of Georgia Press, 1996), 23.

196 Appendix B

70 Edward J. Larson, *Sex, Race, and Science: Eugenics in the Deep South* (Baltimore, MD: Johns Hopkins University Press, 1996), 2; citing Robert Carruth, "Race Degeneration: What Can We Do to Check It?" *New Orleans Medical and Surgical Journal* 72 (1919): 184–5.
71 Dave Unander, "Race: A Brief History."
72 Alan Templeton, "Biological Races in Humans," *Studies in the History and Philosophy of Biology and Biomedical Sciences* 44 (2013): 271.
73 Antony Alumkal, *Paranoid Science: The Christian Right's War on Reality* (New York: NYU Press, 2019), ch. 2, 65ff.
74 E.g., Barbour, *Issues in Science and Religion* (New York: HarperCollins, 1971 [1966]); Clayton, *Religion and Science*; Christopher Southgate et al. *God, Humanity, and the Cosmos: A Textbook in Science and Religion* (Harrisburg, PA: Trinity, 1999); Alister McGrath, *Religion and Science*; Holmes Rolston, *Science and Religion: A Critical Survey* (West Conshohoken, PA: Templeton Press, 2006); Mark Richardson and Wesley J. Wildman, eds. *Religion and Science: History, Method, Dialogue* (New York: Routledge, 1996).
75 Philip Clayton, *Science and Religion: The Basics*, 2nd edition. (New York: Routledge, 2019), xi. I added a "to" before "relate" in the quotation, which was missing in the original.
76 Clayton, *The Basics*, 182.
77 American Association for the Advancement of Science (AAAS), "Climate Change Communication," retrieved June 25, 2019, https://www.aaas.org/pes/climate-change-communication.
78 See Greg Cootsona, "Christian Faith and Sustainability: Friends or Foes? Christian Theology and Stewardship of Creation," unpublished paper presented at Chico State University Sustainability Conference, November 10, 2008.
79 Lisa Hendry, "*Homo erectus*, Our Ancient Ancestor," Natural History Museum, November 7, 2018, retrieved June 29, 2019, http://www.nhm.ac.uk/discover/homo-erectus-our-ancient-ancestor.html.

Bibliography

Alumkal, Antony. *Paranoid Science: The Christian Right's War on Reality*. New York: NYU Press, 2019.

American Association for the Advancement of Science (AAAS). "Climate Change Communication." Retrieved June 25, 2019. https://www.aaas.org/pes/climate-change-communication

American Society of Human Genetics (ASHG). "ASHG Denounces Attempts to Link Genetics and Racial Supremacy." *The American Journal of Human Genetics*, 103, Issue 5 (2018): 636. Retrieved June 25, 2019. https://www.ncbi.nlm.nih.gov/pmc/articles/PMC6218810

Bagir, Zainal Abidin. "The 'Relation' between Science and Religion in the Pluralistic Landscape of Today's World." *Zygon*, 50 (2015): 403–417.

Barbour, Ian. *Issues in Science and Religion*. New York: HarperCollins, 1971 [1966].

Barrett, Justin. "Exploring the Natural Foundations of Religion." *Trends in Cognitive Sciences*, 4, vol. 1 (2000): 29–34.

Barrett, Justin. *Born Believers: The Science of Children's Religious Belief*. New York: Free Press, 2012.

Black, Edwin. *War Against the Weak: Eugenics and America's Campaign to Create a Master Race*. New York: Thunder's Mouth Press, 2003.

Bolger, Daniel, Robert A. Thomson Jr. and Elaine Howard Ecklund. "Selection versus Socialization? Interrogating the Sources of Secularity in Global Science." *Sage* 2019. https://journals.sagepub.com/doi/pdf/10.1177/0731121419835507

Bostrom, Nick. "Transhumanist Values." *Review of Contemporary Philosophy*, 4, no. 1–2 (2005): 87–101.

Boyer, Pascal. *The Naturalness of Religious Ideas*. Berkeley, CA: University of California Press, 1994

Boyer, Pascal. *Religion Explained: The Evolutionary Origins of Religious Thought*. New York: Basic Books, 2001.

Brooke, John Hedley. *Science and Religion: Some Historical Perspectives*. The Cambridge History of Science Series. Cambridge, UK: Cambridge University, 1991.

Brooke, John Hedley and Ron Numbers, eds. *Science and Religion Around the World*. Oxford, UK: Oxford University Press, 1991.

Cantor, Geoffrey and Chris Kenny. "Barbour's Fourfold Way: Problems with His Taxonomy of Science-Religion Relationships." *Zygon*, 36 (2001): 765–781.

Cha, Ariana Eunjung. "CRISPR Babies Spur NIH Director to Call for Public Debate, New Oversight." *Washington Post*. December 28, 2019. Retrieved June 29, 2019. https://www.washingtonpost.com/health/2018/12/20/crispr-babies-spur-nih-director-call-public-debate-new-oversight/?utm_term=.ec721662601e

Clayton, Philip. *Science and Religion: The Basics*. 2nd edition. New York: Routledge, 2019.

Collins, Francis. *The Language of God*. New York: Free Press, 2006.

Collins, Francis. "Why This Scientist Believes in God." *CNN*. June 6, 2007. Retrieved June 25, 2019. http://www.cnn.com/2007/US/04/03/collins.commentary/index.html

Collins, Francis. "What do YOU Believe, Doctor?" April 19, 2019. BioLogos 10th Anniversary Conference. Retrieved June 25, 2019. https://biologos.org/resources/what-do-you-believe-doctor

Cootsona, Greg. "Christian Faith and Sustainability: Friends or Foes? Christian Theology and Stewardship of Creation." Unpublished paper presented at Chico State University Sustainability Conference, November 10, 2008.

Cootsona, Greg. "How Nature and Beauty Can Bring Scientists and Theologians Together." *Theology and Science*, 9, no. 4 (2011): 379–393.

Cootsona, Greg. "Some Ways Emerging Adults Are Shaping the Future of Religion and Science." *Zygon: Journal of Religion and Science*, 51, no. 3 (September 2016): 557–572.

Cootsona, Greg. *Mere Science: Bridging the Divide with Emerging Adults*. Downers Grove, IL: InterVarsity, 2018.

Cootsona, Greg. "Science and the Sensus Divinitatis: The Promise and Problem of the Natural Knowledge of God." Matthew Nelson Hill and Wm. Curtis Holtzen, eds. *Connecting Faith and Science: Philosophical and Theological Inquiries*. Claremont, CA: Claremont School of Theology Press, 2018.

Coyne, Jerry . *Faith Versus Fact: Why Science and Religion Are Incompatible*. New York: Penguin, 2016.

Dalai Lama. *The Universe in a Single Atom: The Convergence of Science and Spirituality*. New York: Morgan Road Books, 2005.

Dalai Lama, Herbert Benson, Robert Thurman, Howard Gardner and Daniel Goleman. *MindScience: An East-West Dialogue*. Boston, MA: Wisdom, 1999.

Davis, Jake H. and Owen Flanaga. *A Mirror is for Reflection: Understanding Buddhist Ethics*. Oxford, UK: Oxford University Press, 2017.

Dawkins, Richard. *The Selfish Gene*. 2nd edition. Oxford, UK: Oxford University Press, 1989.

Delbanco, Andrew. *The Real American Dream: A Meditation on Hope*. Cambridge, MA: Harvard, 2000.

Dictonary.com. "Big Data." Retrieved June 25, 2019. https://www.dictionary.com/browse/big-data

Dukas, Helen. *Albert Einstein the Human Side*. Princeton, NJ: Princeton University Press, 1981.

Ecklund, Elaine Howard and Christopher P. Scheitle. *Religion vs. Science: What Religious People Really Think*. Oxford, UK: Oxford University Press, 2018.

Evans, John H. *Morals Not Knowledge: Recasting the Contemporary U.S. Conflict Between Science and Religion*. Oakland, CA: University of California Press, 2018.

Ferngren, Gary B. *Science and Religion: A Historical Introduction*. Baltimore, MD: Johns Hopkins University Press, 2002.

Finke, Roger. "Religious Deregulation: Origins and Consequences." *Journal of Church and State*, 32 (1990): 609–626.

Gaustad, Edwin and Leigh Schmidt. *The Religious History of America: The Heart of the American Story from Colonial Times to Today*. San Francisco, CA: HarperCollins, 2004.

Guardian, The. "Five Markers of Adulthood Millennials Have Had to Give Up On." Retrieved June 13, 2019. https://www.theguardian.com/lifeandstyle/2016/mar/10/five-markers-of-adulthood-millenials-have-had-to-give-up-on

Guthrie, S.E. *Faces in the Clouds: A New Theory of Religion* New York: Oxford University Press, 1993

Ha, Minsu, David L. Haury and Ross H. Nehm. "Feeling of Certainty: Uncovering a Missing Link between Knowledge and Acceptance of Evolution." *Journal of Research in Science Teaching*, 49 (2011): 95–121.

Haidt, Jonathan. *The Righteous Mind: Why Good People Are Divided by Politics and Religion*. New York: Vintage, 2013.

Ham, Becky. "Religious and Scientific Communities May Be Less Combative Than Commonly Portrayed." February 17, 2014. Retrieved June 25, 2019. http://www.aaas.org/news/religious-and-scientific-communities-may-be-less-combative-commonly-portrayed

Harmon, Amy. "Why White Supremacists Are Chugging Milk (and Why Geneticists Are Alarmed)." *New York Times*. October 17, 2018. Retrieved June 25, 2019. https://www.nytimes.com/2018/10/17/us/white-supremacists-science-dna.html?module=inline

Harmon, Amy. "Geneticists Criticize Use of Science by White Nationalists to Justify 'Racial Purity'." *New York Times*. October 19, 2018. Retrieved June 25, 2019. https://www.nytimes.com/2018/10/19/us/white-supremacists-science-genetics.html

Hasian, Marouf A. *The Rhetoric of Eugenics in Anglo-American Thought*. Athens and London: University of Georgia Press, 1996.

Hendry, Lisa. "Homo erectus, Our Ancient Ancestor." Natural History Museum. November 7, 2018. Retrieved June 29, 2019. http://www.nhm.ac.uk/discover/homo-erectus-our-ancient-ancestor.html

Hodges, George. *Faith and Social Service*. New York: Thomas Whitaker, 1896.

Huang, Aric. "A Holistic Approach to AI." Retrieved June 26, 2019. https://www.ocf.berkeley.edu/~arihuang/academic/research/strongai3.html

Iqbal, Muzaffir. "Scientific Commentary on the Quran." Seyyd Hossein Nasr, general editor. *The Study Quran: A New Translation and Commentary*. San Francisco, CA: HarperOne, 2015.

Jeevan, Manu. "50 Amazing Big Data and Data Science Quotes to Inspire You." Retrieved June 26, 2019. https://www.edvancer.in/50-amazing-big-data-and-data-science-quotes-to-inspire-you

Keller, Catharine and Laurel C. Schneider, eds. *Polydoxy: Theology of Multiplicity and Relation*. New York: Routledge, 2010.

Kinnaman, David with Aly Hawkins. *You Lost Me: Why Young Christians Are Leaving Church … and Rethinking Faith*. Grand Rapids, MI: Baker Books, 2011.

Kinsley, David. *Ecology and Religion: Ecological Spirituality in Cross-Cultural Perspective*. Englewood Cliffs, NJ: Prentice, 1995.

Krauss, Lawrence. "All Scientists Should Be Militant Atheists." *The New Yorker*. September 8, 2015. Retrieved May 23, 2019. https://www.newyorker.com/news/news-desk/all-scientists-should-be-militant-atheists

Kurzweil, Ray. *The Singularity is Near*. New York: Penguin, 2005.

Lajka, Julian Quinones Arijeta. *CBS News*. August 14, 2017. "'What Kind of Society Do You Want to Live in?' Inside the Country Where Down Syndrome is Disappearing," August 15, 2017. Retrieved June 29, 2019. https://www.cbsnews.com/news/down-syndrome-iceland

Larson, Edward J. *Sex, Race, and Science: Eugenics in the Deep South*. Baltimore, MD: Johns Hopkins University Press, 1996.

Lawson, E.T. and R.N. McCauley. *Rethinking Religion: Connecting Cognition and Culture*. Cambridge, UK: Cambridge University Press, 1990.

Ledford, Heidi. "CRISPR Deployed to Combat Sickle-Cell Anaemia." *Nature News*. October 12, 2016. Retrieved June 26, 2019. https://www.nature.com/news/crispr-deployed-to-combat-sickle-cell-anaemia-1.20782

Lewis, C.S. *Mere Christianity*. New York: MacMillan, 1952.

Longest, Kyle and Christian Smith. "Conflicting or Compatible: Beliefs About Religion and Science Among Emerging Adults in the United States." *Sociological Forum*, 26, no. 4 (2011): 846–869.

Machuga, Ric. *Three Theological Mistakes*. Eugene, OR: Wipf and Stock, 2015.

McGrath, Alister. *Religion and Science: A New Introduction*. 2nd edition. Oxford, UK: Wiley-Blackwell, 2010.

Moritz, Joshua M. *Science and Religion: Beyond Warfare and Toward Understanding*. Winona, MN: Anselm Academic, 2016.

Mumford, Charles. "Causal Dispositionalism." *Properties, Powers, and Structures: Issues in the Metaphysics of Realism*. Edited by Alexander Bird, B.D. Ellis and Howard Sankey. New York: Routledge, 2012.

NASA. "Exoplanet Exploration." Retrieved June 25, 2019. https://exoplanets.nasa.gov

Pascal, Blaise. *Pensées*. Translated by A.J. Krailsheimer. Penguin Classics. New York: Penguin, 1995.

Pellissier, Hank. "Do all Transhumanists Want Immortality? No? Why Not?" Institute for Ethics and Emerging Technologies. August 12, 2012. Retrieved June 26, 2019. https://ieet.org/index.php/IEET2/more/pellissier20120801

Peters, Ted. *Playing God? Genetic Determinism and Human Freedom*, 2nd edition. London: Taylor & Francis, 2014.

Peters, Ted. "Theologians Testing Transhumanism." *Theology and Science*, 13, no. 2 (2015): 130–149.

Peters, Ted. "Astrobiology and Astrochristology." *Zygon*, 51, no. 2 (2016): 480–496.

Peterson, Michael L., William Hasker and Bruce Reichenbach. *Philosophy of Religion: Selected Readings*. Oxford, UK: Oxford University Press, 2014.

Pinker, Stephen. *How the Mind Works*. New York: W.W. Norton, 1997.

Regalado, Antonio. "EXCLUSIVE: Chinese Scientists are Creating CRISPR Babies." *MIT Technology Review*. November 25, 2018. Retrieved June 29, 2019. https://www.technologyreview.com/s/612458/exclusive-chinese-scientists-are-creating-crispr-babies

Richardson, Mark and Wesley J. Wildman, eds. *Religion and Science: History, Method, Dialogue*. New York and London: Routledge, 1996.

Rolston, Holmes. *Science and Religion: A Critical Survey*. West Conshohoken, PA: Templeton Press, 2006.

Rosen, Christine. *Preaching Eugenics: Religious Leaders and the American Eugenics Movement*. Oxford, UK: Oxford University Press, 2004.

Scheitle, Christopher P. "U.S. College Students' Perception of Religion and Science: Conflict, Collaboration, or Independence? A Research Note." *Journal for the Scientific Study of Religion*, 50, no. 1 (2011): 175–186.

Schleiermacher, Friedrich. *The Christian Faith*. Edited by H.R. Mackintosh and J.S. Stewart. Edinburgh: T&T Clark, 1989.

Schmidt, Leigh Eric. *Restless Souls: The Making of American Spirituality*. Berkeley, CA: University of California Press, 2012.

Science Daily. "Artificial Intelligence." Retrieved June 25, 2019. https://www.sciencedaily.com/terms/artificial_intelligence.htm

Setran, David P. and Chris A. Kiesling. *Spiritual Formation in Emerging Adulthood: A Practical Theology for College and Young Adult Ministry*. Grand Rapids, MI: Baker Books, 2013.

Smith, Christian with Patricia Snell. *Souls in Transition: The Religious and Spiritual Lives of Emerging Adults*. Oxford, UK: Oxford University, 2009.

Smith, Christian, Kari Christoffersen, and Hillary Davidson. *Lost in Transition: The Dark Side of Emerging Adulthood*. Oxford: Oxford University, 2011.

Smith, Huston. *The World's Religions*. San Francisco, CA: HarperOne, 1991.

Southgate, Christopher et al. *God, Humanity, and the Cosmos: A Textbook in Science and Religion*. Harrisburg, PA: Trinity, 1999.

Stanford Encyclopedia of Philosophy. "Religion and Science." Retrieved June 24, 2019. https://plato.stanford.edu/entries/religion-science

Stanford Encyclopedia of Philosophy. "Occasionalism." Retrieved June 26, 2019. https://plato.stanford.edu/entries/occasionalism

Statista. "Number of Smartphone Users in the United States from 2010 to 2023 (in Millions)." Retrieved June 26, 2019. https://www.statista.com/statistics/201182/forecast-of-smartphone-users-in-the-us

Templeton, Alan. "Biological Races in Humans." *Studies in the History and Philosophy of Biology and Biomedical Sciences*, 44 (2013): 262–271.

Templeton, Alan. *Human Population Genetics and Genomics*. Cambridge, MA: Academic Press, 2018.

Test of Faith. Retrieved June 25, 2019. http://www.testoffaith.com

Turing, A.M. "Computing Machinery and Intelligence." *Mind*, 49 (1950): 433–460. Retrieved June 27, 2019. https://www.csee.umbc.edu/courses/471/papers/turing.pdf

Unander, Dave. "Race: A Brief History of its Origin, Failure and Alternative." February 21, 2018. Retrieved June 25, 2019. https://biologos.org/articles/race-a-brief-history-of-its-origin-failure-and-alternative

Vainio, Olli-Pekka. *Cosmology in Theological Perspective*. Grand Rapids, MI: Baker, 2018.

Wallace, Alan B. *Buddhism and Science: Breaking New Ground*. New York: Columbia University Press, 2003.

Watt, Nick. "Stephen Hawking: 'Science Makes God Unnecessary'." September 7, 2010. Retrieved June 26, 2019. https://abcnews.go.com/GMA/stephen-hawking-science-makes-god-unnecessary/story?id=11571150

Whitehead, Alfred North. *Process and Reality: Corrected Edition*. Edited by David Ray Griffin and Donald W. Sherburne. New York: Free Press, 1978 [1929].

Whitehouse, Harvey. *Modes of Religiosity: A Cognitive Theory of Religious Transmission. Cognitive Science of Religion*. Walnut Creek, CA: AltaMira Press, 2004.

Wright, Robert. *Why Buddhism is True*. New York: Simon & Schuster, 2018.

INDEX

2001: A Space Odyssey 110

Agassiz, L. 49, 73
agnosticism, rise in 160–1
Ahlstrom, S. 43, 109
American Association for the Advancement
 of Science (AAAS) 51, 66, 84, 119,
 120, 149
American Dream 7, 32–3, 138, 156
amillennialism 74
Anderson, M. B. 67
anthropology 127
Apollo 11 moon-landing (1969) 109
Armstrong, N. 109
Arnett, J. 5, 137
artificial intelligence (AI) 147–8
atheism 57, 61, 66, 130–1; rise in 160–1
atomic/nuclear physics and technology 93,
 94; atom bomb 99, 101; Cuban Missile
 Crisis 110; Three Mile Island power
 plant 113

Bacon, F. 48, 67, 131–2
Baptists 53, 78, 88
Barbour, I. 17, 96, 106, 107–8, 112, 117
Barth, K. 79–80
Barzan, J. 76
Bayes, T. 43
beauty, concept of 38–9, 169
Beecher, H. W. 75
Behe, M. 120
Bellah, R. 126; et al. (*Habits of the Heart*
 team) 34, 35, 49–50, 138, 139

biblical interpretation and criticism 77–8;
 antebellum period 49; post-Darwin 65,
 66, 67; Puritans 33–4, 77; Scopes trial
 (1925) 85–7
Biblicism 34, 77
Big Bang cosmology 93, 94–5, 118
Big Data 147
Bill of Rights 46
Biologos 128, 132
Bixby, J. T. 4
Black, E. 81–2, 83, 113
Bohr, N. 93, 94, 96, 99, 115
Bozeman, T. 48–9
bricolage 138, 139, 140–1
Brooke, J. H. 19, 62
Bryan, W. J. 84–7, 88
Buddhism 52, 145, 146
Butler Act (1925) 84

Calvin, J. 19, 30, 74
Capra, F. 114–15
Carroll, P. and Noble, D. 59
Carson, R. 110
Carter, J. 113
Carus, P. 74
Catholicism 19, 33, 64–5, 100–1, 110;
 colonial era 30, 31–2; immigration 76;
 Vatican Observatory 116, 119
Center for Theology and the Natural
 Sciences (CTNS) 116, 119
CERN, Switzerland 127

202 Index

Challenger space shuttle 116
Chauncy, C. 44
Chinese Exclusion Act (1880) 76
Chinese immigrants (1849) 52
Christian History 68
Christianity 23–4; decreasing influence
  and splintering of religious life 157–9;
  see also Catholicism: Protestantism;
  evangelicalism; revivalism; *specific
  Protestant sects*
Christianity Today 38
church and state, separation of 46
Civil War (1861–5) 58–9
Clayton, P. 149, 164
Clergy Letter Project 127
climate change 149
Clinton, B. 126
Clustered Regularly Interspaced Short
  Palindromic Repeat (CRISPR) 146
Codrescu, A. 35
cognitive science of religion 146
Cold War 101
collaboration/integration 17, 19; Eighties
  (1980s): growth and 116–18; *see also*
  Collin, F.
Collins, F. 19, 67, 126, 128, 131–2, 146
Columbus, C. 29, 31
Common Sense Realism 46–8
complementarity, concept of 93, 96–7, 114
complexity thesis 19
computer technology, internet, and social
  media 113, 127, 138, 139, 143
conflict/"conflict thesis" 4, 17–18; emerging
  adults 141, 142–4; future perspective
  162–4; *see also* Dawkins, R.
Copernicus, N. 30
Coronado, F. V. de 31
cosmology: and astrobiology 146–7; Big
  Bang 93, 94–5, 118; and physics 127
counter-culture (1960s) 109
creation *ex nihilo*, doctrine of 59–60, 95
creationism/creation science 6, 101, 110,
  117, 128; day-age 63; intelligent design
  (ID) 117–18, 120; Islamic 128
cultural forces 5, 6–7, 65
cultural-linguistic model of religion 15
culture, definitions of 21–2
Cuvier, G. 43

Damasio, A. 20
Darrow, C. 84, 85–7
Darwin and post-Darwin era 21, 51–2,
  118, 130; conflicting perspectives 63–5;
  impact on religion 59–63; reconciliation
  and rejection 65–8; setting the break with

Origin of Species 57–9; social Darwinism
  81, 82, 85; *see also* evolution
Davenport, C. B. 81–2, 83
Dawkins, R. 17, 44, 57, 67, 130–1, 145
Declaration of Independence 44,
  53–4
deism: "Moralistic Therapeutic
  Deism" (MTD) 140; of Thomas
  Paine 43–6
Delbanco, A. 7, 32–3, 138, 156, 159
Deloria, V. 116
design in nature 66, 68
determinism to indeterminacy 97
dialogue 17; Seventies (1970s): broadening
  113–16
digital natives 139
Dirac, P. 93
divine action 119, 145
Dixon, T. 13, 112
DNA: structure of 94; *see also* genetics and
  genetic technologies
Dorrien, G. 106, 107
Douglass, F. 54
Douthat, R. 102
Draper, J. W. 63–4, 65
Drees, W. 16
Du Bois, W. E. B. 99–100
Dupree, A. H. 68
Durkheim, É. 15

eastern religions 52, 114–15; *see also specific
  religions*
Ecklund, E. H. and Scheitle, C. 17–18, 19,
  141–2, 160, 162, 169
Edwards, J. 36–9, 43, 45, 66–7, 169
Edwards v. Aguillard 117
Eighties (1980s): growth and collaboration
  116–18
Einstein, A. 21, 93, 94–5, 99
Eisenhower Revival 100
emerging adults 135–7; accelerating
  tradition 134–5; signs pointing in
  opposite directions 141–4; streaming
  spirituality vs LP religion 135, 137–41;
  top eleven topics today and for the future
  144–9; *see also* future perspective
Emerson, R. W. 50
emotions and rationality 20–1, 44
Enlightenment 37, 39, 43, 50; Reformation
  and conquest 29–31, 33; Scottish 47
environmentalism 110, 114; climate change
  149; energy conservation 113
episteme 22
Epperson v. Arkansas 110
essentialism 16, 165–6

ethics: of beauty 39; conflict of 5, 6; *see also entries beginning* moral
eugenics: and genetic editing 146; movement 74, 81–3, 85; and race 148
evangelicalism 43–4, 48–9, 102; fundamentalist/right-wing/white 77, 117, 143, 157–8
Evans, J. H. 5–6, 17
evolution 73, 74–5, 80–1; and Catholicism 100–1, 119; as contemporary issue 127–8, 145–6; and race 99–100; theistic 132; *see also* creationism/creation science; Darwin and post-Darwin era; eugenics; Scopes trial (1925)

Faraday, M. 48
Feyerbend, P. 14
Finke, R. 46
Fischer, I. 82
Fisher, R. 80–1
Fleming, D. 63, 64
Fosdick, H. E. 79
Foucault, M. 22, 31
Founding Fathers 44, 45
Fowles, S. M. 14
Franck, J. 4
Franklin, B. 43, 45
functional Magnetic Resonance Imaging (fMRI) 146
fundamentalism 77–8, 65, 87; -modernist split 78–81, 88; Islamic 113; right-wing/white evangelicalism 77, 117, 143, 157–8
future perspective: decreasing influence of Christianity and splintering of religious life 157–9; nones/religiously unaffiliated 160, 161–4; perils of prediction 156; rise in atheism and agnosticism 160–1; towards new modes and models 164–6; towards a truly pluralist model 166–7

Gaia hypothesis 114
Galileo Galilei 29–30
Galton, F. 81, 82
Gaskin, S. 114
Gaustad, E. and Schmidt, L. 44, 52–3, 108–9, 111, 117, 140
Geertz, C. 22
general relativity theory 93, 94–5
genetics and genetic technologies: Human Genome Project 126, 128, 131; medicine and eugenics 146; race and eugenics 148; and reproductive technology 113; structure of DNA 94
Gilbert, J. 20, 21, 116, 168

Gordon, P. 6
Gould, S. J. 5, 18, 80, 129–30
Graham, B. 100, 120
Gray, A. 66, 67–8, 73
Great Awakening 35–6, 38, 39; Second 47
Great Depression 98
Guyot, A. H. 63

Habermas, J. 158
Habits of the Heart team 34, 35, 49–50, 138, 139
Hammond, P. 111
HarperCollins Dictionary of Religion 5
Harrison, P. 14–15, 16, 52, 166
Harvard University 1, 3, 4, 67–8, 73, 99–100
head/heart dichotomy 20–1
Heisenberg, W. 93, 94, 95–6, 97
Hermann, W. 80
Hinduism 99, 146
Hodge, C. 36–7, 48, 52, 57, 65–7
Hovecamp, H. 57
Hubble, E. 93, 95
Hudson, W. 35
Human Genome Project 126, 128, 131
human origins 127
Hume, D. 47, 60
Hunter, G. W. 85
Hutcheson, F. 39
Hutchinson, A. 34

immigration 52, 76, 83, 98–9
in vitro fertilization 113
independence/independent co-existence 17, 18; *see also* Gould, S. J.
indigenous/Native Americans 14, 32, 116
individualism 35–6, 45, 111, 138, 165; and tinkering *see* emerging adults
inerrancy of the Bible 77
Ingersoll, R. 44, 46, 63
inner world of human thought 74
integration *see* collaboration/integration
intellectual history 6; periods of 22–3
intelligent design (ID) 117–18, 120
internet and social media 127, 138, 139, 143
Iranian Revolution (1979) 113
Islam 109; creationism 128; fundamentalism 113

James, W. 36, 75–6
Jammer, M. 97
Jastrow, R. 95
Jefferson, T. 3, 35
Jehovah's Witnesses 76
Jenson, R. 20, 37
Jewish immigration 76, 98–9
John Templeton Foundation (JTF) 117

204 Index

Johnson, P. E. 118

Kant, I. 106–7, 108
Kellogg, J. H. 82
Kelvin, Lord 48
Kennedy, J. F. 109
Kepler, J. 29–30
King, Jr., M. L. 108, 109
Kingsley, C. 61–2
Kinnaman, D. 143
Kitzmiller v. Dover trial 120
Kuhn, T. 14, 107
Kurzweil, R. 147–8

Lakatos, I. 14
Lamarck, J.-B. 48
Laplace, P.-S. 96, 97
Larson, E. 60, 84, 87, 165
Lawrence, D. H. 82
LeConte, J. 73–4
Lemaître, G. 93, 95
Lewis, C. S. 22–3, 57, 100, 107, 111,
    131, 145
light: in quantum theory 95; in special
    relativity theory 94, 98
Lincoln, A. 53, 58
Lindbeck, G. 15
Lipton, P. 14
Lovelock, J. 114
Luther, M. 30

McCauley, R. 21
McCosh, J. 48, 67
McGrath, A. 14
Machen, J. G. 88
MacIntyre, A. 3, 7
Malcolm X 109
Marsden, G. 33, 37, 38–9,
    62, 88
materialism 118
Matthews, S. 73
Mead, S. 46
Mencken, H. L. 6
Methodists 36, 53
Milken, R. A. 80
millennialism 74, 76
Millennials 161–2
Miller, P. 37–8, 39
Miller, W. 50–1, 76
mindfulness 146
Mitchell, L. J. 39
"Moralistic Therapeutic Deism" (MTD) 140
morality 5, 6, 118
Moritz, J. 68, 87
Mormons 50

Moseley, H. 93
multiperspectival and polycontextual model
    166–7
mysticism 114–15

Napier, J. 29–30
National Academy of Science (NAS) 18,
    58, 143
Native Americans 14, 32, 116
natural philosophy 13, 38, 39, 51
natural science 51
natural theology 60
Nazi Germany 83, 98–9, 100
neuroscience 146
New England *see* Puritans, colonizers
New Mexico 31–2
Newton, I. 29, 30, 38
Newtonian to quantum worldview 96–8
Niebuhr, H. R. 80, 112
Niebuhr, R. 80, 100, 112
nineties (1990s): consolidation and
    counter-narratives 118–20
Nixon, R. M. 113
Nobel laureate scientists 33, 99
Noll, M. A. 43, 44, 47–8, 49, 85
Non-Overlapping Magisterial Authority
    (NOMA) 18, 80, 129–30
nones/religiously unaffiliated 160, 161–4
Nuclear Age *see* atomic/nuclear physics
    and technology

Oñate, J. de 31–2
Oppenheimer, R. 99
Orsi, R. 15

Paine, T. 44–6
Paley, W. 59–60, 130
Parker, C. 98–9
Parsons, T. 22
Pascal, B. 147
Pauli, W. 94, 99
Penzias, A. 94, 95
Pessoa, L. 20
Pew Research Center 142, 160, 161–2,
    163–4
physics and cosmology 127; *The Tao of
    Physics* (Capra) 114–15; quantum 93, 94,
    95–8, 115, 119; *see also* atomic/nuclear
    physics and technology
Plank, M. 94, 95
pluralism *see* religious diversity/pluralism;
    religious modernism and pluralism
Polkinghorne, J. 76, 97, 98
polycontextual and multiperspectival model
    166–7

Pope John Paul II 116, 119
Pope Paul II 19
Pope Paul VI 110
Pope Pius XII 100–1, 119
Popper, K. 14
post-Darwin era *see* Darwin and post-Darwin era
postmillennialism 74–5
premillennialism 74, 77
Presbyterians 48, 53, 77, 88, 112–13
present: 1966–2000 106–20; third millennium 126–32
Princeton University 48, 62, 63, 67
Princeton Theological Seminary 48, 62, 65, 67, 88
Principe, L. 4, 13, 51
Protestant Reformation 30
Protestantism: mainline/liberal 88, 98, 100, 102, 119–20; schisms 53; *see also* evangelicalism; religious modernism and pluralism; revivalism; *specific sects*
Prothero, S. 14, 15
psychedelics 114
psychology 146
Puritans: amillennialism 74; colonizers 32–4, 77; loss of influence 49–50, 102

quantum physics 93, 94, 95–8, 115, 119

race: and eugenics 148; and evolution 99–100; scientific racism 81, 148; and slavery 49, 52–4
rationalism/rationality 43, 45–6; and emotions 20–1, 44; and faith 145
Rauschenbusch, W. 78–9
Reagan, R. 102, 117
realism, naïve to critical 96–7
reductionism 96, 98
Reeves, J. 16, 107–8, 165–6
Reid, T. 47, 48
relativity, general and special theories of 93, 94–5, 98
religion, definitions of 14, 15–16, 17, 36, 52
"Religion of Science" 74
religious diversity/pluralism 108–9, 116, 128, 134–5, 137–41, 166–7
religious freedom 34, 45
religious modernism and pluralism 73–6; eugenics movement 74, 81–3, 85; *see also* fundamentalism; Scopes trial (1925)
reproductive technology 113
revivalism 44, 77; Eisenhower 100; Great Awakening 35–6, 38, 39; Second Great Awakening 47

Revolutionary period to 1859: Common Sense Realism 46–8; deism of Thomas Paine 43–6; early 1800s and brewing discontent 48–51; key words and critical shifts 51–2; race and slavery in antebellum period 49, 52–4
Ritchie, A. D. 14
Roberts, J. 73, 74
Roberts, J. H. 80
Rosen, C. 74, 85
Ruse, M. 117–18
Russell, R. J. 116
Rutherford, E. 93

Scheitle, C. and Ecklund, E. H. 17–18, 19, 141–2, 160, 162, 169
Schleiermacher, F. 107
Schneider, H. W. 47, 75
Schrödinger, E. 93, 94, 95
science: definitions of 13–14, 17, 51; and shifting worldview 96–8; *see also* technology
science and religion: in America 19–24; definitions and their limitations 13–17; relationship of 17–19
"science of religion" 76
Science for Students and Emerging Young Adults (SEYA) project 136, 137
scientific discoveries/developments: eighteenth century 43; nineteenth century 48; twentieth century 93–6, 113, 116, 118–19; twenty first century 126–7
Scientific Revolution (sixteenth and seventeenth centuries) 29–30
scientist: coining of term 14, 51
Scopes Trial (1925) 6, 84–8, 165
Scottish Enlightenment and Common Sense Realism 46, 47–8
secularization thesis 158–9
Sedgwick, A. 51
Seventh Day Adventists 50–1
Seventies (1970s): broadening dialogue 113–16
sex and sexuality 148–9
Sheilaism 138, 139
Sibley, M. 111
Silliman, B. 48–9
Sixties (1960s): turbulence 109–13
slavery 49, 52–4
Smith, C. and Longest, K. 141, 142; and Snell, P. 140
Smith, J. 50
social Darwinism 81, 82, 85
"social gospel" 78–9
social media and internet 127, 138, 139, 143

206 Index

Sommerville, M. 51
Soviet Union 101
Spanish conquest 31–2
special relativity theory 93, 94, 98
"spiritual bricoleurs" and bricolage 138, 139, 140–1
spiritual communities 114
spirituality 16; atheists and agnostics 160; eastern religions 114–15; Native American 116; nones 162, 164; streaming vs LP religion 137–41
Spirituality in Higher Education (SHEP) survey 141–2
Stanford Encyclopedia of Philosophy 111–12, 134
Stephenson, D. 114
sterilizations, eugenic 82–3
Sunday, B. 60
supernatural beliefs 15–16

The Tao of Physics (Capra) 114–15
technology: AI and transhumanism 147–8; computer, internet, and social media 113, 127, 138, 139, 143; definition of 17; and science 16–17; warfare 58–9; *see also* atomic/nuclear physics and technology; genetics and genetic technologies
telescopes 29
Temple, F. 61, 62
Templeton Prize 117
Tevelyan, G. M. 23
Thomas Aquinas 15, 60, 94
Thoreau, H. D. 50
Tillich, P. 100
Tocqueville, A. de 159
Transcendentalist movement 50
transhumanism 147–8

Troeltsch, E. 74
Truman, H. S. 4
Trump, D. 157, 158, 164–5
Turner, J. 49, 52, 57
uncertainty principle 93, 96, 97
United States v. Seeger 110
University of California, Berkeley 73, 109
Updike, J. 65

Vatican Observatory 116, 119
virtue 39

"warfare thesis" *see* conflict/"conflict thesis"
Warfield, B. B. 67, 77
Weber, M. 158
Wedge Document 118
Weiss, E. 99
Welch, C. 21, 62, 78
Welker, M. 166–7
Wherwell, W. 14, 51
Whitcomb, J. and Morris, H. 6
White, A. D. 64–5
Whitefield, G. 35, 38
Whitehead, A.N. 36, 57, 107, 166, 167; challenge and response 1, 2, 3–4, 5–8, 20, 23, 82, 115, 135, 164, 169; definition of religion 36
Williams, R. 34
Wilson, R. W. 94, 95
Witherspoon, J. 47–8
women leaders 128
World Parliament of Religions (1893) 76, 108
Wuthnow, R. 136–7, 138, 140–1

Zimmerman, M. 127